Intellectual Pr
A Manager's Guide

Editor
Vivien Irish

McGRAW-HILL BOOK COMPANY

London · New York · St Louis · San Francisco · Auckland
Bogatá · Caracas · Hamburg · Lisbon · Madrid · Mexico · Milan
Montreal · New Delhi · Panama · Paris · San Juan · Sao Pãulo
Singapore · Sydney · Tokyo · Toronto

Published by
McGRAW-HILL Book Company (UK) Limited
Shoppenhangers Road, Maidenhead, Berkshire, SL6 2QL, England
Telephone 0628 23432
Fax 0628 770224

British Library Cataloguing in Publication Data
Intellectual property.
1. Intellectual property. Management
I. Irish, Vivien
658.575
ISBN 0-07-707356-0

Library of Congress Cataloging-in-Publication Data
Irish, Vivien
  Intellectual property : a manager's guide / Vivien Irish.
    p. cm.
  Includes index.
  ISBN 0-07-707346-0
  1. Intellectual property--Great Britain. 2. Intellectual
property. I. Title.
KD1269.I75 1991
346.4104'8—dc20
[344.10648]   90-44668

Copyright © 1991 McGraw-Hill Book Company (UK) Limited. All rights reserved. No part of this publication may be reproduced, stored in a retrieval system, or transmitted, in any form or by any means, electronic, mechanical, photocopying, recording, or otherwise, without the prior permission of McGraw-Hill Book Company (UK) Limited.

1234   94321

Typeset by BookEns Limited, Baldock, Herts.
and printed and bound in Great Britain at the University Press, Cambridge.

Contents

Contributors		vii
Foreword		xi
Introduction: using this book		xiii

1   Confidential information   *Vivien Irish*   1
Introduction—What is confidential information?—What is excluded?—Confidential disclosures: when do they occur?—Third party relationships—Visitors—Employees—Legal remedies—Computer software and escrow—Disadvantages of confidentiality—Unrecorded confidential information—Unsolicited technical suggestions—Summary

2   Trade marks   *Richard Gallafent*   15
What is a trade mark?—Types of trade mark—Protection of trade marks—UK trade mark registration law—What marks can be registered?—Application procedure in the United Kingdom—Other objections to registrability—Using your mark—Infringement: using your registration—Passing off—Letting others use your mark—International aspects—Trade mark personnel—Trade mark selection—Summary

3   Technical copyright and information technology   35
Roger Broadie
COPYRIGHT: Introduction—The nature of copyright—The concept of the 'work'—Conditions for copyright to subsist—Authorship and ownership—Infringement—Copyright in three-dimensional articles—Administering copyright—INFORMATION TECHNOLOGY: Protection of computer programs under copyright—Other copyright works in the field of information technology—Restricted acts and infringement—Administering copyright in the IT field—Summary

4   Industrial design   *Clifford Lees and*   61
Keith Weatherald
The sources—The ingredients of design—REGISTERED DESIGNS—Registrability of a design—What to do to get

protection—DESIGN RIGHT—What can be protected by design right?—The benefits of protection—Relationship between registered designs, design right and copyright—Summary

5   Protection of semiconductor products   89
    Robert J. Hart
    Introduction: integrated circuits and their protection—Protection in the United Kingdom—Protection outside the United Kingdom—Summary

6   Patents   *Jacqueline Needle*   99
    Introduction—What can be protected by a patent?—Exclusions from patentability—Novelty—Obviousness—Other intellectual property rights—Applying for a patent—Protection in other countries—Keeping and using patents—Maintaining a patent—Summary—**Case study**

7   Ownership of intellectual property   *Tibor Gold*   133
    Introduction: the terminology—The general rule—Formalities—Trade marks—Co-ownership—Consultants, R & D contracts—Directors—Employees and IP—Summary—**Case studies**

8   Licensing and other exploitation   *Harry Shipley*   151
    Introduction—Nature of rights and litigation—Assignment and licensing—Choosing the exploitation path—Sole and exclusive licences—Compensation—Special types of licence—Licensing agreement formats—Risk—Developments, modifications and grant back—Anti-trust and EC restrictions—Financial aspects of licensing—Summary

9   Strategy and litigation   *Alan Burrington*   171
    Introduction—IP STRATEGY: Three different industries—What policy for patents?—Managing an intellectual property portfolio— LITIGATION: Introduction—Why litigate?—The UK legal system—UK litigation and the European Community —Summary

    Useful addresses   205

    Index   207

Contributors

All contributors are Chartered Patent Agents, Fellows of the Chartered Institute of Patent Agents (CIPA), and European Patent Attorneys.

Roger Broadie read Natural Sciences at Cambridge and is Head of Patents and Licensing at International Computers Limited. He recently rejoined the company after leaving its former parent STC PLC, where he had held the same position. He is Chairman of the Software Protection Working Group of the Electronics and Business Equipment Association and a member of the British Computer Society Intellectual Property Rights Committee. During the passage through Parliament of the Copyright, Designs and Patents Act 1988 he took part in the consultations between the Government and industry that led to significant changes in the provisions on information technology.

Alan Burrington holds degrees from London University in physics and law. A significant proportion of his career has been spent in industry, with ITT, STC, Ford Motor Company and British Leyland twice holding the position of Head of an Intellectual Property Department. His special interests lie in technology transfer/licensing and in litigation. He has also spent a significant number of years in private practice and is currently with Beresford & Co. Alan is a member of the Council of the CIPA and chairs its Legal and Licensing Committee.

Richard Gallafent has a physics degree and realized that he did not wish to research or teach physics, which inclined him to a career in patent agency. He has his own practice in London, is a member of the Council of the CIPA and was President in 1989/90. He is currently Treasurer of the Community Trade Mark Office Committee which lobbies to locate that office in London. He co-authored the book *Intellectual Property Law and Tax* now in its third edition.

Tibor Gold was born in Budapest, read physics at Oxford and entered patent agency in 1964. After cutting his professional teeth on jet engines and electronic watches, he set up on his own in 1970. Despite the growth of his practice, he has found time to acquire a law degree and fluency in four Continental languages. He acted for Professor Rubik throughout the rise and fall of the cube craze. He specializes in employer–employee disputes, is a committed teacher in aspects of intellectual property law, and, having chaired the Education Committee of the CIPA, is now a member of the Joint Board of Examiners of that Institute and the Institute of Trade Mark Agents.

Robert J. Hart was until 31 December 1989 the Intellectual Property Development Manager of the Plessey Company PLC and is now the Managing Director of Intellectual Property International Limited, a management consultancy company specializing in intellectual property. He is Chairman of the Intellectual Property Committee of the British Computer Society, a member of the CIPA Software Protection Committee, and also a member of the editorial panel of Computer Law and Practice. He was a consultant to the World Intellectual Property Organization on the legal protection of semiconductor products.

Vivien Irish after graduating from Durham University with a degree in physics, worked in industrial research at BICC Limited. Moving to the Ministry of Defence to train as a Chartered Patent Agent, she achieved her aim of broadening the technical scope of her work, and a transfer to the National Research Development Corporation added the interest of seeing patents put to commercial use. Several years at British Telecom widened her intellectual property experience to contractual aspects, especially software licences, and to the interpretation of intellectual property law for engineers and managers. This broad background is highly relevant at Laytons, Solicitors, where she now advises clients on all aspects of intellectual property. She is a Director of FAST, the Federation Against Software Theft.

Clifford Lees, after a traditional engineering apprenticeship, was employed as a draughtsman at David Brown Gears and the then English Electric Company, so that he has first hand experience of design. Entering the patent profession in 1952, he has remained with the same firm (now Appleyard Lees of Halifax) and is now senior partner. Clifford is the author of a book, *Patent Protection*, published in 1965 which is still used by some as a primer to the profession. He has given numerous lectures on intellectual property especially on patent and design matters. As Chairman of the Home Laws Committee and a member of the Design and Copyright Committee of the CIPA, he was involved in discussions with the DTI leading up to and during the progress of the bill which became the Copyright, Designs and Patents Act 1988.

Jacqueline Needle is a graduate in electrical and electronic engineering from the University of Leeds. She has worked in a number of firms of patent agents since joining the profession in 1969, and is now a partner of W.H. Beck, Greener & Co., of Lincoln's Inn. As well as advising clients generally in all areas of intellectual property, she has a varied patent practice covering a wide area of technology, and is a specialist in design and copyright. In 1987, she became the first woman to be elected to the Council of the CIPA. She is currently an enthusiastic Chairman of the Press and Public Relations Committee of the Institute and is concerned to make British industry more aware of the value of intellectual property laws in general, and of the specialist patent agent in particular.

Harry Shipley read Natural Sciences at Cambridge, and after working for BICC and the Institution of Electrical Engineers he joined the General Post Office in 1968. He trained and qualified as a Chartered Patent Agent within the Intellectual Property Unit of British Telecom, and for some years has specialized in licensing, including the licensing of software and the intellectual property aspects of taxation. He has written various articles on licensing and lectured both internally and externally on the subject. Harry has now been appointed Manager, Licensing with British Steel plc.

Keith Weatherald, armed with a BSc degree in physics and mathematics from Queen Mary College, London, did a graduate apprenticeship with the BICC group, and then joined the Patent Department of BICC. After a few years, he went into private practice with D. Young & Co., London then to IBM (UK) Limited, The British Oxygen Co. Limited, and on to his present job as Patents Manager of the Xerox Corporation's London Patent Operation.

He has spent many years on the Council of the CIPA, was its President in 1986/87, and is on the Council of the European Patent Institute. Being committed to education he is a co-organizer of, and lecturer on, the Queen Mary and Westfield College course leading to the Certificate in Intellectual Property Law. He also lectures on technology transfer at the Centre International d'Etudes de la Proprieté Industrielle, Strasbourg, and is the Chair of the Board of Supervisory Examiners of the CIPA.

Foreword

The concept of intellectual property has recently acquired much prominence. Industrial managers have long appreciated the value of ideas, but their exploitation has largely been a fringe consideration. Patenting has more often been intended as protection of a domestic market rather than as a springboard for growth. The internationalization of trade and the growing need for collaboration in research with other companies, including potential competitors, has forced all those seriously involved in the business of innovation to examine their procedures.

Not everyone finds this easy. Patent law is complex, varying from country to country, and the choice between licensing and exploitation abroad requires fine judgment. Moreover, few seem to understand how the Treaty of Rome, with its insistence on the removal of barriers to free competition, can complicate the establishment of friendly cooperative agreements between like-minded companies. It has also to be confessed that innovators rarely want to spend the time necessary to understand the problems of those entrusted with the protection of the inventions.

This situation will certainly be made more tolerable by the publication of this Guide. Though written by legally-trained contributors, the words set the scene simply. The contents also make clear that IP is not just a matter of patents. The balance of importance between computer hardware and software is rapidly shifting, and those who are not aware of the need to protect computer programs that are truly the key to their novel systems will surely live to regret it. In industry we are often asked to sign, or have others sign, confidentiality agreements without knowing our legal responsibilities. The more one ponders on the complications that stem from successful research, the more one recognizes the need for professional help. There are organizations that are apparently oblivious of the problems. Those in UK universities who call for freedom to license their patents might well read the section on litigation, and appreciate that your patent is only as strong as your will to fight infringements, and your resources to carry the fight through the courts.

Everyone interested in the interplay between innovation and exploitation will welcome this addition to the literature. It provides a helpful guide to the way forward, carefully avoiding pedantry and obscurity, the twin weapons of many lawyers, and will ease the task of operating successfully in the developing world of IP.

C Hilsum
Director of Research GEC plc
June 1990

Introduction: using this book

Intellectual Property (IP) is the general term for different types of ideas protected by different legal rights. The law recognizes that the time spent on originating new concepts is an investment which needs to be protected so the originator or owner has the opportunity to benefit. IP is not limited to technical ideas, although this is a major application; trade marks cover all types of product or service; confidential information includes strategic plans and marketing data; copyright covers every business document.

The aim of the authors is to help managers in industry in the broadest sense of that word: service industry as well as manufacturing industry, indeed any technical business. Innovation is not limited to large research laboratories, any improvement to a product or service generates IP to some extent.

A manager needs to know what to look out for in most circumstances so as to give appropriate protection to new ideas and to avoid being sued. This book considers the position that applies perhaps 95 per cent of the time. Inevitably detail is glossed over. The 'ifs and buts' are ignored. It is not a book for practitioners and is not intended to replace practitioners, rather it helps a manager to decide when to call in an expert.

For the six different intellectual property rights (*confidential information, trade mark, copyright, registered design, design right* and *patent*) each chapter explains the type of idea which the right protects, the legal benefits and limitations, and goes on to explain how to get the right and how to keep it in force.

The general assumption is that an idea is generated by an employee in a UK company, so the nationality rules which limit availability of some types of protection are ignored. In some cases, such as patents, the position abroad is covered in some detail; in others it is not. Readers should be aware that the law overseas may be quite different from UK law.

Two technical areas are highlighted, computer software and semiconductor chips, because they are so central to British industry. The specialized field of biological innovation is mentioned only in Chapter 6, on patents, although many general principles explained elsewhere will apply to it. Copyright applied to non-business literature, or to fine arts or music, is touched on only briefly.

References to and quotations from statute law and regulations are minimized and decided cases are included only if they are crucial. Some cases, which are relevant but not vital, are placed in annexes at the end of some chapters for readers interested in more detail.

The chapters are centred on the type of legal right, but to guide the reader in approaching legal protection from the practical position, the matrix in Table I.1 shows which chapters may be relevant to different types of record of an innovative idea.

Table I.1 Which chapter?

Protection needed for: / Protection that may apply	Confidential information Chapter 1	Trade marks Chapter 2	Copyright Chapter 3	Design right Chapter 4	Topography right Chapter 5	Registered design Chapter 4	Patents Chapter 6
Many words on paper	✓	—	✓	—	—	—	—
Name of company, product or brand	—	✓	—	—	—	—	—
Pictorial design or logotype	—	✓	✓	—	—	—	—
Technical drawing on paper	✓	—	✓	✓	✓	✓	✓
Mechanical device with moving parts	—	—	—	✓	—	✓	✓
Mechanical device with no moving parts	—	—	—	✓	—	✓	✓
Electrical device	—	—	—	✓	✓	—	✓
Computer program	✓	—	✓	—	✓	—	✓
Test method	✓	—	—	—	—	—	✓
Manufacturing method	✓	—	—	—	—	—	✓
Chemical process	✓	—	—	—	—	—	✓
Chemical compound	—	—	—	—	—	—	✓

Once an idea has been generated the question of ownership of the rights in it arises, and is dealt with in Chapter 7 for all types of IP. When the IP is protected, by registration if appropriate, using it may involve licensing and Chapter 8 covers the general principles. The assumption is made that two commercial parties are involved, and the special user right of the Crown is not considered. Chapter 8 also considers the effect of EC law and regulations, and the taxation position on payments received. Chapter 9 deals with IP strategies, and the ultimate position, litigation.

All of the authors are chartered patent agents and European patent attorneys. This means that we all started with a technical training and then learned the law relevant to the protection of technology, as part of our professional qualification. We believe this enables us to understand the innovation process, and the practical concerns of innovators and their managers. This book addresses those concerns.

1 Confidential information

Vivien Irish

Introduction

All businesses have information of value to their competitors, varying from technical specifications through pricing information to customer address lists. Few businesses are totally self-sufficient, so there is frequently the need to disclose information to sub-contractors or to independent experts for services such as marketing. In most businesses, employees come and go—and some information goes with them.

This chapter covers the law relating to control of information which is in any degree confidential, and sets out what cannot be controlled. It also includes the obligations of employees with respect to confidential information belonging to their current or previous employer, and the rights of ex-employees to continue to work in the same field.

Since this is a book primarily for managers, it does not cover personal confidences, nor artistic or literary confidences, and does not extend to government or defence secrecy.

What is confidential information?

Some types of information can be kept totally secret for decades, such as the recipe for a liqueur which can be limited to a very small number of people at any time and stays secure. Most business information is not important for so long and is not capable of such a degree of security, but the English courts have recognized that information should be protected provided that it is of the right type.

There is no statute law of confidentiality in England, so there are no overall definitions as to what can be included. The current position has developed through decisions made by the courts in various types of legal dispute, as judges considered whether the material in question merited protection and what the equitable position was. The effect of this process is that the legal position can change substantially because of one particular case which comes to court and the decisions made on it.

The aim has always been to find a balance and to reach a reasonable position. The word 'reasonable' has been used by several judges as they considered what a reasonable person would believe and do. The rights of the owner of information have been balanced against the rights of other parties who should be constrained only to a reasonable degree for a reasonable length of time, or not at all.

The sort of information which has been considered by the courts to be confidential has in the last few decades included the design of a carpet grip, a formula for gold ink, test results on pharmaceuticals, a card index of client names and addresses, and an idea for a television programme; another case was based on the details of a manufacturing process for making leather punches. In other words, 'know-how' is protectable. The technology range has varied from a method of constructing a brassiere to a method of constructing an above-ground swimming pool.

The scope has been set less by the type of material than by other factors such as the need for effort to duplicate the information—the originator's investment of thought, time and effort deserves protection. A simple method of cleaning ships' hulls which saved time and money was held confidential—simplicity was not a disqualification. Negative information can also be valuable, such as the knowledge that one line of research has failed. Information can be available to a few people, rather than truly secret, and still be protected.

Almost invariably the type of information held to be confidential is specific and well defined. It is often technical, but business information—such as marketing and sales details—is also clearly included if it is of sufficient importance to a company.

What is excluded?
Information which is easily available to the public cannot be protected, although a selection from it involving effort and expenditure can be valuable and therefore protectable. If the information never was secret, such as an incident occurring in a public place (perhaps misbehaviour by a well-known person), it cannot be 'made' secret to restrain its publication.

There may also be a public duty to disclose a public wrong, for example knowledge of a crime, but that is outside the scope of this book, and so is the legal position of information acquired by illegal means such as electronic eavesdropping.

If the information can be discovered by analysis, such as chemical analysis applied to an ointment for treating blisters on horses, the owner of the recipe cannot prevent that analysis, or manufacture and sale of an identical product. This also applies to a liqueur recipe but other intellectual property rights, such as trade marks and reputation, could make the duplication commercially unattractive.

For engineered products put on the market, competitors are permitted to take them apart, analyse them and use the results of analysis to design a similar product—this is called *reverse engineering*—but there is no automatic permission to use other types of intellectual property rights which might be involved, such as patents or design rights.

Confidential information cannot be used to place constraints on genuinely independent research and development. It is quite possible for two research workers to reach the same result at about the same time, for example in the last century Swan and Edison both developed the electric filament lamp. Apparent breach of confidence can be no more than sheer coincidence.

The general approach is that if you have put effort into generating information, you can stop others benefiting from it by merely taking it, but you cannot place unreasonable constraints on others, especially ex-employees, see page 10 below.

Confidential disclosures: when do they occur?

There are two main types of disclosure of confidential information. The first is when an independent third party needs to have it, probably in a business different from, but complementary to, that of the discloser; the second relates to employees who learn something relating to a business—and employees sometimes generate confidential information themselves during their work.

In both cases there can be an explicit agreement when the parties know and agree in advance that the information in question is confidential. While there is no law to say that such an agreement should be in writing, a record of it minimizes the risk of disagreement later.

Confidentiality can also be implied: if the circumstances of the transfer to a third party are such that a reasonable person should have realized that the information was not being given away, there will still be an obligation not to misuse it. Employees also have a duty to keep their employers' proprietary information confidential.

Third party relationships

Examples of planned disclosure for a particular purpose will, typically, involve a consultant or expert of some kind having a skill in another field such as marketing or a particular technical area; specific information will be supplied so that the expert can plan a project or solve a problem. If another company is to manufacture a component for your product, it will need specifications and drawings which may disclose important details. There may be disclosure to several other companies, for example when there is a competitive tender—all tenderers will need the information but the intention is that while the winner of the contract may use it, the others must not.

Major disclosures also take place when a company is negotiating with a prospective licensee to make a product or provide a service in different markets and pay royalties for use of the information. Even at the preliminary stages of discussions the other party will need information to decide whether to negotiate or pull out.

There are many other examples of a need to disclose, for example to a potential financial backer, or a potential business partner. A computer bureau may have the company sales figures or the customer address list. If your product needs installation or maintenance services, which you do not yourself provide, a distributor or a maintenance company will need product details to carry out its work.

The common link is that confidential information must be transferred. The information is known, the recipient is known, and there is usually time to record the position in a written *confidentiality agreement*.

Written agreements with third parties
A confidentiality agreement can be as short as one paragraph in a letter, or it can be lengthy and formal. There are few standard terms for such agreements, it is more a question of negotiating the wording. The agreement can last forever, but will usually last for a specified time—often the period during which information will be of importance, plus a safety factor. A paragraph may refer to the receiving party treating the confidential information as carefully as that company treats its own valuable information—provided you are sure you are dealing with a reputable business. There may be a promise to make the information available to employees on a need-to-know basis only, and for very important information a request for specific warnings to employees, or even individual agreements with them. There may be a promise to return all records after the permitted use is finished; this would be particularly important in competitive tenders to permit retrieval of information from those who fail in the bidding.

The aim of the agreement will be twofold: to prevent further disclosure of the information and to prevent it from being misused.

Prohibited disclosure
In all agreements, however brief, there should be a clause stating that the confidential information must not be published and must not be disclosed to others in any other way. This need not be a deliberate disclosure, carelessness can be just as damaging. In one case an accountant left an instruction letter from a client where it could be read by another visitor, and this was held to be misuse of confidential information in the letter. (The letter contained a libellous statement but protection was still given to it even though the author did not have 'clean hands'.)

Prohibited use
The general principle that the receiver of confidential information may not use it for his own benefit was established in the case *Terrapin Limited* v. *Builders Supply Company (Hayes) Limited* which can be found in *Reports of Patent Cases 1967*, p. 375.

Terrapin had designed a portable building which was manufactured by Builders Supply under contract. When the work was completed, Builders Supply started to make a similar portable building using Terrapin's design information. Terrapin took legal action.

In court, Builders Supply argued that the construction of the building was evident from dismantling it so any purchaser could have found out what the design was. The court held that anyone analysing the structure in this way would have had to generate plans and specifications and would have needed to build a prototype and test it. Builders Supply had avoided all this by using the information from Terrapin: this was wrongful. Builders Supply could not use the confidential information as a springboard for an unfair start over companies which had to do their own preparatory work. Builders Supply was stopped from proceeding further.

This 'springboard' principle has been widely applied ever since and conditions which prevent recipients of confidential information from using it to gain an unfair head start are common.

The agreement might limit use of the information to manufacture for the discloser or the preparation of a tender or marketing survey. The use should be defined carefully and as narrowly as possible, either in positive terms (the information is to be used only for manufacture and supply to this company) or in negative terms (there must be no manufacture or provision of service to any other organization), or both.

Exceptions

Because the law has developed as excluding material which is already public, the longer formal agreements often include releases from confidentiality. If the information is made public through no fault of the recipient, or if it is received legally by another route, or even generated independently if this can be proved, then the information ceases to be constrained by the agreement. Typical release phrases are given in Box 1.

Box 1 Confidentiality release clauses

The ABC company will keep the information confidential unless:

1. it comes into the public domain through no fault of the ABC company; or
2. it is already in the possession of the ABC company; or
3. it is disclosed to the ABC company by a third party; or
4. it is generated independently by the ABC company

and the ABC company can provide documentary proof thereof.

Third parties and implied confidence
Unfortunately not all disclosures of information are made after signing a confidentiality agreement, or even after a verbal reference to confidence. Fortunately the law has developed so that an obligation to protect the material can be implied from the circumstances in which it changes hands. This applies to professional relationships such as medical, financial and legal advisors, and also in direct business meetings.

If a reasonable person would realize that information had been given in confidence then the recipient has an obligation to protect it. When some of Queen Victoria's etchings were sent to a printer, he was expected to keep them confidential. When you discuss a possible joint venture with a potential partner and disclose details of your product and pricing, the other side should realize that this is a confidential discussion. If you supply a mould to a moulding firm for production of your product, it is reasonable to assume that you do not intend it to be copied or to be used to supply your competitors.

If there is no written agreement before information is handed over, it may still be possible to argue implied confidence and record the agreement later in a document signed by both sides. If the recipient of the information refuses to be bound, litigation may be the only solution.

Visitors
Meetings which have exchange of information as their object clearly need confidentiality conditions, but details of a product or service or commercial plans can be acquired, deliberately or involuntarily, by visitors to a factory or office and particularly to research and development

---

Box 2   Visitors' Confidentiality Agreement
This very short agreement is suitable for use at a research and development facility:

I, ... (insert name)
of
....
(insert address of self or employer)
visiting the premises of the XYZ company for the purpose of
....
(insert brief reason)

acknowledge that during my visit I may have access to information which is confidential to the XYZ company. I agree that I will not disclose this information to any third party without the prior written consent of the XYZ company nor use it in any way (except for the purpose of ....
................................) (either insert narrow definition or delete words in brackets).

laboratories. A written reminder of the visitor's obligations can be helpful. A short Visitor's Confidentiality Agreement, to be signed on arriving at Reception, can help to avoid unauthorized disclosures (see Box 2).

Employees

Employees have freedom to change their jobs, so there is also a need for their ex-employer to control the company's confidential information while not interfering with the ex-employee's freedom. This section begins by considering the obligations during employment, then looks at the rights and obligations of ex-employees, then returns to the employment situation to draw lessons for both sides.

Current employees

All employees have a duty to their employer not to disclose confidential information obtained during their employment or as a result of their employment. Even if there is a contract of employment and it does not mention confidence, there is an implied obligation of 'faithful service'— an employee must not use the employer's information for his or her own benefit or give it away. An employee must also disclose relevant information to the employer and not conceal, for example, the existence of a patent relevant to the employer's business and owned by another company—the employee is certainly not free to leave the company and negotiate patent rights on his or her own behalf.

During employment, employees build up their skill and knowledge and the business benefits from their greater effectiveness. Typical words used by the courts relating to an employee's skill and knowledge are 'information which is part of the workman himself', the employee's 'skill and dexterity, manual or mental ability'. The employer has no right to control this skill, which belongs entirely to the employee.

Also during employment, employees will learn how the business is run and may have access to what are undoubtedly trade secrets, such as secret recipes or processes. They may themselves generate such information on behalf of the employer. The day comes when an employee wishes to leave. The employer sees the departing employee as confidential information personified, especially if the ex-employee is about to set up in competition. The ex-employee wants to earn a living. Confidential information is the battleground. The grey area between the employer's trade secrets on the one hand and the employee's skill and knowledge on the other gives scope for disagreement.

The courts recognize that an ex-employee has every right to compete with an ex-employer and also has the right to continue to use general skill and knowledge. But trade secrets must not be carried away and there is no implication that the employee is free to use information just because it has been memorized.

A recent important case in the Court of Appeal has clarified several points in this area and indicates lines of good management practice. It is known as *Faccenda Chicken* v. *Fowler* and can be found at *1986 Fleet Street Reports*, p. 291.

The Faccenda Chicken case

Faccenda Chicken Limited bred, reared and slaughtered chickens and chilled them for supply to the wholesale market. Mr Fowler, Faccenda's Sales Manager, developed the concept of supplying the chilled chickens direct to retailers using refrigerated vans covering different geographical areas. Mr Fowler was familiar with the customers' names and addresses, their usual requirements and the prices charged. He then left Faccenda Chicken and set up in competition supplying many of the same customers using identical delivery routes, and he was joined by other ex-employees of the Company.

Faccenda Chicken applied for an injunction to stop Mr Fowler using confidential information obtained during his employment, that is the customers' names and addresses, the supply routes and the pricing information. Faccenda lost in the High Court, appealed, and lost again.

The Court of Appeal confirmed the long-held position that an employer can protect his or her trade secrets and information of similar importance but that a departing employee may still use his or her skill and knowledge.

In the middle ground, the judgment makes it clear that a current employee has greater obligations to keep information confidential than a former employee. Some information, which a current employee could disclose only by breaching these obligations, cannot be controlled by the employer once an employee leaves.

To determine whether there is an implied obligation on the ex-employee to keep information confidential, the court ruled that all factors of the case must be considered, including:

1. The nature of the employment—was the job of high status and such that access to confidential information was frequent? If so, the ex-employee has a higher obligation to keep it secret than if access was rare.
2. The nature of the information—was it a trade secret, or was it of a highly confidential nature equivalent to a trade secret? If so, then the ex-employee must not use or disclose it.
3. Did the employer notify the employee of the confidential nature of the information? The employer's attitude helps to determine the degree of protection given by confidentiality.
4. Could the information be easily isolated from other information?

Again, the way the employer deals with the information throws light on the level of protection which should be accorded to it.

The customer lists, delivery routes and pricing information at issue in Faccenda Chicken failed at least tests 2, 3 and 4. The court held that the sales routes were not confidential, they were well known to the salespeople responsible for the areas who referred to them frequently and were also known to van drivers and to secretaries. There was no question of knowledge of the routes being restricted to higher level staff. The pricing information might have been considered as a trade secret but it was not kept separate from the other information. The management of Faccenda Chicken had not instructed their employees that the information was confidential.

Thus the various items of information could not be classified as trade secrets and Mr Fowler and the ex-employees could not be restrained from using them.

Even after the Faccenda case, the words 'trade secret' are still undefined. Probably the full range of technical or commercial, written or unwritten, information can still be protected by confidentiality if it is of sufficient importance to a company. It was not the nature of the information which caused Faccenda to lose its case but its lack of crucial importance—pricing information can still be of the same nature as a trade secret, for example when it relates to the price of a new model of car, or the price of different grades of oil in a very competitive market, and ex-employees would then be unable to use it.

Further, the names and addresses of Faccenda's customers were not excluded from protection on the grounds that the list could be memorized but, at least in part, because the way that the material was handled by the Company was not in line with its alleged importance. However, the court indicated that employees must not deliberately memorize customer lists for further use.

How to manage confidential information
Some of the Faccenda Chicken tests for trade secrets are parallel to good business practice. If information is of great importance to a firm, it should be treated appropriately. Employees should be told that it is confidential, especially if they rarely handle secret material. Access to it should be restricted, for example on a 'need-to-know' basis, and the information should be kept separate from non-confidential information to maintain its identity and integrity. On the other hand, no amount of careful handling will boost relatively unimportant information to 'trade secret' level.

The earliest warning which can be given to employees is in their contract of employment on joining the company. A general warning that the work may involve use of confidential information and of the need to handle it correctly can be included. But the restraint should be fair. There should be no promise to keep *all* information of the company a secret, the courts would not uphold such an unreasonably restrictive condition.

Even with an express reference to confidentiality in all employment contracts, another lesson of Faccenda Chicken is that reminders to staff about particularly important items will help an employer's arguments that the material should be protected.

One way of warning staff is to mark the information, for example 'commercial in confidence' (this distinguishes the material from the Ministry of Defence classification of 'confidential'). The information should be kept carefully, and not merged with other less important material, and made available only to staff who need it.

Similar treatment should be applied to information received in confidence from third parties, with reminders to staff of its nature.

Notice period
The obligations of an ex-employee are certainly much less onerous than those of a current employee. Ex-employees can use their skill and knowledge for the benefit of competitors; they could not do that while employed. As the Faccenda Chicken case sets out, an ex-employee can use information of a previous employer, provided it is not a trade secret, while a current employee must not breach his duty of good faith by disclosing the employer's confidential information which is of lower status.

What should management do when an employee gives notice? First, the obligation of good faith still applies until the contract of employment terminates. An employee is not allowed to start collecting information for use in the future; in one case a departing employee was ordered to deliver up records of confidential information. But in another case, a court found nothing wrong with an employee, in the notice period, setting up a competing business although he was not permitted to solicit existing customers. Therefore there is an implication that the obligations of an employee may be less after giving notice.

To clarify risks and minimize them, a practical step is to set up an exit interview. This can be with the line manager or personnel department. The interview should review what 'trade secret' information (using the Faccenda Chicken tests) has been made available to the employee and is an excellent time for reminders about obligations to keep it confidential.

Restrictive covenants
Whatever the difficulties of defining the middle ground between the rights of employers and employees, there has never been any doubt that a business can protect its trade secrets. Employees can be restrained even after they leave a firm and one way of placing specific limitations is in the

form of a *restrictive covenant*, in other words, a legal agreement setting out what the employee can and cannot do after leaving employment.

There can be an explicit prohibition on using trade secrets. (In fact, there is no need for a covenant because such a limitation is implicit anyway but the covenant acts as a reminder.) To limit loss of customers, it may be possible in appropriate circumstances to prevent an employee taking a job with a specific competitor for a given period, perhaps one year, or to restrain him or her from competing in a specific geographical area; these limitations are broader than the restrictions without a covenant, but may be justifiable to protect the employer.

As with all matters relating to confidential information, the restrictive covenant must be reasonable, given all the circumstances. A sales representative can be restrained from soliciting previous customers, but an ex-employee cannot be prevented from earning a living and the limitations cannot last for ever.

In the Faccenda case there was no restrictive covenant binding Mr Fowler. If there had been one, he would probably have been forbidden to set up business so close to Faccenda and from approaching Faccenda's customers for a reasonable period.

Because there is a need to strike a delicate balance between the rights of both sides, drafting 'reasonable' restrictive covenants is notoriously difficult. Since the covenant will be drafted on the instructions of the employer, there is a strong possibility of too tight a restraint. While the existence of this form of protection for an employer needs to be noted, it should only be used when the risk of the loss of a secret to a competitor or the loss of customers outweighs the considerable risk of the whole covenant being held invalid by a court.

Legal remedies

While many disagreements about confidential information can be settled by negotiation, there are times when more forceful action is felt to be necessary and formal legal proceedings are begun. There are three basic requirements: the information must be confidential; it must have been disclosed in circumstances which impose an obligation on the receiving party to keep it confidential; and that obligation must have been breached.

Legal remedies generally are discussed briefly in Chapter 9.

Computer software and escrow

A special case of disclosure of confidential information arises with computer programs in source code, in other words, the form of the program which is written and can be read by human beings. Access to it is essential for a program to be altered or corrected and then converted into the computer-comprehensible object code form.

A frequent situation is that a small software house writes a special program for a large company to use under licence. The user finds the program crucial to the business, either technically or commercially, and starts to wonder what happens if the small company goes out of business and stops maintaining the program. The large company asks for the source code so it can maintain the program in-house, the small company resists, fearing the information will fall into the hands of its rivals.

The solution is an escrow agreement in which an independent third party holds the code in secure conditions and releases it to the licensee if the software house does come to an untimely end. While any third party, such as a bank, can provide the service, knowledge of proper storage of computer media is advisable. The National Computing Centre runs a service with standard charges and conditions. It also has a scheme for a program licensed to a large number of companies, each of which would have access if the owner of the source code was unable to maintain it.

Disadvantages of confidentiality

As protection for valuable information, confidentiality has three main disadvantages. If the obligation of confidence is breached, the information can never be made truly confidential again. There is no protection against independent generation, and the third difficulty, following from the first, is that if information is disclosed in breach of confidence to an innocent third party, that party cannot be stopped from using it or making further disclosures.

A management system which ensures proper dealing with confidential information can be onerous and expensive, and must walk a tightrope between making sure staff are aware of the need to protect the information and avoiding blurring the message by repeating it too often.

Unrecorded confidential information

Most transfers of confidential information involve a record of some sort: of words, figures or diagrams on paper, film, tape or disk. Records are not an essential factor, information can be given verbally, and it can be received by looking and listening.

A special category of confidential information occurs when information cannot be recorded and can only be demonstrated. Even recordable information can sometimes be transferred far more quickly and effectively by demonstration. In a licence agreement, training of the licensee's personnel may be an important part, and some of the information transfer may be by watching others use a machine or control a process. If this type of information is to be protected, extreme care will be needed; it should be clear that by its very nature it is likely to form part of an employee's skill and knowledge, and therefore be uncontrollable by the originator. This is one of the reasons why a substantial downpayment is normal when confidential information is transferred as part of a licence grant—it helps to cover the risk to the discloser.

Demonstrable information is sometimes called 'show-how', perhaps because Common Market regulations on know-how require it to be 'secret, substantial and identified in any appropriate form', that is, the know-how must be recorded.

Unsolicited technical suggestions
Companies known to the general public often receive suggestions for improving their product or service. The suggestions are mostly impractical, but sometimes they are useful. What does the company do if it is already working on the idea? This is often the case when there is a substantial research and development function. If the company turns a suggestion down and then later appears to use it, accusations of stealing ideas will be made, probably in the popular press.

One solution is to return the material to the originator, agreeing to look at the idea in detail only if a patent application is filed. The patent specification then acts as a disclosure document and has an official date. This does not work if the originator is not prepared to pay for the application, or if the idea is very simple.

Another solution is to send the material back and agree to look at it only if it is submitted on a non-confidential basis. This avoids the technical argument of breach of confidence, but not necessarily the claims of unfair treatment.

Neither method avoids the basic difficulty—the company has seen the original letter and therefore to some extent has unavoidably received confidential information. One method of dealing with this is for all suspect mail of this type to be dealt with by non-technical staff who immediately send out a standard letter, explaining that no technical person has looked at it. The letter can be short and friendly if the company wants to attract ideas and keep potential customers happy, or long, complex and legalistic if the aim is to discourage further contacts.

Summary
English law recognizes the rights of a business to protect its trade secrets, and also other information generated by expending time and effort. Third parties wishing to use it can be stopped from publishing it or disclosing it to others, and limited to using it for specified purposes. Preferably a written agreement records the position before the confidential information is disclosed. If this is forgotten and a reasonable person would realize

from the circumstances that disclosure was made in confidence, then similar obligations can apply. If the information is easily available to the public, its use cannot be restricted and it is not confidential.

Employees have a duty of good faith to their employer, and must not use trade secrets or their own skill to the employer's disadvantage. When employees leave, they may then use their skill and even set up in competition, but they cannot use any trade secrets or similar highly confidential information.

An employer should treat confidential information carefully, warning employees it is confidential, keeping it separate from other information, restricting access to it and, perhaps, marking it. Employers can also consider including a paragraph on confidentiality in contracts of employment and setting up an exit interview system.

2 Trade marks

Richard Gallafent

What is a trade mark?
Since antiquity it has been the practice of manufacturers to mark their goods with an identifying and unique mark. Providers of services, most notably stonemasons, have also adopted the practice for centuries. It is done, in essence, to distinguish the goods or services of one provider from those of another.

This simple concept is most valuable in a highly developed market with a number of competing suppliers providing essentially the same product. From the point of view of the consumer, there is little to choose between one sort of breakfast cereal and another or one sort of washing powder and another. Both may be made essentially of the same raw materials and do much the same job. They may not even differ much in price. What differentiates them, particularly in a modern consumer market economy, is the trade mark applied by the manufacturer.

In many areas, it is quite obvious when a trade mark *is* a trade mark. However, other markings appear associated with goods and it is useful to contrast some of them with trade marks in order to focus on the distinctions between them. Thus quality marks, marks required by law, for example, to indicate hazardous ingredients, handling precautions, or compliance with accepted standards (for example a DIN or BS marking) are not trade marks. Neither is a varietal name, applied, for example, to a type of flower or vegetable or to a type of beer or wine. Nor again is a statement of origin a trade mark, for example 'Printed in the USA' or 'Appellation Controlée' accompanied by the particular 'Appellation'.

Between a brand name and the various other types of marking there is a middle ground, most easily identified by the following simple test: is the mark one which is clearly free for use by anyone, albeit that certain conditions may need to be met to enable its legitimate use, or is it a mark which can be legitimately monopolized by one person or company? If the former, it is not a trade mark. If the latter, it is. The middle ground, sometimes referred to as that of the 'collective mark', is where a group of people can monopolize a particular mark.

The various kinds of marking just noted have different functions in practice. The basic function of a trade mark is to associate whatever the mark is used on with a particular source. In the case of a mark used on goods, that source is often the manufacturer, though it need not be so. The most obvious case where it is not so is that of 'own brand' goods, which are not made by the retailer in question but which are made for the retailer, assumedly to certain standards of quality which the retailer sets down and the purchaser can trust. The same approach can operate in connection with services. The services provided by a franchisee are not generally provided by the owner of the mark used to identify the particular service, but the franchisor is assumed to control the quality of the service provided and ensure it comes up to the same standards everywhere.

The UK Trade Marks Registry (of which more below) regards a trade mark as a mark which is used on goods and a service mark as one which is used in association with services. The same mark can, of course, be used both as a trade mark and as a service mark, using this terminology. In this chapter, the term *trade mark* will be used as covering marks applied to goods or used in association with services, or both.

In both cases, the function of the mark is to identify goods or services connected with the mark owner and distinguish them from others. Promotion of the trade mark by means of advertising is designed to fix the mark in the mind of the potential customer for the goods or service in question so that that particular brand is chosen in preference to others. If the goods or service are satisfactory, the consumer assumes that he or she will be able to secure the same again by sticking to the same brand.

Thus, both in order to attract business and to continue with repeat business, a trade mark or identity is important.

Equitably, the adoption and use of a particular mark builds up reputation. That requires investment in time and effort. Once that investment has been made, it is clearly inequitable that it should be stolen by others or that others should improperly take advantage of it. One way in which others may take advantage of reputation built up by a manufacturer or trader is by adopting and using in connection with their goods and services a mark built up by others. Clearly, this principle should apply not only to use of the identical mark, but to use of a mark so close or similar to the original that customers will be deceived.

Types of trade mark
Trade marks may take many different forms. The most obvious is the word mark. This is often an invented word, that is, a made-up word with no meaning, but need not be. An alternative mark is a two-dimensional symbol. This is sometimes called a design or device mark. Intermediate between these two types are marks which are predominantly a word or words but which have pictorial characteristics to them. These are often called logotypes. Also there is a wide range of marks which combine both pictorial elements and words. One example of this is the so-called label

mark. Figure 2.1 shows examples of these various types of mark. The figure does not show a three-dimensional mark (such as the carved mouse running up the leg of a chair), or a traditional 'mason's mark' carved into stone, nor does it show other marks not so easily represented in book form, for example a sequence of musical notes or advertising 'jingle' or a container shape.

The classification just set out and illustrated in Figure 2.1 classifies marks according to intrinsic type. Sometimes marks are classified internally in an organization by the way in which they are used. Thus, a mark which is used in connection with everything the company does may well be called a 'housemark' while marks which are only used on individual brands or product lines may be called a product mark or brand. Sometimes there is the use of a further mark to indicate affiliation with a large group, which may be called, for example, a group housemark or (if it is in logotype form) a group logo.

Protection of trade marks
It has long been felt that people who build up reputation in trade marks should be protected against others misusing their marks or something very similar to them. There are two ways in which protection is given.

The first way is non-statutory in many countries and is a sort of 'common law' protection. The second way is by a statutory system of registration. Before looking at either in detail, they should be contrasted.

Protection at common law is reactive. Protection by trade mark registration is proactive. In the first case, if circumstances arise in which damage is being done to a legitimate business by the use of a mark which has been used in the business, or something very similar to that, and all the circumstances are such that there is some form of confusion or misrepresentation, then such damaging action by third parties may be restrained. Action which is not damaging may sometimes be quite unrestrainable. Much depends on the circumstances and prevailing conditions in the trade at the time. In particular, the effects on the consumer are often given much greater weight than any feelings of the protagonists. In the United Kingdom, cases of this nature tend to be lumped together under the heading 'passing off '; in the United States, the same term is used or the allied term 'palming off '; and in many continental jurisdictions case law under so-called 'unfair competition' statutes has developed on the basis that the misappropriation of the trade mark of another, or of something very similar to it, in circumstances which give rise to confusion or deception, is an act of unfair competition.

In contrast to this, trade mark registration, in connection with which the trade mark owner is proactive, has to take some positive action, provides a different scenario. Registration of one's trade mark gives a statutory

Word mark (invented) **QACA**

Word marks (not invented) **ADMIRAL** **SHIRLEY**

Device marks

Logotypes

  **MAXISTORE**

Composite (device + words)

Label mark

Monogram mark

Figure 2.1 Various types of trade mark

right to stop other people using the mark, or a very similar one, in circumstances which could give rise to confusion or deception and which could be damaging. As will appear below, this broad approach is not without its provisos and limitations, but trade mark registration enables the owner of the mark to take the high ground against competitors who misappropriate the mark, or adopt something improperly close to it. In many cases the owner of the mark may succeed in stopping activities of which the owner does not approve before those activities reach the stage at which they are actually damaging.

Indeed, trade mark registration, because it requires a claim to protection to be staked in a publicly available place, open to inspection, has a substantial deterrent effect. Anyone contemplating legitimately starting a business in a given area of services, or adopting a trade mark on particular goods, can look to see what marks have already been registered in order to see whether any party holds a registration which could be exerted against the proposed use. If there is no such registration, and no one with unregistered but substantial reputation in the same or a similar mark (and thus no threat of a passing off action), it makes good sense to adopt the mark proposed. If, on the other hand, the mark proposed or something very similar to it is already registered, the would-be user knows to choose another mark or, possibly, acquire the mark that has been registered from its registered owner whose name can, of course, be found out from the Register.

UK trade mark registration law
For over 100 years UK statute law has provided for a Register of Trade Marks kept by the Patent Office under a 'Registrar'. The Register he keeps provides a publicly accessible, searchable list of marks.

The current UK statute is the Trade Marks Act 1938. This, and the 'secondary legislation', the Trade Mark Rules, provide the basis on which the UK trade mark registration system operates. Since 1938 there have been a few changes in the law by amendment of the Act, but the basic structure has remained unchanged for 50 years. The most important change, in 1986, was the extension of the Register to enable marks to be registered for services as well as for goods. A more recent change (in 1989) is to make the fraudulent use of a registered mark (e.g. when one is applied as part of the production of counterfeit goods) a criminal offence.

The basic function of the Registrar, under the statute, is to maintain the Register, that is, the list of marks registered with the relevant details of each registration. The statute also sets out the rights of the proprietor or owner of the registration, once the mark is on the Register. The owner of the mark is given the right to stop other people using the mark or something confusingly similar to the mark. There is a further qualification: the right is only to stop the use of the mark, or a closely similar mark, on goods or services covered by the registration. Quite clearly, there is no problem in practice if two people use the same mark in entirely different areas of trade. TOOTLEBUG could happily be used by one manufacturer for agricultural chemicals and a different manufacturer for musical instruments. Thus, associated with each mark on the Register is a so-called 'specification' of goods or services in respect of which that mark is registered.

The Register is divided in two ways. First it is divided into two parts called Part A and Part B. The historical reasons for this and the technical detail of the division are beyond the scope of this work. Generally speaking, however, Part A is for stronger, more distinctive marks, while Part B registration is available for marks which have a lesser degree of distinctiveness but still have some distinctiveness or capacity to distinguish. In both cases, the registration enables the assertion to be made that the mark is registered (which may itself be enough to put plenty of people off) and, in both cases, the existence of the registration enables the mark to be found by those checking to ensure they do not infringe the rights of others. The rights against third parties provided by Part A registration are, however, wider. Part A registration allows the owner to stop third parties using the mark in most circumstances. Part B registration, on the other hand, enables use to be stopped only if the use would be confusing and deceptive. This is easiest seen the other way round: wholly non-deceptive use of a Part B mark cannot be stopped. Such a non-deceptive use might be, for example, in comparative advertising.

Secondly, the Register is divided up into 42 sections or classes. These 42 classes are made up in turn of 34 classes of goods and 8 of services. Dividing the Register up in this way makes it easier to search for a particular mark proposed for use on particular goods or services. The division is arbitrary, but follows a standard system agreed internationally some time ago. Problems always arise as to whether particular goods should fall into one class or another, so to preserve order, the Registrar has absolute discretion as to where particular goods or services fall. This ensures that (providing the Registrar always stays consistent) the Register stays consistent. In a changing world, however, perfection in this area is not achievable, as the most appropriate class for a given item can change. Last decade's scientific electronic gizmo (normally class 9) can be next year's best selling toy (class 28). For best protection, registration in more than one class may be needed. If you make signs for inside buildings, you will probably have both metal parts (class 6) and plastic ones (class 20), and if you are ambitious you may even have the wonderfully named 'luminous and mechanical' signs in your range—which go into class 9! The 34 goods classes do not have a 'dustbin' class for miscellanea otherwise unclassifiable, though the services classes include class 42, 'Miscellaneous', for services not included in other classes.

What marks can be registered?
Particularly because of the strong rights given by trade mark registration in the United Kingdom, and the protection against infringing the rights of others conferred by registration, UK statute provides that registration is not achieved automatically. Rather, a system of examination of applications is operated to ensure, to the extent reasonably practical, that the marks which are put on the Register are entitled to registration.

In order to be registrable, a mark must be distinctive or, at least for Part B, capable of distinguishing. Two differing types of test are applied by the Trade Mark Office to assess distinctiveness, conveniently thought of as intrinsic and extrinsic distinctiveness. Intrinsic distinctiveness relates to the mark itself; extrinsic to the relationship of the mark in question to the marks of others, usually those that are on the Register, but not exclusively so.

Distinctiveness is conveniently thought of as contrasted with descriptiveness. It must also be considered in relation to the goods or services in respect of which it is to be used. Thus the mark *Black Velvet* is purely descriptive and non-distinctive for cloth of that type coloured that colour. It may, however, be entirely distinctive when applied to agricultural chemicals or cigarettes. A picture of a sailing dinghy is descriptive of such boats but may be distinctive for a range of board games or pickles. A signature is inherently distinctive for goods or of services of any nature whatever.

Extrinsic or external distinctiveness is judged against the marks of others. The similarity may be verbal such as *marwan* and *maruan* or allusive such as *kangaroo* and *wallaby*. The name of an animal may clash with a picture obviously of that animal. Language may be important: *sweetskin* might be considered too close to *peaudouce*.

Application procedure in the United Kingdom
Application procedure is essentially straightforward though the time from application to registration may be long, particularly if problems are encountered during examination or an opposition is filed (see below). Application is made to the Trade Marks Registry (part of the Patent Office, in turn part of the DTI) and an application fee is paid. The application must state the name of the mark owner, provide representations of what the mark is (simply typewritten if it is a word mark, or, e.g. printed or photographs if otherwise) and give an indication of the goods or services in respect of which registration is sought. The specification of goods or services needs to be carefully worded, since the protection given depends

on it and the scope of the wording cannot be broadened beyond that sought at the application date. If you make oboes but want sensible protection against your competitors who make clarinets, you apply to register your mark in respect of woodwind instruments or perhaps just wind instruments or, even more broadly, musical instruments, not just oboes.

The Registry then examines the application. First of all, the application is checked to see if it seems sensible. A covetous approach to the scope of goods or services to be covered can be questioned and will be cut down by the Registrar. A broad specification of goods or services may have to be justified, for example by filing some sort of proof such as a catalogue, price list or (in the case of intention to trade over a wide variety of goods or services) a business plan. If satisfied that the approach is not covetous, the Registry proceeds to examine the application from the intrinsic and extrinsic points of view noted above. It looks at the mark to evaluate its intrinsic distinctiveness and a search of the Register is carried out to see if anything identical or similar is already registered in respect of goods or services identical with, or overlapping or very similar to, those in the application. If such a registration is found, the Registry may 'cite' that earlier registration (or an earlier dated application meeting the same criteria) against the application in question. Sometimes citations may be avoided by argument; other times the specification of goods or services sought may be restricted to avoid the clash or overlap. Sometimes, particularly if a prior search has not been carried out, the citation cannot be overcome in this way. It is then said to be 'fatal' and the application is either not pursued by the applicant or refused by the Registrar. A 'fatal' citation does not always mean that the intended mark cannot be used. The cited mark may be removable from the Register for non-use (see below), or purchasable, or it may simply cease to exist if its registration is not renewed.

In terms of intrinsic registrability, the Registry attempts to see whether the mark applied for is descriptive rather than distinctive. It thus checks to see whether the mark, if it is a word mark, is a mere translation into a foreign language of something which is descriptive about the goods or services in question, as well as looking at the normal English meaning. Device marks, that is, marks with a pictorial content or, indeed, consisting solely of non-verbal material, are likewise assessed. Further tests are made: for example, a surname or a geographical name is assumed to be intrinsically non-distinctive. The thinking behind this is that anyone with a given surname ought to be able to use that surname to identify his or her services or goods, and, likewise, anyone in a particular geographical location ought to be able to draw attention to that fact as well.

These various rules, however, tend to be applied relatively rather than absolutely. Thus, a very rare surname may be more easily registered in respect of goods or services than a relatively common one. It also helps if, although something is a surname, it also has a non-surname significance (e.g. Swift, Castle). In terms of geography, the name of a very small and remote location may be acceptable, particularly if there is little likelihood that the goods would ever be made there or services provided there. On the other hand, names of cities cannot be monopolized.

Sometimes a mark which may not have a great deal of intrinsic distinctiveness, nor even a great deal of capacity to distinguish, can be registered if, in practice in the trade, the mark has become distinctive of the goods of a given proprietor. Thus, in practice, long and extensive use may even render something as inherently undistinctive as a letter of the alphabet acually distinctive of the goods of a particular manufacturer, and if such distinctiveness acquired by a user can be demonstrated by evidence, the Trade Marks Registry will allow the mark to be registered.

Turning now to the question of extrinsic registrability, this is considered essentially in two stages: first of all, the Trade Marks Office itself looks at the existing marks on the Register and decides whether any of them so closely resembles the mark applied for that problems of confusion or deception are likely. The marks themselves are compared as are the goods or services in respect of which one is registered and the other is applied for. The Registry tends to err on the side of caution, often suggesting that there is conflict when in practice there may be none. Conflicts can be removed, sometimes simply by persuasion, at other times by reducing the scope of goods or services applied for, and at others reducing the scope of the goods or services of the already existing registration. The Registrar is partly cautious because if a mark is registered which is too close to an existing registration, the Registrar may be very unpopular with the earlier registrant as the later registration acts to legitimate the use of the mark registered on the goods or in respect of the services for which it is registered, that is, the use of your registered mark does not by statute infringe any other registration. This is a further incentive to registering your mark. Not only can you sue infringers, other registrants cannot sue you in respect of such registered use.

Sometimes, the Registrar will allow two similar marks to be registered if the owner of the existing registration consents to the later registration.

Other objections to registrability
Sometimes, an applicant will wish to register a mark which neither clashes with anything already on the Register or used by others, nor fails to be distinctive. However, there are certain circumstances in which registration can still be refused. Principal among these is where the use of the mark would be deceptive. Thus, the registration of mock Italian wording for wines, for example *Lungareto di Vitalo*, would be refused on the basis

that it would be deceptive to use such words, for example, on German or French origin wines. Such objections may often be overcome, however, by restricting the goods or services in respect of which the mark is proposed to be registered, in the example just noted to Italian wines. On a more severe note, the Trade Marks Registry may even impose conditions on a registration. In one case, the Registry imposed as a condition of registration of a mark for contraceptives, which included the word *duo*, that the products should not be sold in packs of two!

Once the Trade Marks Registry is convinced that there is no real clash, and assuming that any intrinsic objections have been dealt with, the Trade Marks Registry publishes details of the application in a weekly publication called the *Trade Marks Journal*. Owners of trade marks rarely subscribe to this, but their professional advisers or commercial watching services do so, and those parties sound the alarm if a mark is advertised for opposition purposes which would appear to conflict with something their client does or wants to do. It is not necessary that the conflict arises on the basis of an existing registration held by an existing registrant, though that is normal. Other grounds can be asserted and sometimes are. There is a one-month period for objections. Normally nothing happens and then the registration fee is paid and the Trade Marks Registry enters the details of the mark in its (these days electronically maintained) Register, and issues the applicant with a Certificate of Registration giving the details. The mark is then said to be registered. Registration lasts initially for a period of seven years (calculated from the day you applied) and thereafter can be renewed each time (under current law) for a period of 14 years. That term is likely to be standardized in future to 10 years.

If opposition proceedings actually occur, then it is rather like proceedings before an arbitrator. Both sides, the person who wants to register a mark and the person who does not want to see it registered, at least not in the form advertised, have a chance to set their respective cases down in writing and a Hearing Officer in the Trade Marks Registry will make a decision. That decision can be appealed against either into the High Court or before a specialist arbitrator, usually a Queen's Counsel, appointed for the purpose by the Board of Trade (part of the DTI).

Oppositions are, however, relatively rare and people who see problems arising from marks of others advertised for opposition can often resolve those problems by negotiation and agreement. This is much more amicable and far less expensive.

Once any opposition is settled in favour of the person wanting registration, the registration fee is paid and the Registration Certificate then issued.

Using your mark

The first thing to observe here is that trade marks are meant to be used. It is not permitted to adopt a dog-in-the-manger attitude and, for example, try and stop your competition using a good mark for their (and your) goods because you have thought of it and registered it simply to try and stop others using it. An application to register a mark which is not based on an honest desire to use the mark on the goods, or in respect of the services in question, is an application falsely made and any registration which results from that application may be attackable by a third party if it comes to a fight. Likewise, even if you wait to ensure that you are going to secure registration before you put a mark into use (a perfectly legitimate exercise, though sometimes one requiring very long-range planning having regard to the time the registration procedure can take), then if you do not put the mark into use once registered, after a period of five years the registration becomes vulnerable in the sense that an interested third party can remove the mark from the Register (or at least ask the Trade Marks Registry to do so) for non-use.

Sometimes, such applications are successful, though other times, even if there is no use, there is a legitimate excuse for it and the Trade Marks Registry will not remove the mark even though asked to do so. Mostly, however, the situation is self-adjusting: a mark which is valuable and used is not vulnerable to removal and others may well keep clear anyway. A mark which is not used and thus becomes vulnerable to removal clearly does not generally constitute anything very important to its owner, so often an attack on such a mark results not in its removal from the Register, but in the owner of the mark agreeing to sell the registration to the attacker.

As noted above, in order to be registrable a mark must be distinctive. In order to stay properly as a registered trade mark on the Register, a mark must remain distinctive.

Distinctiveness, in fact, can change with time. With proper use and everyone else steering clear, a not very distinctive mark may in time become very distinctive of particular goods or services. The reverse can also happen: a very distinctive mark can, by misuse, become non-distinctive and rather descriptive or generic. Some words have indeed become so generic that it is startling to remember that they were once trade marks. The most obvious example is *petrol*. The classic examples of marks which are liable, if their owners do not take great care (and sometimes if they do), to become generic, are those of highly successful household or commercial products. The obvious ones to choose (without wishing to exempt many other obvious candidates) are Hoover, Xerox and Yale.

Companies which own trade marks which are in danger often spend very considerable sums of money in advertising and promotion and other activity designed to stop their marks becoming generic. The most important thing to remember is not to allow the mark to be used by itself. If you use a mark by itself, others will do so too and the mark will be used in substitution for the goods or services in question. This applies more often to goods than to services. The way to avoid this is to ensure that the mark is accompanied by the right word for the goods in question. This may be vacuum cleaner, copier, lock, or many others. Using the trade mark as an adjective and not as a noun is the first and important step to stopping the mark becoming generic. Reminding people of what the noun is deters them from using the trade mark as a synonym for the goods in question. Closely allied to this is avoiding using a trade mark as a verb. Substantial efforts are devoted to stopping people 'xeroxing' and 'hoovering' things.

Another useful technique is to remind both your own employees and your competitors and the consumers when marks are registered. This can be done by the use of symbols, for example ™ or the ® symbol, or by the use of wording, for example, 'The Blue Bull Device is a Registered Trade Mark of Bovo Industries Inc.' In continuous text, word marks should be written either all in capital letters or with initial capital letters.

Infringement: using your registration

In an ideal world, the fortunate trade mark owner does not need to use his registration (though he does need to use his mark). Clearly, registration provides a firm sign to other people saying 'keep off '. If the sign is effective and everyone else keeps away, that is highly satisfactory. If, on the other hand, whether by inadvertence or design, someone comes too close, the trade mark owner may feel aggrieved and take action. In most cases, this will be because the registration is being 'infringed'.

Infringement is simply the unauthorized use by another of the same or a similar mark on goods or services covered by the registration. In the United Kingdom, the coverage extends only to those goods or services which can be said to fall within the wording of the specification of goods or services for which the mark is registered (see remarks above with respect to wind instruments). In most other countries, coverage includes in addition similar goods or services. The use must be as a trade mark rather than in some other way. For example, if a manufacturer had registered 'Spectrum' for computers, it would not be an infringement for another computer maker to send out an invitation to a sales meeting which said that their 'Novixx™ computers were designed to appeal to a wide spectrum of business and professional users'. Usually, though not always, the use will be one tending to lead to deception or confusion in the mind of the ultimate customer—he or she will either be deceived as to the origin of the goods or services, or confused as to whether they are from the same source as before or not.

If as a mark owner you learn of a possible 'infringement', the first action to take is to draw the attention of the person whose activities you suspect are unauthorized to your registration and ask politely for the use to stop. The 'innocent' infringer may well do so. If so, good. If not, more vigorous forms of persuasion may be called for. Sometimes, for example, in the case that use of your trade mark is only one of a variety of identifiable infringements of your rights, such as where the activity is one of counterfeiting, prior polite request may be inappropriate.

The protection against infringement given by registration may be enforced through the courts. In the United Kingdom, action is generally commenced (if other avenues to deal with the problem have failed) by starting straightforward legal proceedings before the High Court, Chancery Division.

In recent years, a vigorous practice of granting temporary orders in litigation has grown up. In particular, applied to trade marks, the owner of a long-standing registration in Part A of the Register is assumed, prima facie, to have an incontestable right to stop others using that mark, or one closely similar to it, in respect of the goods or services for which that mark is registered. If a lawsuit is commenced and the court is asked at an early, so-called interlocutory, stage to order the party being sued to stop, that order is often successful, the so-called balance of convenience being, generally speaking, in favour of preserving the *status quo* between the parties. The moral of this is that if you want to exert your protection, you must be vigilant to see that people do not use your mark, or something very similar to it, in undetected fashion: it is necessary to 'police' your mark.

Passing off

Whether or not your mark is protected by registration, the use of a similar or identical mark by someone else may be such that consumers who know the genuine goods bearing the mark are misled into thinking that the new mark used by a third party is in some way connected with the owner of the mark. Sometimes the activity is deliberate and classically is seen as an attempt by the second comer to pass off goods or services as those of the original owner or user of the mark.

In the United Kingdom, unfair trade activity of this sort is not covered by a specific statute, but is dealt with under the common law. Accordingly, what is important is not whether any particular activity does or does not meet wording in a statute, but rather whether or not the activity complained of is one similar to others judged unauthorised or otherwise in earlier cases. Thus comparison with earlier cases, that is, precedent law, operates in this field.

In common law cases, the courts try and set down in words what the law is in the area. A few years ago, in the United Kingdom, a case reached the House of Lords which was vigorously contested and which gave the House of Lords the opportunity of restating the modern law of passing off. Fundamentally, the judgment was that in order for passing off to be present, five characteristics must exist. There must be:

1. a misrepresentation,
2. made by a trader in the course of trade,
3. to prospective customers of his or ultimate consumers of goods or services supplied by him,
4. which is calculated to injure the business or goodwill of another trader (in the sense that this is a reasonably foreseeable consequence), and
5. which causes actual damage to a business or goodwill of the trader by whom the action is brought or (in a *quia timet* action) will probably do so.

A *quia timet* action is one where the person suing is not suing on the basis of what has happened but on the basis of what may happen. This can occur, for example, where a product launch to distributors takes place before the release of the product to the general public or the advertising campaign takes place, and the owner of the mark is tipped off by a friendly distributor that rights in the mark are about to be infringed. In those circumstances, it is commerically often very desirable to act before the product arrives at the consumer level and while damage can still be repaired.

Passing off is something that happens sometimes at the same time as infringement of a registered trade mark is taking place. In those circumstances, a claim against passing off may be a relatively unimportant part of what is basically an action to stop infringement of the registration. However, where a mark is not registered, the passing off action comes into its own. Sometimes it is the only possibility since the mark in question may not be one which can, under the Trade Marks Act, be registered. A recent example of this is the lemon-shaped container in which lemon juice has been sold for some considerable while. The shape of the container was not registered as a trade mark but had been used for a very long time by one party. An attempt by another party to sell lemon juice in similar lemon-shaped lemon-coloured squeezy plastic containers was restrained, despite the fact that the containers which had been on the market for years had always borne the trade mark of their manufacturers and that the proposed sales by the newcomer to the market bore a different trade mark. The court held that the proposed container and the one on the market were sufficiently close that people would be misled into thinking that they were buying the product that had been on the market for years. Figure 2.2 shows the two 'lemons' in question.

Letting others use your mark

This is a very difficult area. Classically, the object of using a mark, viz. to identify goods or services with a particular source or origin for those goods or services, is clearly undermined if there is more than one source for those goods or services. In order to stop that happening, clear arrangements need to be made which will ensure that the essential capacity of the trade mark to distinguish the legitimate from the illegitimate is not lost. If it is lost, the registration may become quite worthless and the efforts that have been put into its protection and, indeed, the efforts invested in providing the mark with reputation, may be utterly wasted.

There are two major areas where trade marks are licensed from one party to another: one is internally in a group of companies, where, for example, different manufacturing subsidiaries in different countries may make the same product and sell it under the same mark, and the rather different state of affairs where one company wishes to license the use of a trade mark along with the license of other technology, whether that is know-how, marketing expertise, copyright, designs, or even patents. In such circumstances, where the parties are essentially at arm's length one from another, very considerable care needs to be taken in formulating and monitoring licensing arrangements. Generally speaking, however, the crucial thing to remember is to ensure that the licensor, the original mark owner, has control over the goods which bear the mark or the services which are provided in connection with it. Not only should the agreement between the parties provide for control, but the activities of the parties subsequent to coming to the agreement should actually include positive control measures. Thus, for example, it is common that the trade mark owner is provided at regular intervals with samples of the goods bearing the mark, and also has the right to go and inspect the place of manufacture or, in the case of a service, to inspect when the service is being carried out. Regular reports may be called for. The central object of that sort of activity is to ensure that the standards of quality, or standards of performance, which are laid down from time to time by the owner of the mark, are being adhered to. The conditions are recorded in a 'registered user' or 'permitted user' agreement.

In recent years, there has been much concern expressed in connection with franchise operations and with merchandising operations as to whether these are always operated in accordance with the principles just stated. In fact it varies, some trade mark owners being very vigorous to ensure that their rights are maintained and not subjected to threats, while others adopt a less rigorous attitude.

International aspects

The above discussion of trade mark law and trade mark practice has con-

Jif: yellow cap, green and yellow label

Infringement: green cap, green printing

Figure 2.2 Protected and infringing plastic lemons

centrated, at several points, on the practice in the United Kingdom. The practice in many other countries is similar, though there are some major distinctions to be observed. The important aspect, which should be remembered, is that at the time of writing there are very few international arrangements related to trade marks. This situation is changing but the basic position remains that each country runs its own Register. The notable exception is the combined Register for the Benelux countries which was formed originally by combining the individual Belgian, Netherlands and Luxembourg Registers and which, ever since, has provided a unitary registration system effective throughout the three countries.

A European registration system for the European Common Market countries is in prospect but not yet in operation. It may come into operation in 1992.

A clearing house system also exists (the 'Madrid' system), enabling one registration to act as a basis for a family of like registrations based on it. This system has worked well for many years for some countries, but several major countries are not members and this has inhibited its usefulness. However, the arrangement has shown itself to be of such value that a slightly modified form of it has attracted widespread support, both from countries of the existing 'Madrid' arrangement and from others, notably the United Kingdom and the United States. It is possible that a modified Madrid system will become operational within the next few years.

The existence of individual national Registers poses a major problem for the business which wishes to introduce a new trade mark. Unless the goods are to be sold over a very narrow geographical area, or the services provided only locally, it is necessary to search in more than one Register to see if a mark is clear for use without running the risk of infringing the rights of others. For an international company wishing to launch an international brand, this can be a major expenditure, both of money and of time. There are specialist companies which consult specifically in the field of international brand name selection. It is a highly skilled business.

Trade mark personnel
Trade marks is a skilled and specialist field. Some professionals who work almost exclusively in it are known as trade mark agents. They obviously have that specialism. However, there are other professionals who also have substantial and developed skills in the field. Patent agents and patent attorneys very often have substantial experience in trade marks. Certain solicitors and barristers also specialize in the field. The simplest way of finding a trade mark agent if you want one is to look in the Yellow Pages. The best way is to ask a friend for a recommendation. Larger companies have their own trade mark personnel and, indeed, very large companies have their own trade marks departments which may be

staffed by qualified trade mark professionals. Those departments may form part of a marketing department or they may form part of a central function, for example attached to the company secretarial function. Yet again, they may be integrated with a patents department.

Trade mark selection
Selecting trade marks for new products is hard work. However much work is put in, there is always an element of uncertainty since one does not know whether the mark and the product will actually fit one another in the marketplace. The same applies to services.

Two general observations can be made: first, the more descriptive a mark you choose, the easier it is for the customers and trade to associate the mark with the goods or services but the harder it is to acquire or defend distinctiveness. If you choose a mark that is 'weak', do not be surprised if it is difficult to establish as your own. Do not be surprised if others choose to use something very similar; they are probably entitled to do so. Do not be surprised either if, in examination countries, it proves difficult to register the mark. Likewise, do not be surprised if you do choose a weak mark and register it without difficulties in countries where there is no effective examination procedure, that you have difficulties if someone else then uses something very similar and you try and sue them in the courts. Although by that time the strength of the initially weak mark may have been much improved by virtue of actual use and acquired reputation, no amount of use can rescue an irredeemably weak mark!

The second aspect to remember is that selecting a trade mark which is usable is a two-stage process. Not only must one find a mark which is going to be usable internally, that is, it can be put on the product and people in the company like it. It must also be usable without risk that someone from outside will cause problems. Thus, once a mark or shortlist of marks has been identified, searches need to be made with a view to ensuring that the mark can be used safely. It is no good relying simply on your own knowledge of your own area of trade in goods or services. Your competitors may have taken the trouble to go and register a mark very similar to the one that you have chosen and they then launch a week before you do. If you have simply failed to check, you will be caught by surprise and you will not receive much sympathy if, when you continue a week later to launch, they sue.

Searching takes time. Although initally it may be possible to carry out searches fairly rapidly, it may then be necessary carefully to assess whether in practice marks found would be a problem and/or, if you find a mark that is registered but apparently not used, in tracking down whether it really is used and/or whether you can purchase it from its owner. The purchase of an existing registration can, in certain circumstances, be a

TRADE MARKS

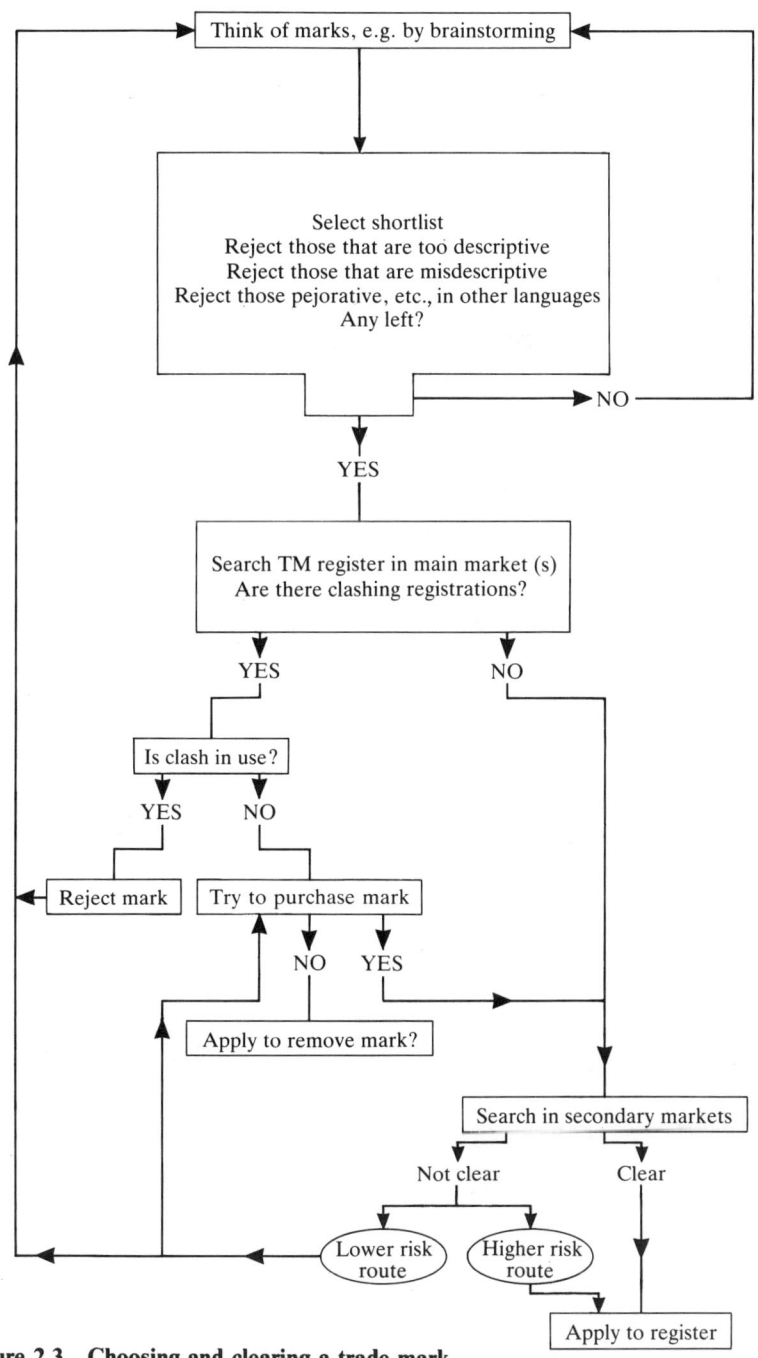

Figure 2.3 Choosing and clearing a trade mark

desirable alternative to choosing another mark. Figure 2.3 is a planning chart showing graphically how to proceed.

Summary
Trade marks are words or symbols used to distinguish one manufacturer's goods from those of another manufacturer or services of one provider from those of another provider. They supply a mechanism for brand loyalty or repeat business. Improper imitation by others can be proceeded against, at common law with some risk and difficulty or much more satisfactorily if the mark is registered with a registration authority, usually simply called a 'Trade Marks Registry'.

Registering trade marks costs a few hundred pounds per country (more if there are difficulties with securing registration) but such cost is more than recouped if you ever have to take action to assert your mark. The fact of registration provides a deterrent for others, which deterrent effect can be enhanced by making clear to third parties that your mark is registered.

Marks which are not used or which are used so sloppily that they become generic can no longer be protected, although even then the fact of a registration may put others off. The cost of litigation invariably exceeds by many times the cost of precautionary registration.

3 Technical copyright and information technology

Roger Broadie

COPYRIGHT

Introduction
Copyright is the most pervasive of all the intellectual property rights. It protects a wide range of the material a company produces: reports, manuals, production drawings, computer programs, publicity materials, even its correspondence. The copyright in materials like these is one of a company's most important intellectual property assets.

This chapter concentrates on those aspects of copyright that concern the normal industrial company and deals only in outline with the more specialized aspects that apply in the entertainment, publishing and general cultural fields. It is concerned with the position in the United Kingdom, where the law is now governed by the Copyright, Designs and Patents Act 1988 (the 1988 Act for short). The 1988 Act introduced some major changes in the law, and some major changes of wording that were probably not intended to change the law. As a result, as with any major piece of new legislation, some of what follows must remain tentative until we start to see how the courts interpret the new Act.

Although the copyright laws of foreign countries are outside the scope of this chapter you can assume that they are mostly similar in principle to the law in this country and that they protect British works in the same way as their own. Similarly, most foreign works are protected in this country in the same way as British works. This regime of mutual protection on a fairly uniform basis arises from various arrangements that the United Kingdom has entered into with other countries, mainly through the two copyright conventions, the Berne Convention and the Universal Copyright Convention. It includes most countries of any size apart from some in the Middle East and Far East.

The nature of copyright
As an intellectual property right, copyright has the great advantage that it arises automatically. It comes into existence as soon as the item concerned—the document, drawing or whatever it may be—is created. You

do not have to take any special steps to apply for copyright as you do for a patent, and you do not need specialized professional assistance to acquire it.

But there are strict limits to the protection copyright affords. Unlike a patent, copyright is not a true monopoly. A patent prevents others making use of the same invention even if they come upon it independently. Copyright, on the other hand, can be infringed only by someone who starts from the original work. An identical work, as long as it is created independently, will not infringe the copyright in the original work.

Copyright does not protect ideas as such. Anyone is free to entertain the idea underlying a work, or to incorporate that idea in a new work. What copyright protects is the form in which the work is expressed. Now this distinction is not always easy to apply. In a novel, the overall idea at the level of boy-meets-girl, boy-loses-girl, boy-regains-girl is clearly not protected, but more must be protected than the exact words, or it would be possible to copy works freely by making trivial changes, and novelists, for example, would have no control over adaptations of their works into other media. The line is drawn somewhere in the region of the fairly detailed plot. But whatever the practical difficulties in applying the test, it remains a helpful indication of the sort of things copyright does and does not protect.

The concept of the 'work'

Copyright protects what are called *works*. British law, in the 1988 Act, defines a number of different types of work, as follows:

1. Literary, dramatic, musical and artistic works.
2. Sound recordings, films, broadcasts, cable programmes and the typographical arrangements of published editions.

These different types of work fall into two broad groups, as set out in 1 and 2 above. Group 1, which we shall term *traditional* works for convenience, is treated in a slightly different way from group 2, which we shall term *non-traditional* works. In the main, the works in this second group are the more modern, technologically based, methods of presenting or communicating information, which may itself be a traditional work. The protection afforded to the non-traditional works is slanted towards protecting the investment made in creating them rather than the creative activity of a human author.

Of the various types of work, the two most relevant to the manager of an industrial company are literary works and artistic works.

Literary works
A *literary work* may be a work of literature in the conventional sense. But

it need not be. As the term is used in the 1988 Act, it applies to any work which can be written either in conventional language or in some other notation or code. So, among works in conventional language, it includes not only novels but also utilitarian works such as reports and instruction manuals. Among works in other forms of notation it includes numerical tables, and material such as football coupons and (as the 1988 Act confirms) computer programs. Computer programs are so important a subject of copyright that they are considered in more detail on page 50.

There is a limit below which material, although 'literary' in the sense described above, does not qualify as a 'work' at all. A single word, even though invented, has been held not to be protected by copyright. And titles of songs, books and plays are also not normally protected, although in these cases the grounds for the decisions tend to be partly based on the related ground, discussed below, that they do not meet the requirement that they are 'original'. That does not mean that every word is free to be taken by a third party: if it is a trade name, there will probably be other ways to stop its misuse, as described in Chapter 2.

For completeness, it should be added that dramatic and musical works (discussed below) are explicitly excluded from the category of literary work, in order to make them types of work in their own right.

Artistic works

The second type of work of interest to the industrial manager is *artistic work*, and in particular one sub-division of this type, *graphic work*. Graphic works include paintings and drawings, but once again there is no connotation of artistic quality, so the category also includes plans and diagrams. Some very simple drawings have been held to have copyright, including drawings of a washer, of a metal bar and of a straight length of pipe. A number of very important items to the industrial company are therefore protected under this heading, for example production drawings and the diagrams included in catalogues and manuals.

The other artistic works are:

- *photographs:* fairly broadly defined to include, for example, holograms;
- *sculptures and collages;*
- *works of architecture:* that is buildings or models of buildings, not architect's plans, which are graphic works;
- *works of artistic craftsmanship:* a rather obscure category applying to the work of a craftsman with, for once, it seems, an implication that there is some artistic intention; items of pottery or jewellery might meet the required standard.

Instruction sheets, catalogues, manuals and publicity material will be primarily literary works. But they will usually also include artistic works such as diagrams or photographs. And drawings, as artistic works, can include significant literary material such as dimensions and tolerances. Too minute an analysis of the category is rarely necessary, since under the 1988 Act the consequences in general are the same and the important thing is to recognize that the item as a whole is protected. None the less the fact that different types of work may be included in a single work is relevant as a reminder that more than one author is likely to be involved and all the necessary rights must be obtained.

Other traditional works
Dramatic works are works that are intended to be performed. They will normally originate as texts or scripts, which might have been expected to be literary works if they had not been specifically excluded from the category of literary work. This distinction becomes significant in defining what is meant by 'adaptation'.

Musical works consist of the notes concerned, dissociated from any accompanying words, which remain a literary work. So a song must contain two copyrights, one for the music and one for the words.

Non-traditional works
The different types of non-traditional work, in more detail, are:

- *sound recordings:* any recording of sound, whether music, words or even a live recording of, for example, bird song;
- *films:* any recording from which moving images can be produced; so not only are cinema films included but also video tapes and, probably for a video game, the computer program responsible for the pictures shown on the screen;
- *broadcasts:* radio and television broadcasts, including satellite broadcasts;
- *cable programmes:* normally items transmitted by cable diffusion services, but the meaning of the term is extended to cover networked database services (this aspect is discussed on page 54);
- *typographical arrangements of published editions.*

The distinction between a non-traditional work and a traditional work it embodies—a novel, say, in the case of a film based on the novel—is important and discussed further on page 39.

The rights in non-traditional works are sometimes less than those in the other categories. They will not be discussed in detail, but will be found summarized in Table 3.1 on page 40.

Conditions for copyright to subsist

Originality
So far we have been considering the different types of work that are eligible for protection. But for copyright in fact to subsist in the work, it must meet other conditions.

The most important is that the work must be *original*. In this context, a work is original if it results from its creator's own efforts. It must embody that person's skill or labour or knowledge or judgment. Paradoxically, there is no requirement that the work should differ from existing works, so long as it is not copied from them. What is required is that the work should originate with its author.

Of course, if you present a publisher with a novel which is word for word the same as someone else's you may have a hard time persuading him or her that you own the copyright or (a closely related point) that it is not an infringement of copyright in the other novel. But if your work is factual, it may very well be similar to an existing work. In some cases, for instance if it is a mathematical table, it may even be identical to it. That will not deprive the work of copyright if it is the result of your own independent work and you will be able to stop others copying it. But you will not be able to stop them generating their own equivalent works independently.

On the other hand the fact that a work is original, in the sense we have explained, does not mean that it must be unconnected with any existing work. There are many works in which the author's contribution justifies the creation of a new copyright in the work, without extinguishing an existing copyright. Two kinds are especially important.

1. *Derivative works* The term 'derivative work' is American, but is useful to describe a work involving some form of transformation or reworking, for instance the adaptation of a literary work to a dramatic work (a novel to a film script, say) or a translation from one language to another. While the contribution of the adaptor or translator can serve as the input of originality that justifies the creation of a new copyright in the derivative work, the copyright of the work on which it is based continues to exist and someone who copies the derivative work will be at risk of an action from both the original author and the author of the derivative work.

2. *Compilations* A 'compilation' is explicitly classed as a literary work. It is a collection of individual items, where originality is earned by the skill and labour put into assembling, selecting or arranging the items. These items may have copyright in their own right, in which case the compiler will need the permission of their copyright owners to include them. That would apply, for instance, to a literary anthology, at least if

Table 3.1 Copyright works and their characteristics

Type of work	Author	Duration	Restricted acts: do the following apply to the type of work?				
			Copy	Adapt	Issue copies to the public	Perform, show, play in public	Broadcast, include in cable programmes
Literary work	Creator	Life of author plus 50 years	Yes—reproduce in material form	Yes	Yes—includes rental of computer program	Yes	Yes
Dramatic work	Creator	Life of author plus 50 years	Yes—reproduce in material form	Yes	Yes	Yes	Yes
Musical work	Creator	Life of author plus 50 years	Yes—reproduce in material form	Yes	Yes	Yes	Yes
Artistic work	Creator	Life of author plus 50 years	Yes—reproduce in material form*	No	Yes	No	Yes
Sound recording	Person undertaking arrangements for making of recording	50 years from release, or from making if unreleased	Yes	No	Yes—includes rental	Yes	Yes
Film	Person undertaking arrangements for making of film	50 years from release, or from making if unreleased	Yes—includes making a still	No	Yes—includes rental	Yes	Yes

Broadcast	Broadcasting organization	50 years from broadcast	Yes—includes making a still	No	Yes	Yes	Yes
Cable programme	Person providing the cable programme service	50 years from transmission	Yes—includes making a still	No	Yes	Yes	Yes
Typographical arrangement of published edition	Publisher	25 years from publication	Yes—but only as a facsimile	No	Yes	No	No
NOTES	If computer generated: the person undertaking arrangements for creation of work	If computer generated: 50 years from creation If the author is unknown, 50 years from publication or (if unpublished) until reasonable to assume copyright expired All periods to end of calendar year	*includes 2D to 3D and vice-versa unless the work is a drawing of the design for a non-artistic work				

it contains modern items. On the other hand, something like a trade catalogue will have copyright as a compilation even though the individual items—the descriptions and possibly product identifying numbers of the different articles listed—will almost certainly not enjoy copyright individually. Many productions of a business will therefore enjoy copyright as compilations.

For non-traditional works (sound recordings, films, broadcasts, cable programmes and typographical arrangements), the requirement of originality is essentially that they do not reproduce another work of the same category. Thus a mere copy of a sound recording does not receive a new copyright.

Fixation
In the United Kingdom, copyright in a work does not come into existence until the work has been recorded in some form. Under the old British law, doubts were sometimes expressed about the status of works composed directly at the keyboard of a computer terminal. Under the 1988 Act, it is clear enough that all such versions count and there is no need for a paper copy.

A literary work can originate in spoken form, in which case a sound recording of the work would count as the fixation necessary to establish protection under copyright.

Duration
Copyright is an extremely long-lasting right. While the copyright in a work does eventually expire, so that the work can be copied freely, the precise duration is likely to be of only academic interest to the industrial managers, since the sort of work with which they are concerned will amost certainly have ceased to have any significance before its copyright expires. Broadly, however, for traditional works copyright expires 50 years from the end of the year in which the last identifiable author dies. Non-traditional works and works with no identifiable human authors have a fixed term of 50 years (25 years for typographical arrangements): for more details see Table 3.1.

Authorship and ownership

The author
Every copyright work has an author. If it is a work of one of the traditional types and has a human creator, that person is, as you might expect, the author. If it is a work of one of the non-traditional types, the 'author' is defined not as the human who makes the creative input, but as the 'person' (probably a non-human legal entity such as a company) by whom the

arrangements necessary for the making of the work are undertaken. So the 'author' of a broadcast is the broadcasting organization and the 'author' of a film is the film production company. Works that have no human author because they are computer generated are treated in the same way. The object of this rather strained definition of authorship for non-traditional works is to put ownership of the copyright in these works in the hands of the entity responsible for the investment leading to the creation of the work.

Works can have *joint authors*, but only where the authors collaborate in such a way that their individual contributions cease to be distinct. If, as is more common in practice, their contributions are distinct, there will be separate works, each with its own separate author and copyright and, possibly, owner of that copyright. There may also be an overall copyright in the work as a compilation. Joint ownership of copyright is a different matter and is discussed separately below.

The owner
The ownership of copyright is covered in more detail in Chapter 7. But, briefly, the copyright in a work is owned by its author unless there is something to change that state of affairs, normally either that the work is one of the traditional types and was created by an employed author in the course of employment (when the copyright belongs to the employer) or that the copyright has been assigned, for instance to someone who commissions the making of the work.

Joint ownership of copyright
Copyright can have *joint owners*. Joint ownership will arise as a consequence of joint authorship in those cases where the copyright does not vest in a single owner such as a common employer. Or it can be created by agreement even in the case of a single author. But the status of joint owner has its pitfalls. For instance, a joint owner cannot exploit a copyright work (e.g. by making copies or by licensing others) without the agreement of the other joint owners. Therefore, in any situation in which joint ownership arises or is created by contract, the rights of the parties to use the work should always be agreed in advance.

Moral rights
The 1988 Act gives the author, for the first time in the United Kingdom, what are called moral rights, though it sets them at such a low level that they are not likely to cause any embarrassment to an industrial company. The two chief moral rights are the right of paternity and the right of integrity.

The *right of paternity* is the right for the author to be identified on published copies of the author's work, or when it is performed or otherwise made publicly available. It does not apply at all to employed authors and in other cases will apply only if the author asserts it in writing. It can be waived.

The *right of integrity* is the right to object to changes that distort or mutilate the work or are 'otherwise prejudicial to the honour or reputation of the author'. Again, it applies only to works that are published or otherwise made publicly available. It can be waived, but in the absence of a waiver applies without the need for the author to assert it. If the author creates the work as an employee, he or she will benefit only if identified as the author, but even then the employer has complete control over any changes, provided there is a 'sufficient disclaimer', that is, a clear indication that the work has been subject to changes to which the author has not consented.

These two moral rights last as long as the copyright, normally 50 years from the end of the year in which the author died, and pass with the estate.

The works subject to these moral rights include all the traditional works other than computer programs or computer-generated works. But among the non-traditional kinds it applies only to films, for which the moral rights belong not to the producer, who is the deemed 'author' for ownership purposes, but to the director, that is, the genuine creator.

Infringement

The most important question for any owner of an intellectual property right is what rights it gives. In the case of copyright it gives the right to stop others carrying out various acts, called *restricted acts*, in relation to the work. The full set of restricted acts is:

- copying the work;
- adapting the work;
- issuing copies of the work to the public;
- performing, showing or playing the work in public;
- broadcasting the work or including it in a cable programme service.

Not all these acts apply to all types of work, and Table 3.1 shows which acts apply to which type.

If you are the owner of the copyright in a work, anyone who, without your authorization, carries out a restricted act which applies to it is an infringer. You can sue the infringer and in the normal course will obtain damages for past infringement and an injunction to prevent continuing infringement.

As with most intellectual property rights, even though you, as copyright owner, have the right to stop others carrying out certain acts, that does not serve as permission for you to carry out these acts yourself if the rights of others are involved. If your work embodies a pre-existing copyright work, as happens, for instance, when a film is based on a novel, you will still need the permission of its owner before you can copy your own work or carry out any of the other restricted acts on it.

The restricted act of copying
Copying is the most basic of the restricted acts. It is defined in a very broad sense. For traditional types of work, it covers 'reproducing the work in any material form', including any form of electronic storage. Copying covers any method of reproducing the contents of the work, even though the form in which it is recorded may be very different from the original. So copyright in a literary work will be infringed if it is copied by hand, or photocopied, or stored on a magnetic disk of a computer.

General principles of infringement
You may sometimes meet the view that someone who wants to copy a work can avoid infringement simply by changing a few words. Clearly, copyright would be of little use if it could be avoided so easily. In fact, it is equally an infringement to take a *substantial part* of the work. This phrase, in the context of copying, covers both the exact copying of less than the whole work and departure from the exact words or other form or expression of the work (or indeed both). It is impossible to lay down a precise quantitative definition of what will, or will not, be found to be substantial in this context—the test is qualitative—but it is worth remembering that courts often find the maxim 'what is worth copying is worth protecting' attractive, and the more someone is seen to have ridden on the back of someone else's skill and labour, the more likely that person is to be found an infringer. Quite a short extract can be a 'substantial part' if it is especially important.

However, there must be a *causal connection* between a work and its alleged infringement. No amount of similarity will make a work an infringement if it was in fact generated independently. On the other hand, the causal connection can be indirect and may be via acts that are not themselves infringements, for instance a sufficiently detailed verbal specification.

Other restricted acts
Adaptation, as a restricted act, has a highly technical meaning. It means transforming a work into a different version, for example by translating into another language, or adapting it for the stage or as a strip cartoon or (if a musical work) arranging or transcribing it. And, as will be seen, the term is further defined for computer programs. If an unauthorized adaptation has been made, it is equally an infringement of the copyright in the

original work to make copies of the adaptation or to carry out other restricted acts on it.

Issuing copies to the public means putting copies into circulation, typically by sale. If the work is a sound recording, film or computer program this restricted act also allows the copyright owner to stop others renting out the work—the so-called *rental right*.

Secondary infringement and criminal offences
The restricted acts we have just considered are sometimes known as *primary infringements*. They are absolute, in the sense that it is irrelevant whether or not the infringer was consciously infringing. There is also a type of infringement known as *secondary infringement*. Secondary infringement applies only if the alleged infringer knows (or has reason to believe) that a primary infringement has been or will be involved. It results from the commercial exploitation of primary infringements, or the enabling of primary infringements. Thus it is a secondary infringement to sell or otherwise deal commercially with infringing copies, to possess them in the course of business or to import them otherwise than for one's own private use. Other acts of secondary infringement include making and dealing commercially with objects such as plates or masters from which infringing copies are intended to be made, and facilitating a public performance of the work in infringement of the owner's rights.

The requirement for knowledge of infringement is to make sure that, for instance, a shopkeeper is not at risk by innocently offering a book for sale which later turns out to be a copyright infringement.

Most commercial dealing with copies, knowing them to be infringing, is also a criminal offence.

Fair dealing
There are times when it is permissible to carry out a restricted act even without the permission of the copyright owner. One important group of such exceptions goes by the name of 'fair dealing'. There are fair dealing exceptions for the purposes of research, private study, criticism, review and news reporting.

Of these, the only one relevant to an industrial company is likely to be *fair dealing for the purpose of research*. There is little direct authority on the scope of this exception, because most of the case law on the meaning of the term 'fair dealing' arises from cases where justification was sought under the different heading of fair dealing for the purposes of criticism or review. None the less, they give some guidance as to where the limits of fair dealing for the purpose of research would be likely to be drawn. Essentially, the more you take the less likely it is to be fair dealing, and it is unlikely to be fair dealing if your purpose is merely to avoid purchasing the original.

Under the 1988 Act, copying that is permissible under a fair dealing exception can be done by photocopying. Previously there was no exception for photocopying and, strictly, any fair dealing copies had to be made by transcription.

Time shifting
Under the 1988 Act it is permissible to record a television programme—or indeed a radio broadcast or cable programme—'for the purpose of enabling it to be viewed or listened to at a more convenient time'. This right to record for time shifting is new: previously most use of a video recorder was a technical infringement of copyright. But it will still be an infringement of copyright to use a video recorder to make a permanent copy. And it remains a copyright infringement to copy audio recordings onto tape.

Transitional provisions
For many years works will exist which were made under previous copyright Acts, all of which give protection in slightly different ways. The transitional provisions of the 1988 Act are therefore very complicated. Infringements that were committed before the 1988 Act came into force continue to be governed by the old law, except that a special kind of damages known as conversion damages, which could be anomalously high, has been abolished for all actions started after the 1988 Act came into force. For actions taking place now in relation to works created under the previous Act the situation is generally as follows. Copyright subsists in the work only if it subsisted previously. If copyright does subsist, infringements committed after the 1988 Act came into force are governed by the 1988 Act. The moral rights of paternity and integrity do not apply in most cases of interest to an industrial company. Where a drawing made before the 1988 Act came into force shows a three-dimensional article, manufacture or copying of the article will still be liable to infringe the copyright in the drawing under the old rules, and the new design right will not apply. But the copyright will be subject to licences of right after five years, (i.e. others may copy on payment of a royalty) and may well not be enforceable to prevent the manufacture of replacement parts.

Copyright in three-dimensional articles

Industrial designs and the design right
British copyright law was for many years sufficiently imaginative to hold that, where a drawing shows an article, it can be an infringement of the copyright in the drawing to manufacture the article. The article was

treated as a reproduction in three dimensions of a two-dimensional original. Developments in this area of the law rendered it increasingly bizarre, and one of the objects of the 1988 Act was to reform it. Protection of three-dimensional functional articles has now been taken out of the scope of copyright and given to the new, unregistered design right described in Chapter 4.

In order to allow room for the design right, in such cases the 1988 Act breaks the infringement link that previously existed between a drawing and the article it shows. The break occurs:

- if the drawing is what is called a *design document*, that is a record of the design of an article (e.g. production drawing) and
- if the article is functional or is not itself an artistic work.

It is then no longer an infringement of the copyright in the drawing to make the article represented, either by using the drawing or by copying an example of the article itself. Nor is it an infringement of copyright to make a new drawing from an example of the article. These acts will be caught, if at all, only as infringements of the much more limited design right.

Interaction between copyright and the design right
Even though making the article from the drawing in this way is now a question of design right infringement, it remains a copyright infringement to reproduce the drawing directly. So normal use of production drawings involves two intellectual property rights: copyright if further copies of the drawing are needed and design right for manufacture of the article. This complex arrangement means that special care must be taken when rights in designs are acquired or licensed.

If a design right is licensed, a copyright licence will normally be needed to support it. And there are special difficulties as to ownership if a design is commissioned from a third party. If nothing is said about ownership of the intellectual property rights in the design, the design right will be owned by the commissioner under the rules that apply to design right. That is the opposite of the rules that apply to copyright, under which the copyright in the drawings will be owned by the designer. The only sensible course is to come to an explicit agreement which ensures that both rights are in the same hands.

Making an article shown in a drawing, or copying an article, may of course also raise questions of infringement of registered designs or patents.

Non-functional articles
The removal of copyright protection from articles made from drawings

applies only if the article is not itself an artistic work. If it is an artistic work, for example because the drawing shows a sculpture or a work of artistic craftsmanship, it will remain an infringement of the copyright in the drawing to make the article shown in it. Works of architecture are also artistic works and the unauthorized construction of a building from an architect's plan or by direct copying of the building will infringe the architect's copyright in the plan. In all these cases, if there is direct copying of the object, there is probably also a separate infringement of the copyright in the object as an artistic work in its own right, although no doubt there would be no extra penalties.

If the drawing is not a design for an article at all, it is not a design document and the previous law should still apply. Therefore, it should still be an infringement of the copyright in a drawing to reproduce—'copy', in the terminology of the 1988 Act—the drawing in three dimensions. Under the previous law it was an infringement of the copyright in a cartoon to make a doll or other three-dimensional representation of a character in the cartoon. That should still be the case, since the cartoon would probably not be regarded as a design for an article, and thus not a 'design document' to which the exclusion applies.

Shortening of term
Where a copyright owner has exploited the copyright in an artistic work (either a drawing or an article) by making on an industrial scale articles that are 'copies' of the work, the term of the copyright is shortened to 25 years from the end of the year in which the articles are offered for sale. This shortening does not apply to some defined categories of articles of a primarily literary or artistic character such as medallions and greetings cards.

Administering copyright
The automatic way copyright arises means that it needs remarkably little administration. The following are pointers to good housekeeping intended to help avoid disputes, or at least put you in a good position to deal with them if they arise:

1. Keep records of the creators of works whose copyright you may need to enforce and, if possible, the conditions under which the works were created so you can demonstrate their originality.
2. Make sure you get assignments of the copyright in works to be created for your company by outsiders or, if that is not possible, be sure your rights in the material are clearly agreed. Consider including a waiver of moral rights.
3. Do not enter into joint ownership of copyright without specifying what rights the joint owners each have to exploit the work.

Notices

It is common for books to carry a copyright notice near the front in the same form as this one, as set out in the Universal Copyright Convention:

Copyright © 1990 McGraw-Hill Book Company (UK) Ltd

That is, it includes the symbol ©, the year of publication and the owner of the copyright. The word 'copyright' is not always included, but helps to explain the purpose of the notice. Although it appears that such a notice is no longer required in any country as a condition for copyright to subsist, it is none the less recommended for all published works and also other works such as reports you give to outsiders and would not want copied. It serves as notice that you claim to be the copyright owner and prevents any suggestion that an infringer is innocent. And in the United States (which used to require the notice) there are still advantages in including it in published works. Technical drawings commonly carry a notice and often include it on the blank.

INFORMATION TECHNOLOGY

Protection of computer programs under copyright

The position in the United Kingdom

Although it was generally accepted for many years in the United Kingdom that computer programs were protected by copyright, that fact was not confirmed by legislation until the Copyright (Computer Software) Amendment Act 1985. One of its purposes was to increase the penalties for commercial piracy of computer programs, but at the same time it confirmed the status of all computer programs, including those existing at that time, as works protected under copyright. They were to be treated in the same way as literary works although, oddly enough, the question of whether they actually were literary works was left undecided.

The 1988 Act has put the exact nature of computer programs as copyright works beyond doubt. They are now stated to be literary works. Consequently, all the general provisions concerning literary works that have been discussed earlier in this chapter will apply to computer programs. Thus, to enjoy copyright, the program must be original in the sense already discussed. It must also be fixed by being recorded in some form. Ownership will normally vest in the programmer or, if the programmer is employed, in the employer, but may be assigned.

The 1988 Act does not define 'computer program', for fear that any definition might exclude forms of computer program that will be developed in the future. Many other countries have introduced a definition; that from the United States is typical: it defines a computer program as 'a set of statements or instructions to be used directly or indirectly in a computer in order to bring about a certain result'. It is probable that British courts will be prepared to interpret the term 'computer program' broadly, and any program judged to meet the US definition would also be found to be a computer program in this country. Both source and object-code programs would be likely to be included—consider the work 'indirectly' in the US definition. Two areas where doubts may arise are microcode and the inputs to modern computer-aided programming systems.

1. *Microcode* Microcode leads to outputs that are supplied as signals to control the operation of the computer's own hardware, rather than, as is the case for a conventional program, passed to external equipment, for instance for display. The status of microcode has already been considered in the United States under the US definition of computer program. The argument that microcode is not a computer program because, in effect, it forms part of the computer itself, was dismissed. It is hard to believe that a British court would take a different view.

2. *CASE systems* The inputs to CASE (computer-aided systems engineering) systems consist of facts and requirements rather than instructions as such, and the designer controls the information flow in the program by manipulating diagrams on a computer screen. It is possible that these inputs do not themselves constitute a computer program, but there is no reason to doubt that the output is a program enjoying copyright, probably as a 'compilation', (using that word in its copyright, not its computer, sense) of existing sections of code.

The international perspective
There is an overwhelming international consensus, confirmed by court decisions and legislation in many countries, that computer programs should be protected by copyright. There are two main reasons. First, copyright gives a suitable level of protection for a work that takes much skill and effort to develop but which can be copied at negligible expense. Second, it ensures a uniform international regime through the requirements of the Berne Convention and avoids the uncertainty which would result from any attempt to develop a special-purpose form of protection.

The latest body to accept this view is the European Commission, which has published a proposal for a directive on the Legal Protection of Computer Programs based on the copyright approach. If the directive is adopted by the Council of Ministers it will lay down the requirements for the laws of member states, including the United Kingdom. The proposal includes a set of restricted acts that are very similar to those in the United Kingdom. But, following the continental tradition, it does not have a fair dealing exception on British lines. This combination has been criticized as too restrictive, and after a long debate it appears likely that there will be a specific exception permitting limited acts of reproduction and adaptation (decompilation) to the extent that they are necessary to discover the information needed to develop interoperable programs.

This topic is one example of what are sometimes called second-generation issues, on to which debate has moved now that the status of computer programs as protected works has been established. The focus of these issues is the appropriate breadth of protection for computer programs. Other second-generation issues include the extent to which protection extends beyond the literal code to the structure of the program—where, in other words, the boundary of the unprotected idea is to be found—and the scope of protection for user interfaces—the 'look and feel' of the screens and commands by which the user communicates with the program.

Other copyright works in the field of information technology

Computer-generated works
Nowadays many works are created with the help of a computer. Examples are designs produced using a computer-aided design package and even documents produced on a word processor. In these cases the computer is acting merely as a tool and the characteristics of the final work derive from the creative decisions and efforts of the user of the computer. Copyright will attach to the work in the normal way, and the author will be the person who uses the computer.

The 1988 Act goes further and for the first time anywhere allows for copyright in what it calls *computer-generated works*. A computer-generated work has a more limited meaning than one might expect. It is defined as a work 'generated by computer in circumstances such that there is no human author of the work'. This definition is intended to exclude the computer-aided case and to encompass works such as weather maps derived from satellite data, where the form taken by the work—the content that gives it its value and distinguishes it from other examples of the same sort—does not derive from human choice. Other examples might be a design for a car produced by a system which alters the design in an unpredictable way to reduce wind resistance, or a program which modifies itself heuristically in response to inputs from the external environment.

The 1988 Act does not take the straightforward course of stating positively that works that are computer generated in this sense are protected by copyright; it provides for such cases by implication by laying down the authorship and the duration of the copyright in a computer-generated literary, musical, dramatic or artistic work. The author is the 'person' (human or other legal entity) 'by whom the arrangements necessary for the creation of the work are undertaken'. In other words this is another case in which it is the investment in the work's creation that is protected. The duration (in a corresponding way to the other cases where the author need not be human) is 50 years from the end of the year in which it was made.

A case decided under the previous law on a preliminary matter illustrates the problems that can arise in deciding if there is a human author. It concerned sequences of letters generated by computer for a newspaper competition and copied by another newspaper. Here, even though the individual sequences were not in themselves selected by a human, the judge held that copyright subsisted and the author was the programmer who wrote the program which generated the sequences. The computer was just a tool. At first sight this case suggests that there can never be a computer-generated work, since there will always be a human author in the form of the programmer. But it is best regarded as one in which the programmer controlled the characteristics of the output by the skill and labour put into ensuring that there were enough, but not too many, winners. At the time, the decision was the only one that allowed a finding that copyright subsisted in something of commercial value that was being copied. Now that judges have an alternative route to holding that copyright can exist in computer output it is to be hoped they will use it, since giving the programmer (or more likely his or her employer) rights in the output is something that suits neither the user nor, in most cases, the programmer or employer. None the less the case shows that the possible contribution of the programmer should not be overlooked.

Some non-traditional works such as sound recordings and typographical arrangements are at least as likely to be computer generated as traditional works. There seems no reason to doubt that they are equally protected. It is true they are not mentioned specifically, but then computer-generated traditional works are mentioned purely to specify the author and duration in terms that already apply to non-traditional works.

Computer-generated design documents
If the output that is computer generated in the sense of having no human creator represents the design of a non-artistic article, the design will be the subject of design right protection as discussed in Chapter 4. The output will be the 'design document'; it may be a graphic representation of the design, in which case it will be an artistic work, but it may equally be a string of numbers, for instance instructions to a numerically controlled manufacturing tool, in which case it will be a literary work. The 'designer' is the person, (human or other legal entity) by whom the arrangements necessary for the creation of the design are undertaken, who is the same person as the author of the copyright in the design document. The owner

of the design right may, of course, be different from the designer, and ownership will be governed by the normal rules for the design right.

If the article is an integrated circuit, its design is particularly likely to be computer generated: even though a human may specify the functions required, the layout of the integrated circuit in a physical sense is likely to be the responsibility of a computer program. The application of the design right to integrated circuits is described in Chapter 5.

Databases
A database, as a collection of items, will normally be protected under copyright as a 'compilation', one of the defined categories of literary work. If there is a human who assembles the data for input into the database he or she will be the author. On the other hand, it is quite likely that the selection and storage will be under computer-program control, in which case the work will be computer-generated and the author will be the person (human or other legal entity) who organizes its creation.

If copyright subsists in a database it will be an infringement to make a copy of the complete database or a substantial part of it. Making a copy of a substantial part of the database is likely to include downloading a section of the database to the user's own computer or terminal, something that is increasingly easy technically, but in normal circumstances would probably not include the retrieval and copying of an individual item. That item may, of course, enjoy its own copyright protection, which may belong to the owner of the copyright in the database, but often will not.

Remote-access databases and cable programme services
If the database can be accessed from a remote point over a telecommunications network, it will probably receive additional copyright protection because it will come within the definition of a *cable programme service*. Although the term is mainly intended to refer to cable systems of the sort that distribute entertainment programmes, it was purposely extended to include remote-access databases.

The copyright work in this instance is not the cable programme service as a whole, but any 'item' included in it which, not altogether appropriately in our context, is called a *cable programme*. The owner of this copyright in this case is the database provider.

Making a copy of material retrieved from a database may therefore infringe two copyrights: that of the database provider in the material as a cable programme, and that of the owner of any original copyright existing in the material before it was introduced into the database.

Since it is an act restricted by the copyright in any work to include it in a cable programme service, a database provider will need permission from a copyright owner not only to include that work in the database itself but to provide remote access.

Documentation
It is worth remembering that the various pieces of documentation produced in connection with a computer program, from the original statement of requirements through program descriptions to the user manuals, are also likely to be protected as literary works.

Restricted acts and infringement
The restricted acts considered previously apply as much to computer programs and other forms of work arising in the field of information technology as they do to more conventional works. It will, for instance, be an infringement to make an unauthorized hard copy of a program by listing it, or even by printing it in a magazine. But besides these applications of the general rules there are some special points that arise from the use of these works with computers.

Electronic storage
The restricted act of copying is defined for literary and other traditional works to include 'reproducing the work in any material form'. That includes 'storing the work in any medium by electronic means' and 'electronic' is defined, more broadly than one might expect, to mean 'actuated by electric, magnetic, electro-magnetic, electro-chemical or electro-mechanical energy'. The consequence is that it is hard to conceive that there is any manner of storing a literary work that does not count as carrying out the restricted act of 'copying'. For a computer program that has impact in three areas.

1. *Distributing a computer program* It requires the licence of the copyright owner to make copies of a program in any of the forms in which they are supplied to users, for instance recorded on a magnetic disk, or a magnetic tape, or a CD-ROM, stored in a semiconductor read-only memory.

2. *Loading a computer program* The copy need not be permanent. The 1988 Act specifically states that, for any type of work, the restricted act of copying includes making *transient* copies and copies that are *incidental* to some other use of the work. It is therefore a restricted act to load the program, either into some form of backing store such as a hard disk, or from there (or directly) into the main store of the computer, and the licence of the copyright owner is needed before the program can be used.

3. *Running a computer program* Running a program involves retrieving individual instructions and copying them one by one into an instruction register. It is likely that this procedure, taken as a whole, would be held to be copying, so running the program itself needs the licence of the copyright owner.

The licence needed to use a program will be given either explicitly by a formal licence or implicitly when a copy is sold without a licence, since the supplier clearly intends the program to be used.

If you buy a copy of a program your right to run the program will be inherited by anyone to whom you transfer the copy unless there are express licence terms which limit the rights of a second owner.

Since the 1988 Act's provisions relating to electronic storage apply to all works, not just computer programs, loading a database or other literary work into a computer is also an act of copying that needs the authorization of the copyright owner. So is displaying the work on a video display unit, since a copy is normally made in a buffer store from which the unit is driven. Another potentially infringing copy is probably made on the surface of the screen itself: if the work is to be visible at all there must be some material change in the surface that would constitute a reproduction in a material form, however transient.

Adaptations

It is a restricted act to make an adaptation of any literary work. For computer programs there is only one relevant type of adaptation, namely a translation, which is specially defined to include 'a version of the program in which it is converted into or out of a computer language or code or into a different computer language or code, otherwise than incidentally in the course of running the program'. That will include converting the source code written by the programmer in a form reasonably comprehensible to a human into the object code that is understood by the computer.

In the other direction, the act of converting the object code as supplied into a more comprehensible version in a higher level language by some form of reverse assembly or decompilation should also be an instance of making an adaptation. Many software developers rely on the fact that they can supply their program in object code and, by withholding their authorization for their customer to carry out the copyright-restricted act of making an adaptation, prevent access to an equivalent to their source code, in which many of their most valuable trade secrets are embodied.

The definition of 'translation' excludes conversions made incidentally in the course of running the program. That appears to take interpretation out of the scope of the restricted act of adaptation. Thus, if a program is supplied in BASIC, even though the user will need the copyright owner's licence to load and run the program, he would not need a further licence to interpret the program into machine code as it runs. This exclusion is perhaps unfortunate. It is a relic of an early stage in the passage of the 1988 Act through Parliament, and there is no logical reason in the Act as finally passed why conversions made in these particular circumstances should be excluded.

Rental right

As has been explained, rental of copies of a computer program to the public is a restricted act. So the owner of the copyright in a program can use that copyright to prevent copies of the program from being hired out.

Transmission

It is a secondary infringement to transmit a work of any type over a telecommunications system if the sender knows or has reason to believe that an infringing copy will be made at the far end. The telecommunications system used can be very short range—the language used appears, on its face, to catch transmission not only in a local network of computers but even within a computer.

Criminal offences

If copyright infringement of a computer program involves commercial piracy, in the sense of the deliberate large-scale copying of the program for supply to third parties, it is a criminal offence as well as a civil wrong. But the criminal law also appears to catch companies which buy one copy of a program and then make multiple copies for use within their own organization, or even companies in possession of an illegally made copy they intend to use.

Copy protection

There are special measures to assist copyright owners who distribute their works in a form which is copy protected. Anyone who sells a device intended to circumvent the particular method of copy protection used, or who publishes information describing how to do so, is treated as infringing the copyright in the work concerned. It will therefore be extremely dangerous to sell anti-spoiling devices for digital recordings or to publish instructions in a computer magazine on how to remove the copy protection from a program, since the damages could be determined by the number of unlawful copies that are made in consequence.

Administering copyright in the IT field

In essence, the rules for administering copyright in the IT field are no different from those in other areas. However, the prevalence of contract programmers means that special care is needed to take assignments for the copyright in the programs they will create. If a contract programmer is an employee of a one-person company it is from that company that the assignment must be taken. It is worth considering whether to seek a warranty that the employee will not infringe the intellectual property rights of third parties (i.e. previous customers). It would not in practice be easy to enforce, and should be backed up by proper workplace disciplines to avoid use of materials from third parties, but would serve as notice of your concern.

If you commission software from a software house the question of ownership of the copyright in the software will normally be a matter for negotiation. The commissioner tends to like to own it, but the software house may be able to do the job more cheaply if it retains ownership and exploits the software on its own account. Software houses normally put stress on being able to reuse individual modules, and also ideas and techniques developed while carrying out the commission.

It is prudent to retain careful records of the programmers involved in the development of a program and the stages of its development to help prove authorship and originality. This information may well be available as part of the normal documentation retained for maintenance purposes.

It is sometimes suggested that redundant lines of code should be included in programs as 'fingerprints' which, if found in a possible infringement, will help prove copying. They can certainly have that effect. But it is normally reckoned that the real problem is keeping redundant code out, not putting it in.

You should consider instituting a regime within your organization to discourage illegal duplication of commercially acquired programs: if such duplication does take place, your organization is likely to be liable as a copyright infringer and possibly for committing a criminal offence.

It is good practice to include a copyright notice in standard form in the source code as a comment near the start, as a literal string in the object code and as a notice shown on any screen each time the program is invoked. Many computer fonts cannot produce ©. The copyright symbol (c) is often used as an alternative, but on its own is probably not effective in the United States (where the form matters most) and the word 'Copyright' (or 'Copr' if space is short) should be used if © is unavailable.

If recorded copies of your programs are issued to the public it is also advisable to include the notice on the packaging. That will allow you as a copyright owner to short-cut the problems of proving ownership, since that fact will be assumed unless disproved.

Summary

Copyright arises automatically for works of various types when they are recorded in writing or otherwise. To enjoy copyright the work must be original in the sense of originating with its creator. Copyright protects the expression of a work and not ideas as such.

Copyright normally lasts until 50 years after the death of the author.

Copyright belongs to the author unless the work is created in the course of employment, when it belongs to the employer, unless it has been assigned to a third party.

Copyright is infringed by anyone who, without the authorization of the owner, carries out any of the restricted acts that apply to the work, either on the work as a whole, or on a substantial part of it (which can include taking only a section or departing from the exact words). Infringement requires copying or otherwise taking from the original: independent generation of an equivalent work is not infringement. Commercial dealing with a copy known to be infringing is also an infringement.

There are various exceptions permitting, for example, copying, etc., that is fair dealing for the purpose of research or private study.

It is not an infringement of the copyright in a drawing to make or copy an article shown in the drawing if the article is functional (non-artistic).

Computer programs are protected by copyright and the protection given to the source code extends to the object code and to use of the program in a computer. Computer-generated works having no human author are protected if original. Databases are protected as compilations, as are cable programme services if available by remote access.

More details are given in Table 3.1.

4 Industrial design

Clifford Lees and Keith Weatherald

The sources

The work of an industrial designer is frequently thought of in terms of putting the aesthetics on a workable article, such as stylizing a car, so that it has eye-appeal. Alternatively, the industrial designer may be the person who considers a traditional product and seeks, by the use of 'state-of-the-art' technology, to produce it more economically. These are both industrial design, but the art goes back almost to the dawn of the industrial age. Indeed, an underlying problem when considering the protection of industrial design is that of distinguishing between design for mere function, so that the 'wheels will go around', and design which is pleasing to the eye.

It is true that the first objective of any designer must be to produce something that will work, no matter how ugly, but it is not very long before, even in relation to the most mundane article, aesthetics will begin to play some part and one of the skills of a good designer is that in aiming primarily for functionality, he or she will at the same time come up with a design that is pleasing to the eye.

Of the traditional industries, metalworking in all its forms from ship building to the work of the silversmith has always been a clear illustration of the need, first to design something that will function and then to produce that something with eye-appeal. Of course, there are fashions even in mechanical engineering: consider the elaborate floral patterns moulded on parts of Victorian cast-iron fireplace surrounds; 'streamlined' cast iron all night burner fire fronts of the 1950s; and the reversion to more elaborate, but often sheet metal and fibreglass, 'coal-effect' gas fires of the 1980s.

Ceramics is another basic industry where the ratio of 'ornamentation' or aesthetics to functionality can vary from just about 0 per cent, in the case of sewer pipes, to 100 per cent in the case of 'Capo de Monte'™ items. In the case of a sewer pipe, function is vital, appearance is just about useless, since no one will see it once it is installed, but for the collector's ornament, appearance is the *sine qua non*. This distinction between the functionality and aesthetics of a design is of great importance from the point of view of the protection available under intellectual property law.

In the case of metalworking and woodworking, the design is often part of the structure of the article, but in some industries, such as textiles and wallpaper manufacture, the design can be considered to be the surface decoration which is apparent on the face of the sheet material. The distinction between a design which appears in the structural shape of the article and that which appears as surface decoration is important when considering protection, because although both structural shape and surface decoration can be registered under the Registered Designs Act, only the structural design can be the subject of *design right*. This chapter explains both types of right and their inter-relationship.

The ingredients of design

The ingredients which typically go into the design of an article may be identified as:

1. *Functional ideas* 'We will produce a rechargeable soda siphon with cartridges each of which will contain a carbonating gas liquefied under pressure; the siphon will have a hollow, hardened steel needle and there will be a cartridge holder with a screw connection between the holder and the siphon so that when the holder and cartridge are screwed on to the siphon, the needle will puncture a cartridge seal to allow the gas to flow through the needle to dissolve in the water in the siphon.' This is pure function: as yet the design is a mere mechanical concept—it has little shape or form.

2. *Parameters* 'The cartridge will have to be designed as a small pressure vessel; that means the thickness of the metal must be calculated; it will be designed with a hemispherical end (to take advantage of the good stress resistance of a sphere); the screw-thread connection should give the necessary mechanical advantage to produce the piercing action when the cartridge holder is turned manually.' These are parameters of design requiring knowledge of the physical forces involved. At this stage, the designer is primarily concerned with *function* (hence the cartridge is made cylindrical and with a hemispherical end). Often there is much reference to tabular information and some calculations. An element of shaping has crept into the process (cylinder; hemisphere) but this is purely incidental.

3. *Attractiveness* The siphon will be on sale in multiple stores; it may figure in mail-order catalogues. Now that there is a workable design, one has to look at its shape and its surface finish to ensure that it has eye-appeal, i.e. something the customers will think will be nice to take out of its packaging. At this point, some degree of artistry is required, although it is not always an artist who is employed to produce it. Also, one progresses from mere function into the realm of aesthetics with the

INDUSTRIAL DESIGN

Figure 4.1 Soda siphon and recharging cartridge

'Indian club' shape of the soda siphon shown in Figure 4.1, which also shows the cartridge and cartridge holder in place to charge the siphon.

4. *Manufacture* Now that the designer has drawn the beautiful siphon body, how on earth is it going to be produced? Metal spinning looks a likely production method, but will it be possible to get the spinning tools in through the opening at the top? Could it be bent and seam welded? This stage obviously requires a grasp of the manufacturing techniques available with their limitations. Of necessity, this stage will interact with stages 2 and 3. In practice, of course, stages 2, 3 and 4 will probably be carried out more or less simultaneously.

5. *Cost* Fine! But if when the design is costed, it is found that the manufacturer will have to sell it at a prohibitive price, the project is dead. So the whole process of design may have to be reworked with a view to cutting cost—while balancing savings against any product liability considerations.

All these stages add up to a considerable investment of thought and capital on the part of the original manufacturer—since the time of the designer(s) directly translates into capital investment. It is this investment which the law sets out to protect, and design can be protected in three ways; by *registered design*, by *design right* and by *copyright*.

REGISTERED DESIGNS

For a design to be registrable, it must have 'eye-appeal'. It is difficult to capture this aesthetic appeal in words, particularly in words to be incorporated in statutes and therefore falling to be interpreted in courts of law, and it is this difficulty which lies at the heart of deciding what design is registrable, and what is not.

Registrability of a design

The registrability of a design in the United Kingdom is governed by the Registered Designs Act 1949 (RDA), of which large parts have been amended by substitutions set out in the Copyright, Designs and Patents Act 1988 (the 1988 Act), most of which came into force on 1 August 1989. The basic criteria for registrability are set out in Section 1 of the RDA, which reads:

1-(1) In this Act 'design' means features of shape, configuration, pattern or ornament applied to an article by any industrial process, being features which in the finished article appeal to and are judged by the eye, but does not include:
    (a) a method of principle of construction, or
    (b) features of shape or configuration of an article which
(i) are dictated solely by the function which the article has to perform, or

(ii) are dependent upon the appearance of another article of which the article is intended by the author of the design to form an integral part.

The 'shape' of an article is usually simple to appreciate but it can cause problems when an openable article, such as a coal scuttle, has a conventional shape when closed, but presents a quite distinctive shape when opened. The procedure of what to do when an article presents several shapes will be discussed below, when the groundwork has been laid.

'Configuration' really refers to the arrangement of the component parts of an article. For instance, one could regard a condiment set as being a single article, in that the salt cellar and pepper pot are usually sold as a pair. It is known to make such sets with the individual containers having abutting surfaces so that together they form a shape appealing to the eye. Whereas 'shape' may apply to each container taken separately, it would be more accurate to regard the set as a 'configuration'. Perhaps also 'shape' means the fundamental shape and 'configuration' the embellishment, but for practical purposes 'shape' and 'configuration' amount to the same thing.

'Pattern' or 'ornament' need to be treated together, because they tend to blur into each other. Both terms imply a relatively superficial treatment of the surface of an article, not affecting its shape, but intended to give the article an attractive appearance. 'Pattern' could focus on the surface treatment, such as stripes or knurling, whereas 'ornament' almost implies that there are bits added on to a basic shape.

Note that a design has to be applied to an article. In other words, a design has no independent existence. Thus a building of a certain shape does not have the same design, as far as protection by a registered design is concerned, as say a cheese dish with a cover in the same shape, but on a smaller scale(!) Thus a design, once registered, can have its property rights infringed only by sale, etc., of a similar article having the registered design applied to it, as will be discussed below.

A registrable design must be 'novel'

In addition to meeting the aesthetic criteria, a design must be 'new', in that the novelty requirements for a design registration to be valid are very similar to those for patents. By the term 'new', the laws of industrial property mean that a design must not have been disclosed to the public before an application for registration has been filed at the Patent Office. Such prejudicial disclosure can take the form of an offer for sale, or any other transaction whereby a member of the public may validly allege that, before the application date, he or she was put in possession of the design without any restraint on further disclosure.

It is not only a disclosure of the exact design which is prejudicial, but one can forgo one's rights by disclosing a design which is similar to the design one wishes to register. Later arguments might well hinge on how 'similar' are the published and 'to-be-protected' designs, but sorting out such problems will involve expense: it is much better not to get into that situation in the first place! Therefore, it makes sound commercial sense to file a design application before there is any risk of publication, and even before one's marketing strategy has been finalized. It is not expensive to file an application, even if it is not proceeded with in the long run, and one should always keep one's options open.

The 'Indian club' body of the soda siphon shown in Figure 4.1 was of unusual shape when it was first put on the market. It was protected by a registered design (No. 931 348); its mode of manufacture, and the valve by which the siphon could be recharged with 'carbonating' gas from a bulb containing liquefied carbon dioxide, were both patented; the siphon itself, and all its associated instructional and publicity material, were marked with the name of its manufacturer, Sparklets (at one time a division of BOC Limited) and/or an invented name, 'Hostmaster', both registered as trade marks.

Design applied to a set of articles
Although most designs are applied to single articles, we are all familiar with sets of articles of common design, such as dinner services or a coffee set (see Figure 4.2). It is often difficult, when considering a decorated plate, say, to decide what might be registrable about its design. One can really appreciate such designs only when put in a position to see the set, which enables one to see how the same decoration or pattern is applied consistently to such different shapes as plates and bowls or sauce boats. In order to allow such articles to be protected, the RDA makes special provision for the registration of sets of articles. One particular requirement is that the representations show sufficient views of each member of the set for their common features of design, be it in the form of pattern or ornamentation, to be appreciated visually.

Textiles, wallpaper and lace
We are all familiar with these articles, perhaps so familiar that we have never thought about the commercial pressures leading their designers and manufacturers to strengthen their copyrights by registering their most important designs. Whereas it might be prohibitively expensive to register, and keep in force, all the output of a manufacturer of these 'flat goods' of indefinite length (for that is what they have in common), it can make good commercial sense to register those designs which differ significantly from standard products, and to keep in force those registrations covering designs that turn out to be popular and profitable. The RDA allows for the registration of such designs, of which the registrability lies

INDUSTRIAL DESIGN

Figure 4.2 A set of articles protectable by design registration

in pattern. Instead of making drawings of the designs, it is generally more convenient to accompany the design applications by specimens, each of enough area to cover the whole of one pattern, plus enough of the bordering areas to show how the pattern links up with itself, both laterally and longitudinally.

Exclusions from registrability
A 'method or principle of construction' is excluded because it is irrelevant to design protection how an article was made: what matters is its appearance. If an aesthetic article is made by a new method, then thought ought to be given to obtaining a registered design to protect its appearance, and a patent for its method of manufacture.

The exclusion from registrability of 'features ... which are dictated solely by ... function ...' is to avoid conflict with design rights (see below). When an article has to have a certain shape, such as a replacement car exhaust system, that is called a 'must-fit' feature, for obvious reasons. The related exclusion of features which 'are dependent upon the appearance of another article of which the article is intended by the author of the design to form an integral part' covers articles such as car body panels, which 'must match' the contiguous panels, etc., of the car of which the replacement panel is intended to form an integral part. Thus the RDA now states that articles of which the design 'must fit' (i.e. the shape is dictated by function) or 'must match' another article (i.e. have a shape dependent on that of another article) may be given protection only by design rights, and not by being able to have their designs registered.

A design must also not be in the class of excluded articles, which are:

1. Works of sculpture other than casts or models ... to be multiplied by any industrial process.
2. Wall plaques, medals and medallions.
3. Printed matter primarily of a literary or artistic nature.

These are protected by artistic or literary copyright.

Identifying registrable designs
Now that the basic criteria for registrability have been discussed, the reader might find it useful to use the flowchart of Figure 4.3. Starting from an article, going through the different 'decision gates', leads one either to a fork indicating that some form of protection other than design registration is more appropriate, or down to the final conclusion that the design of the article is registrable, and that action needs to be taken if one's rights in the design are to be preserved, as by applying to register the design.

INDUSTRIAL DESIGN

```
An article
    │
    ▼
Has the article got eye-appeal? ──NO──▶ Consider other forms of protection
    │
   YES
    ▼
Is its shape dictated by function? ──YES──▶ Consider design right
    │
   NO
    ▼
Is it 'new'? ──NO──▶ Consider value of copyright and design right
    │
   YES
    ▼
Is it to be applied industrially? ──NO──▶ Consider value of artistic copyright
    │
   YES
    ▼
Choose representations. File design application
```

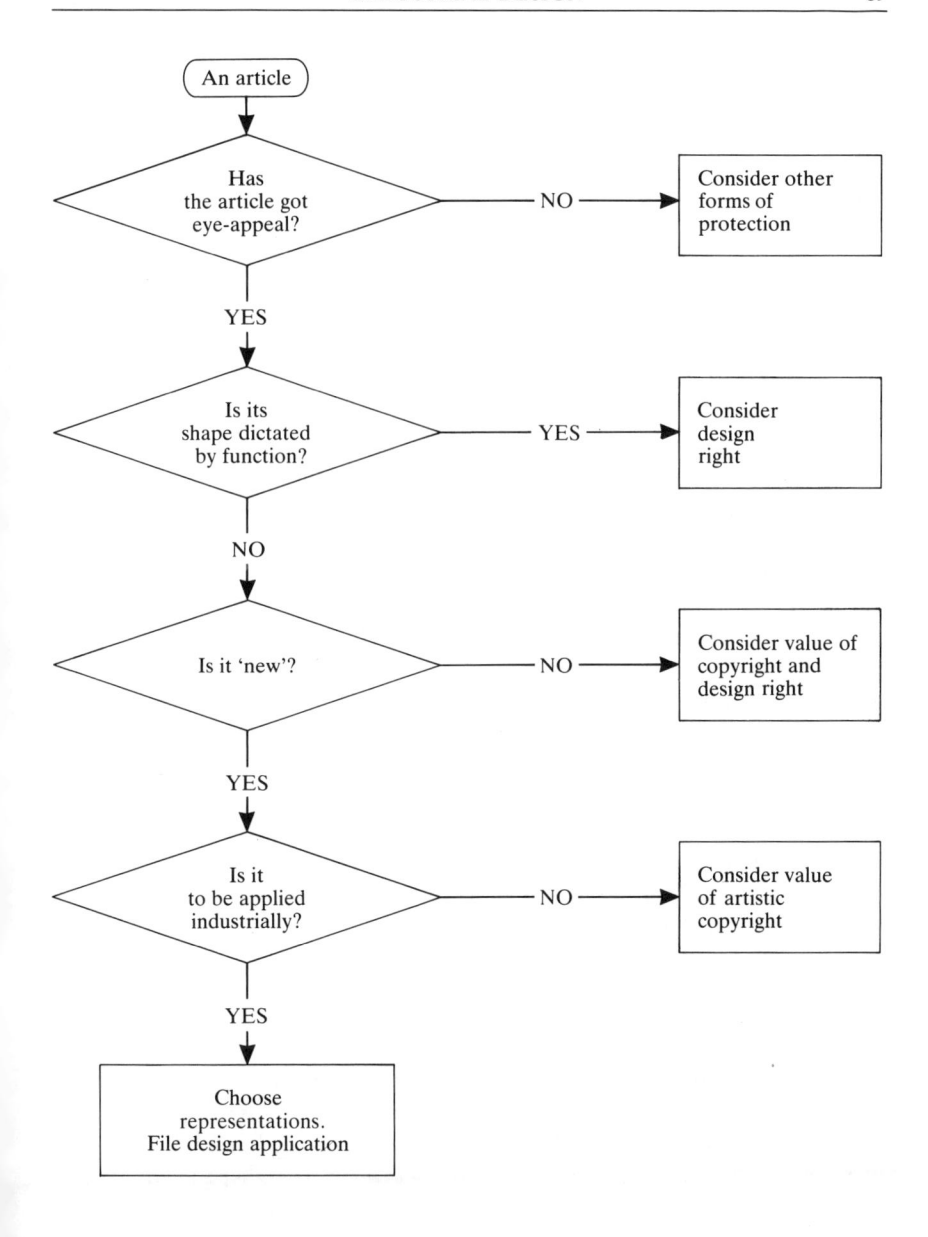

Figure 4.3 Can it be a registered design?

Rights given by registration
Because the rights given by registration are more akin to a monopoly than to copyright, it is not necessary for a proprietor to prove that an infringer had copied the registered article. Instead, it is sufficient for a proprietor to prove that an unlicensed person had put on the market an article of which the design is identical with a registered design, or differs from it only in immaterial aspects. Thus the proprietor has the exclusive right to use the courts to stop anyone from making, using or selling articles made to the registered design for sale or hire or 'for the purpose of a trade or business'. The proprietor has this right also in relation to 'kits of parts' intended to be assembled into an infringing article.

One of the advantages given by the registration is that the infringing article need be compared with only the registered design, so that action can be taken without having to prove that copying had taken place.

What to do to get protection
In order to register a design it must be appreciated for aesthetic reasons, therefore, the first thing to do is to decide on the drawings or photographs, etc., that best show the shape of the article you want to sell under the protection of the registered design. Normally the 'representations' (drawings, photographs, etc.) should show the article in the form in which it will be sold. However, if the article has two or more positions (such as 'open' or 'closed'), the representations should show relevant views of the article in all its alternative configurations.

Frequently an article to be marketed is not entirely new, in that some parts of it will be standard or well known already. In such cases, bearing in mind that the scope of your registered design might fall to be construed by the courts, in order to decide if a competitor has infringed your registration, it is helpful to mark the representations to show which parts of the article are of novel shape, etc. This can be done by encircling the relevant parts, or by applying a coloured 'wash' to them. The accompanying 'statement of novelty' (see below) should then read along the lines of: 'The novelty of this design lies in the shape of that part of the article which is encircled (shown in blue) in the accompanying drawings'.

In order to get a design registered in the United Kingdom, it is necessary to file various papers at the Patent Office (Designs Registry). The papers concerned are:

1. *An application form:* This differs as to whether an article or set of articles is to be registered, and if the design is to be applied to textiles, wallpaper, lace or cutlery. In any case, the form has to be signed by an agent or authorized signatory, and it must give an address for service which is within the United Kingdom. It must also identify the article to which the design is to be applied.

2. *Four identical specimens or representations:* This is required unless the design is to be applied to a set of articles, in which case five are necessary. Except in the case of an application to register designs applied to textiles, wallpaper or lace, each specimen or representation must carry a statement of the features of the design for which novelty is claimed. This 'statement of novelty' may be written or typed on the first sheet of the backing paper or drawings.

If the specimens cannot be stuck to paper for mounting in a flat position, or by being stitched to linen-backed sheets of paper, so as to be able to be stored without damage to other documents, then representations must be supplied in place of specimens.

If a design to be registered consists of a repeating surface pattern, then the representations must show the complete pattern and a sufficient part of the repeat in length and width.

When an application is filed, it must be accompanied by a cheque, etc., in payment of the official fees, to cover the cost of searches (to check that the design is new and not previously registered), publication, etc. These fees vary over a wide range depending on the article to which the design is to be applied. Other fees have to be paid at later stages in the life of the application, and renewal fees have to be paid by specified dates to keep the eventual design registration in force.

After filing, the Designs Registry at the Patent Office will object to any shortcomings in the papers, which usually will be in the representations. These objections have to be overcome within the period of 12 months from the date of application, although this period can be extended up to three months on payment of extension fees.

In a typical case, the cost of filing a design application through a patent agent, including his paying the official fees, might be about £200.

Period of protection
For designs registered under the RDA, the initial registration was valid for five years, and it could be renewed for two more periods of five years each. Under the current law, the registration may be extended for a further two periods, making 25 years in all.

If the necessity to pay a renewal fee is overlooked at the time, then it can still be paid up to six months late, on payment of 'surcharge' fees. Under these circumstances, the registration is treated as if it had never expired.

Registering designs overseas
Similarly to the situation which is discussed in Chapter 6 on patents, the international statute to which most industrial countries are signatories, the Paris Convention, also deals with registered designs. Under its provi-

sions, an application for design registration filed first in the United Kingdom (or any other signatory country) establishes a theoretical filing date for equivalent protection in all signatory countries. If an application is filed in any such country within the so-called 'priority period', and priority is claimed at the time of filing, then the Convention application is treated for novelty purposes as if it had been filed on the same day as the priority application. Because, for a design to be registered, it must not have been disclosed to the relevant public before the date of the first-filed application, the effect of such 'Convention' filings is to ensure that any 'intervening' publication of a similar design after the first filing date, but before the date of the Convention filing, can be ignored. Note that while the Convention period for patents is 12 months, for design applications it is only six months. Thus, if a UK design application were filed on, say, 10 April, the corresponding Convention design application has to be on file by 10 October in order to take advantage of the Convention.

Marking
Although there is no obligation in law for a UK proprietor to mark articles of which the design is registered, or promotional literature relating to them, with the number of the registration, there are commercial reasons for doing so. One of the most important of these reasons is to remove from infringers any defence that they were innocent because they had no reason for believing that the design was registered. Marking an article with the legend 'Registered Design' is not good enough in itself to deprive infringers of this defence: the actual number of the registration should also be added.

It is an offence punishable by a fine to represent falsely that a design applied to an article sold is registered. After a registration has lapsed or expired, then it becomes an offence to imply, by applying the mark 'registered' to an article, that there is a subsisting right in the design under the RDA. Therefore, it makes good sense to mark one's records relating to each design registration, with the product name or other reference, so that when a registration lapses (which can now be in 25 years' time, so that it might be one's successor who has to deal with it), then a process is initiated to ensure that no such marking is applied in the future to such articles being made for sale.

Borderline cases
It usually takes a legal decision to help define a boundary, in this case between registrable and unregistrable designs. These cases have come into case law because patent agents on both sides have been genuinely uncertain just what the words of the statute mean in a particular instance. A few cases might be of interest, in letting you know how legal minds view the law on registered designs.

One of the seminal cases, most quoted in later cases, is that of *AMP Inc.* v. *Utilux Proprietary Limited* (*1972 Reports of Patent Cases*, pp. 103 *et seq.*). The articles in this case were electric terminals to which the bared end of a wire was connected by two sets of integral ears intended to be crimped to the wires to terminate it in a 'flag or battle-axe' connection. It was admitted by AMP that the author of the design chose the shape purely for functional reasons, but it argued for registrability on the ground that the terminals could have been of different shape without affecting their function, so that the shape was not dictated by function. The House of Lords eventually held that the features of the design were dictated solely by function, and that therefore the registrations were invalid. In an observation by one of the judges it was held that if the shape were not there to appeal to the eye, but solely to make the article work, then it was excluded from protection under the RDA. Intent on the part of the designer was not the sole criterion: someone coming up with a functional article could add some features of shape additional to what was functionally needed, to end up with an article having a feature that appealed to the eye. The whole court also held that the eye in question was the eye of the intended customer, and not that of the court.

Two other cases were decided in 1978. The first was *Lamson Industries Limited's* application (*1978 Reports of Patent Cases*, pp. 1 *et seq.*) relating to pre-printed computer printout web (fan-folded paper) on which alternating bands of colour were printed on white paper. The question of registrability hinged on whether or not such bands of colour were features of pattern or ornament. The application was rejected by the Designs Registry on the ground that the article was primarily of a literary or artistic character, and was therefore unregistrable. On appeal, the application was again refused registration, but on different grounds. The Appeal Tribunal held that the article did not consist of printed matter primarily of a literary or artistic character, but that, although the bands of colour were features of pattern or ornament, the design did not qualify for registration because the bands were not features which in the finished article would be judged solely by the eye.

The second case was that of *P. Ferrero's* application (*1978 Reports of Patent Cases*, pp. 473 *et seq.*) in which the Italian confectionery firm tried to register a filled egg with inner and outer layers in contrasting shades or colours (remember gob-stoppers?). Registration was refused on the ground that features for which novelty was claimed could be seen only when the article was broken (or partially consumed) at which time it would no longer be a finished article within the meaning of section 1(2) of the RDA. The subsequent appeal was successful on the ground that the RDA required only that the features claimed should be features in the finished article; there was no requirement that the features should be able to be judged at the time the article was bought, and so the design was registered.

The case of *Cook and Hurst*'s design application (*1979 Reports of Patent Cases*, pp. 197 *et seq.*) hinged on whether the design of an England football shirt was new or original. The application was initially refused on the grounds that the design did not display enough originality, in that striped bands on such a shirt were typical in sports garments and constituted only a trade variant, and that the use of the England colours did not impart sufficient novelty to justify registration. Perhaps the judge hearing the appeal was impressed by the national importance of the shirt for, although agreeing that the variations in stripes had become commonly used on sports garments, he held that it would not be appropriate to refuse the application. Instead, the statement of novelty was required to be limited to football shirts and to 'the particular stripes of colour applied to the article in the manner shown in the representation'.

The final case, that of *K. K. Suwa Seikosha's* application (*1982 Reports of Patent Cases*, pp. 166 *et seq.*) related to an 'invisible' design in that the article was a display panel for a digital watch, of which its features were visible only when connected to the watch circuitry and battery. The alleged novelty was in the configuration and pattern of the article, one of the examples being the sound and bell symbols, together with two parallel lines. The application was refused on the ground that the symbols were not features which in the finished article appealed to the eye. The appeal was allowed along the same lines as Ferrero's application, in that the features of the design, although not necessarily visible at the time of purchase, became visible when the article was used for its intended purpose.

DESIGN RIGHT

The Copyright, Designs and Patents Act 1988 ('the Act') which formulates design right opens with the statement that it is a property right 'which *subsists* . . . in an original design'. This means that, unlike registered design, the protection is rather like an invisible cloak which descends on the design when it is created, unsought by the designer. Because design right does not require registration, it follows that no *decision* is required. There will rarely, if ever, be anything which either the designer or management can do about a design which will induce protection where it would otherwise not exist.

What can be protected by design right?
The broad initial definition is in the following terms:

'. . . design is the design of any aspect of the shape or configuration (whether internal or external) of the whole or part of an article'.

It is only concerned with 'shape or configuration', a phrase which has been taken from the Registered Designs Act 1949, because that way the lawyers at least might know what the words mean. In practice, there is no difference between 'shape' and 'configuration'.

Even at this basic level, however, much design skill is not protected. Take the cartridge for a rechargeable soda siphon: some painstaking work may have been necessary to choose the correct material, but that will not be protected by design right, whereas the cylinder with a hemispherical end could be protected in that it is the external shape of the article.

However, note that it is any aspect of the shape which can give rise to protection, for instance the external or the internal shape, so that if, for instance, the inside and outside shapes of a form of soft drinks bottle were quite different, the 'inside' design right could be infringed by a competitor even if the outside shape of his bottle were totally different.

The section of the Act which defines what features attract design right also excludes from protection 'surface decoration', which is a part of the limitation to shape. The obvious candidates for exclusion in this way are wallpapers and textile fabrics. (Fine worsted manufacturers may protest that their 'decoration' goes right through, but that argument is unlikely to persuade the courts that it is not surface decoration.) Also excluded from design right protection are decorative patterns such as those which appear on crockery, etc.—so a store which markets 'interiors', that is curtains, wallpaper, wastebaskets, and crockery all in one matching design, will receive no protection for its efforts under the design right. Most of these products will be protectable by registered designs and the basic pattern will receive copyright protection.

Providing one remembers the strict limitation to shape, almost all industrially produced articles can give rise to design right.

Inherently excluded features
It is now appropriate to consider some of the exclusions from design right.

A method or principle of construction People have sometimes sought to obtain protection by the relatively cheap door of registered design for things which really ought to have been the subject of patents. For instance, in one early case it appears that a particular method of manufacturing baskets had been registered. This was never the intention and therefore the various registered designs Acts excluded, among other things, 'methods or principles of construction'. The same exclusion applies to design right protection. The main effect of this is simply to reinforce the limitation already in the broad definition that only shape (or configuration) is protected.

It is not easy to cite examples of the features excluded in this way. Perhaps one can consider a carpet fastening strip which comprises a metal plate with teeth punched out of it, so that there is a small triangular hole where each tooth is bent out of the plate. If design right were claimed for the plate the protection would not extend to the 'method or principle' of forming teeth out of the parent metal by a punching process.

In an action for infringement of the design right, the court would look to see if the particular design had been copied, but would subtract from its consideration the *concept* of punching the teeth, so that the mere fact that the defendant's plate had a triangular hole at the root of each tooth would not be considered to give rise to infringement.

Anyone engaged in manufacture may find the idea of looking at an article and notionally removing from it what could be regarded as a design feature somewhat artificial, if not comical—but in relation to intellectual property in general, and design right in particular, such mental gymnastics are part of the stock-in-trade of the practitioner.

'Must-fit' and 'must-match' feature
Features which

1. enable the article to be connected to, or placed in, around or against, another article so that either article may perform its function, or
2. are dependent upon the appearance of another article of which the article is intended by the designer to form an integral part.

These exclusions can only be understood in the light of the fierce debate about design copyright, in the mid-1980s. Previous copyright law gave protection to components such as the piston of an internal combustion engine, providing such articles were made from drawings. By a quirk in the law, if the article was completely functional and devoid of eye-appeal, so that it could not be registered under the Registered Designs Act (maximum protection 15 years), it had copyright protection for the life of the person who made the drawing and 50 years after that person's death!

This was good news for the people who made original functional designs, particularly in the case of a machine with rapidly wearing parts where spares were necessarily copies. The big clash came in the motor industry, where certain parts, such as exhaust systems, require replacing several times in the life of the vehicle, and there was a large and influential spare parts industry.

On the basis that anyone should be able to compete with the original manufacturer in the supply of spare parts, the definition quoted above is intended to ensure that design right does not protect the features of a design which the manufacturer of spare parts is compelled to copy.

MUST FIT   It has been said the wording of the first exclusion was written around an exhaust pipe! Certainly, an exhaust pipe is 'connected to' the engine manifold and various parts of the chassis; it is sometimes 'placed in' mounting brackets; it usually passes 'around' or 'lies against' other parts of the engine and the whole purpose of so fitting it is to allow it to 'perform its function'. But there are much simpler examples of this exclusion, viz:

- a splined shaft fitting into the splined bore of a coupling;
- the flanges on a valve to enable it to fit the flanges on pipes;
- the pattern of holes in a printing plate to enable the plate to fit on the printing roller . . .

The list is endless and runs throughout manufacturing industry. Because these features are all concerned with one article fitting another, this has come to be known as the 'must-fit' exclusion.

A simple illustration of the effect of the 'must-fit' exclusion is the brush roller of a domestic vacuum cleaner. Each end of the roller must sit in a bearing. Therefore, these features of the design of the roller do not give rise to design right because they are 'features which enable the article', that is the roller, 'to be connected to or placed in . . . another article' (i.e. the bearing), 'so that either article' (the roller) 'may perform its function' (i.e. brush the carpet). There are some manufactured articles where virtually every feature is designed to fit another article, so that design right is lost by this exclusion. This is certainly true of some very simple components such as nuts and bolts or the balls of a ball bearing. This is a wide ranging exclusion which must be seriously considered before action is contemplated to enforce design right. Every feature of the shape of the article must be considered separately and every one which is shaped to fit something else must be discounted.

MUST MATCH   The second leg of the 'spare parts' exclusions is that there is no design right in those 'features of the shape' (we are getting familiar with this phrase by now) which 'are dependent on the appearance of another article of which the article is intended by the designer to form an integral part'. Now it is relatively easy to envisage that the shape of a car body panel is within this clause (and therefore excluded from protection). After all, if one takes a battered wing off a car, there is really only one shape of replacement wing which is going to suffice: the shape of the edges of the replacement wing are determined by the fact that they have to fit exactly to the adjacent parts of the car body and the general shape must be such that the wing is a mirror image of the opposite wing. This exclusion is known by the abbreviated title of 'must match'.

However, this clause may prove to be very limited because if one took, say, the bonnet of the car, which of course does not have an exactly matching part, although the shape of the edges of the bonnet is determined by the rest of the car, the shape of everything between the edges is a matter of choice. On that basis, the original car manufacturer would not lose design right in the shape of the bonnet—except for the peripheral shape which it might well be argued is a question of 'must fit' not 'must match'.

The concepts of 'must fit' and 'must match' are shown as applied to a gearbox (Figure 4.4(a) and (b)) designed solely for this book.

'Original' Another exclusion is a design that is not original. 'They cannot have protection for that, everybody does it!' An exclamation heard frequently in relation to intellectual property rights in functional designs. But they might! It is most important therefore to understand what is meant by a design being 'original'. Basically, it could be characterized as the 'blank-sheet-of-paper' definition, meaning that the designer set out to

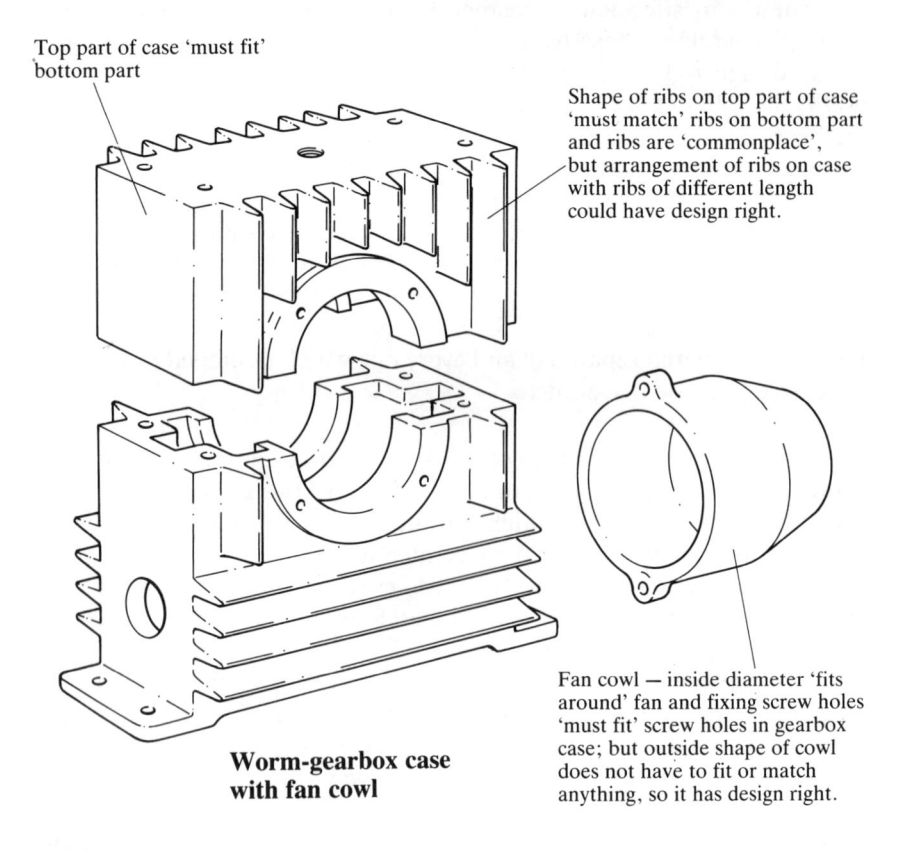

Top part of case 'must fit' bottom part

Shape of ribs on top part of case 'must match' ribs on bottom part and ribs are 'commonplace', but arrangement of ribs on case with ribs of different length could have design right.

Worm-gearbox case with fan cowl

Fan cowl — inside diameter 'fits around' fan and fixing screw holes 'must fit' screw holes in gearbox case; but outside shape of cowl does not have to fit or match anything, so it has design right.

Figure 4.4 (a) The 'must fit' and 'must match' concepts of design rights

INDUSTRIAL DESIGN

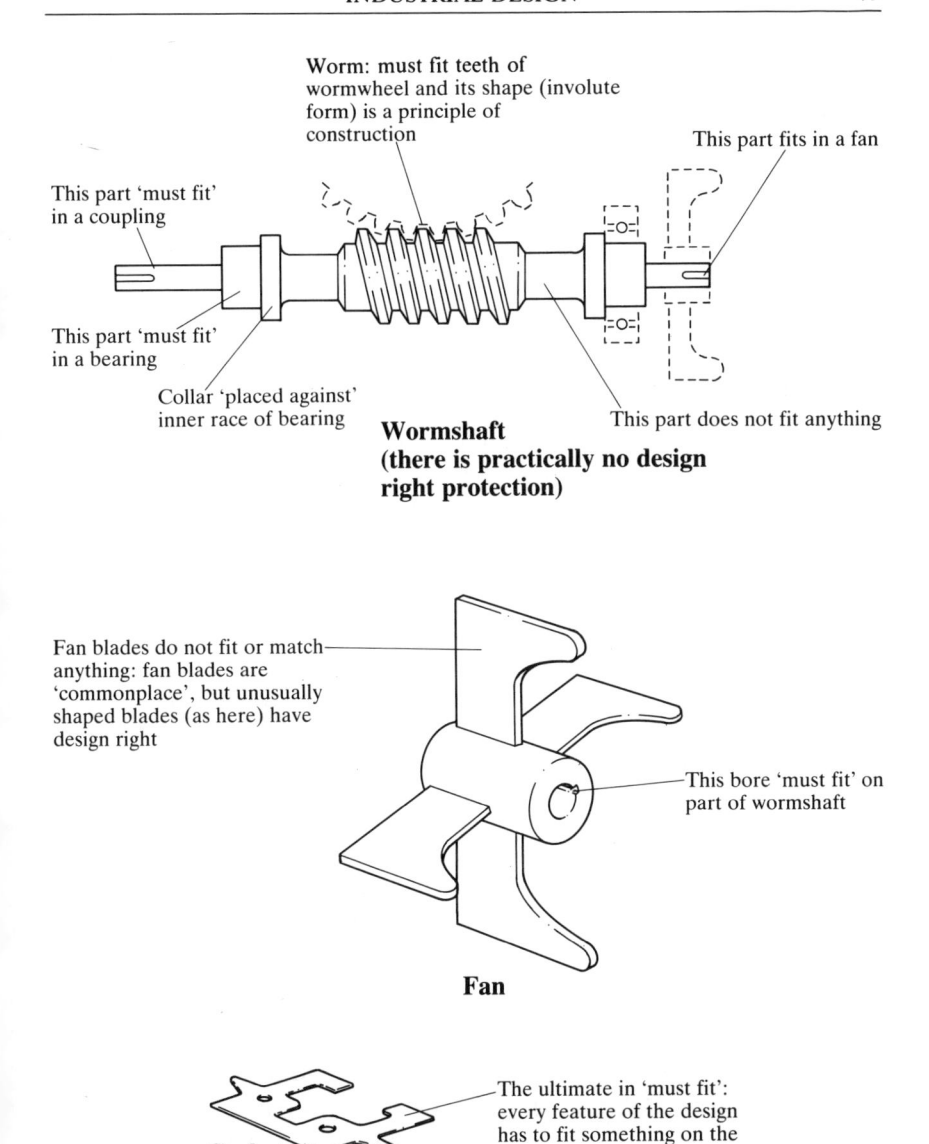

This part 'must fit' in a coupling

This part 'must fit' in a bearing

Collar 'placed against' inner race of bearing

Worm: must fit teeth of wormwheel and its shape (involute form) is a principle of construction

This part fits in a fan

This part does not fit anything

**Wormshaft
(there is practically no design right protection)**

Fan blades do not fit or match anything: fan blades are 'commonplace', but unusually shaped blades (as here) have design right

This bore 'must fit' on part of wormshaft

Fan

Gasket

The ultimate in 'must fit': every feature of the design has to fit something on the case

Figure 4.4. (b)

design the article, starting with an empty sheet of paper on which to draw some ideas. The moment the designer takes either an article, a drawing or a picture of an article and begins to use that as the model, originality is lost at least for those features copied from the model.

Taking this principle to its extreme, it means that two designers working independently could come up with exactly the same design: but in each case the design would be 'original' and therefore capable of attracting design right protection, even if one had been published before the other, so long as the second designer did not copy the first-published design.

The comparison between the monopoly given by a registered design and copyright arising from design right is in itself sufficient to show that where a design is thought to be completely novel, the proprietor ought to consider whether he can obtain patent or registered design protection, since that protection will be so much wider than the protection given by design right.

The concept of originality is simple enough, but, pushed to its extreme, it gives rise to the plea with which this section began: surely no one could have protection for a hexagon nut just because he made a drawing of one without copying anything else?

There is in fact a definition of 'originality' in the 1988 Act which says that something is not original if it is *'commonplace in the design field in question at the time of its creation'*. This brings our query into the real world of the 'design field in question', for example manufacture of belts, cars, pegs or whatever is being considered, which allows the manager for this purpose to concentrate on what is known in the industry. For precisely that reason, it is not possible to generalize about what does not get protection because it is commonplace.

The humble football boot stud has assumed a new importance in modern sports footwear. No longer secured by its own nails, four studs to the sole and two to the heel, it appears in a variety of patterns, each one having much the same sort of function as the latest 'magic' ingredient in a detergent—to increase the performance of the wearer in a particular sport. Some of the stud patterns doubtless involve much thought, but does that mean the designer of a new stud arrangement has design right protection? Probably not. Now that studs are frequently arranged in fancy patterns, it may well be argued that the design is commonplace—this will almost certainly be a matter of degree. (If the pattern is novel, the designer would probably be better advised to attempt to register it under the Registered Designs Act, because the question of 'not commonplace' does not arise there.)

Will it have design right?
It is now possible to summarize by setting out in the flowchart of Figure 4.5 the questions which must be asked about the design of any article to test whether it has design right protection.

INDUSTRIAL DESIGN 81

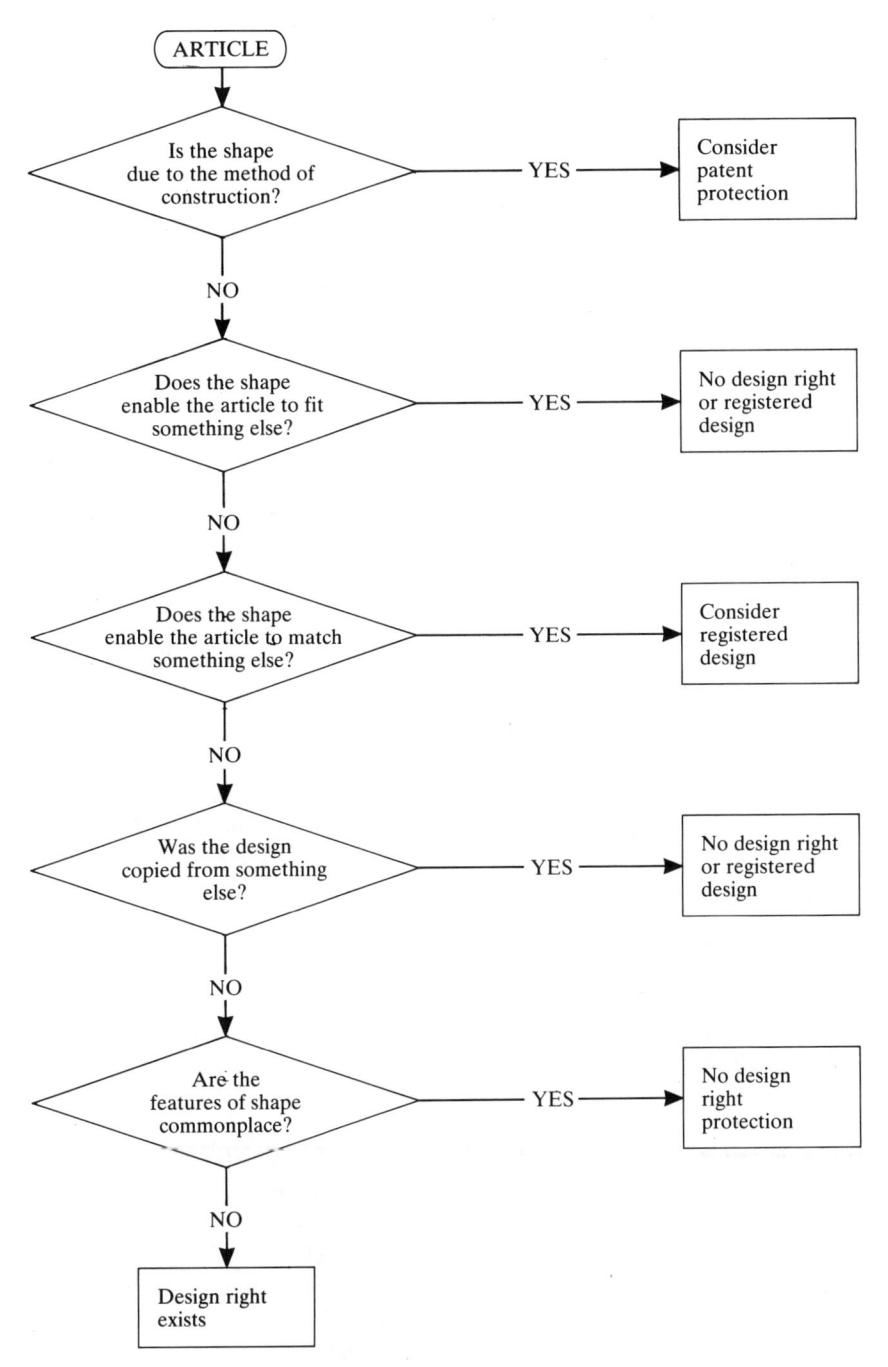

```
                    ARTICLE
                       │
                       ▼
              ┌─────────────────┐
              │  Is the shape   │                    ┌────────────┐
              │ due to the method│──── YES ────────▶│  Consider  │
              │ of construction?│                    │   patent   │
              └─────────────────┘                    │ protection │
                       │                             └────────────┘
                      NO
                       ▼
              ┌─────────────────┐
              │ Does the shape  │                    ┌──────────────┐
              │enable the article│─── YES ────────▶ │No design right│
              │to fit something │                    │ or registered│
              │     else?       │                    │    design    │
              └─────────────────┘                    └──────────────┘
                       │
                      NO
                       ▼
              ┌─────────────────┐
              │ Does the shape  │                    ┌────────────┐
              │enable the article│─── YES ────────▶ │  Consider  │
              │ to match something│                  │ registered │
              │     else?       │                    │   design   │
              └─────────────────┘                    └────────────┘
                       │
                      NO
                       ▼
              ┌─────────────────┐
              │  Was the design │                    ┌──────────────┐
              │ copied from     │──── YES ────────▶│No design right│
              │ something else? │                    │ or registered│
              │                 │                    │    design    │
              └─────────────────┘                    └──────────────┘
                       │
                      NO
                       ▼
              ┌─────────────────┐
              │    Are the      │                    ┌────────────┐
              │ features of shape│─── YES ────────▶ │ No design  │
              │   commonplace?  │                    │   right    │
              │                 │                    │ protection │
              └─────────────────┘                    └────────────┘
                       │
                      NO
                       ▼
              ┌─────────────────┐
              │  Design right   │
              │     exists      │
              └─────────────────┘
```

Figure 4.5 Will it have design right?

The term of design right
Because design right begins to subsist from the creation of a design, it is more difficult to determine the commencement date of the protection than it is with registered rights, such as patents or registered designs.

Where the mental concept of a design is changed into a drawing or some such precursor of the manufactured article, the 1988 Act refers to this as the design being 'recorded in a design document'. Design right does not subsist until the design has been *either*:

- recorded in a design document; *or*
- an article has been made to the design.

This gives us the starting date for design right protection.

It would of course be perfectly possible to define a shape entirely in numerical data comprising all the coordinates of the shape, and this would constitute a design document. It is to be stressed however that design right can subsist even if there never is a design document, as is the case when an artisan 'knocks up' an article without making a drawing first.

So we have a starting date for the protection, but what of its end? The formula which enables the term to be calculated works as follows. From the starting date (as established above) either:

- the term goes to the end of the calendar year 15 years after the year containing the starting date, *or*
- if articles embodying the design are put on the market (and that includes hiring as well as selling) within 5 years from the starting date, the term goes to the end of the calendar year 10 years after the year containing the first marketing date.

What appears from this rather involved method of calculating the term is that the proprietor never gets more than 11 years' protection after first marketing, even if that occurs on 1 January. Also, it will be apparent that, if possible, the event which determines the termination date should be as early in the year as possible.

The benefits of protection
It is convenient at this point to look at what the proprietor of design right can do with unsought protection. The answer is that the proprietor has the exclusive right to *reproduce* the design, but since the word 'reproduce' is capable of various interpretations there is a definition that the exclusive right to reproduce the design is infringed by anyone who *copies* the design. Therefore, the proprietor of design right does not have a monopoly in that design but only the right to prevent *copying*. Thus, in terms of protection, design right is nearer to copyright than to a registered design.

In practice, this means that someone who has a design right and finds a copy on the market must try to ascertain how the 'copy' article was produced. Not only must its source be traced, there must be at least prima facie evidence that the other person has actually copied the design for commercial purposes. There are many instances where the history of the case is such that the prima facie case is readily established; for instance, if the parties were at one time in some kind of trading relationship (e.g. a customer may think that it is possible to get the article made cheaper elsewhere, in which case the alternative manufacturer will be asked to copy the original design).

Taking the point of view of the company that knows of a competitor's product, which we will assume has design right, and that wishes to market something similar, the only safe ways of avoiding infringement are:

1. To employ a designer who is totally unaware of the protected design and then use the resulting design—since no matter how close it comes to the 'protected' design, it will not have been copied.
2. To design something which, while retaining the principle of operation of the 'protected' design, is so far removed from the shape of the 'protected' design that it could not possibly be regarded as a reproduction.

Infringement

Design right is infringed by a person who, without the licence of the design right holder, does, or authorizes another to do, anything which is the exclusive right of the design right owner. That exclusive right is the right to prevent copying by any person:

- making articles to the design; or
- making a design document, drawings, written description, etc., for the purpose of enabling such articles to be made for commercial purposes.

Anyone who breaches these rights is called a *primary infringer*.

However, there is another category of person who is considered to be an infringer, that is anyone who, again without licence from the design right holder:

- imports into the UK for commercial purposes; or
- possesses for commercial purposes; or
- sells, lets for hire or offers or exposes for sale or hire in the course of a business

an article which is, and which that person knows or has reason to believe is, an infringing article.

Such a person is referred to as a *secondary infringer*. Of course, the primary infringer may not be in the United Kingdom and therefore be very difficult, and sometimes impossible, to sue before the UK courts. Hence, in order to give the proprietor effective rights against infringement by importation, the Act allows the design right proprietor to sue the importer. But the law goes further than that: it permits an action to be brought against anyone selling the articles, irrespective of whether they were imported or not. This is a useful weapon for the proprietor because in some cases, although it may be obvious who is selling the articles (secondary infringer), it may be almost impossible to ascertain who is the manufacturer (primary infringer).

In order to prove infringement by a secondary infringer, it will be necessary to show that the importer or person offering the articles for sale had reason to believe that the articles were infringing. There are in fact provisions to protect an innocent infringer, but one way of depriving a party of the innocent infringer defence is for the proprietor to send the party a letter drawing attention to the claimed design right, and the alleged infringement of it. This should be drafted by an expert to avoid giving grounds for legal action.

In practice, if an article, which appears to be a copy, appears on the market then, if it turns out that the manufacturer cannot be sued because he is outside the United Kingdom, the proprietor will have to sue the importer or whoever is selling the article in the United Kingdom.

Licences of right

In one sense, design right differs from all other forms of intellectual property in that for the last five years of its term licences to copy are available 'as of right'. This means that during the last five years of the protection, anyone can approach the proprietor of the design right and demand a licence to do anything which is an infringement of the design right in that work. There is no record of such licences of course, because there is no design right register to endorse.

The terms of the licence will be settled by the comptroller unless the parties can agree. As to what level of royalties will prevail under the licences of right provisions, each case will have to be taken on its merits.

Besides, design right cannot, by definition, protect the only practical method of manufacture, so that usually a competitor will be able to make a *similar* article without a licence.

Consider someone selling a special spanner with sales of £5000 per annum. If the royalty likely to be awarded by the comptroller is only 3 per cent and the would-be licensee is only likely to sell £2000 worth per annum, the *total* royalties throughout the period of licences of right will £300. The costs of a contested application to the comptroller would greatly exceed that, so that there would be little point in the proprietor contesting the case, that is, in practice he or she will get nothing.

All this emphasizes the necessity for the proprietor of design right to be vigilant. Marking the goods with the proprietor's own name should abort the danger of a free licence from the comptroller and 'jumping on' infringers at the earliest possible moment will deprive competitors of the defence of 'innocent infringement'.

Transfer and voluntary licensing of design right
Since design right is a 'property right', it can be transferred (assigned) or voluntarily licensed like any other property. In general the rules relating to assignment and licensing follow those for other forms of intellectual property. However, there are some particular points to consider:

1. An assignment must be in writing.
2. It is possible to *assign* (but presumably not to license) future design right (i.e. a design not yet created) and this may be in respect of a specific design or a whole class of designs.
3. If a design is registered under the Registered Designs Act, then an assignment of the registered design *automatically* assigns the design right as well.

Relationship between registered designs, design right and copyright
The law seeks to draw a boundary between copyright and design right, while allowing for duplication of design right and registered design protection for the same article.

Generally speaking, design right is intended to give protection to functional designs which are not sufficiently aesthetic to be registrable. If a design is registrable, but is not in fact registered, the design will still have its design right. (Strictly speaking, it will retain its design right even if it is registered, but that will not normally be of any significance since the rights under the Registered Designs Act are both wider and of longer term than design right.)

A practical effect of this overlap between registered design and design right is that many plaintiffs in infringement actions will sue under both rights in the hope that if they fail on one, they will succeed on the other.

When it comes to copyright, the law states that if there is both copyright and design right in an article then it is not an infringement of the design right to do anything which infringes the copyright. Thus, the copyright is to predominate and designers who think their designs have been copied must sue for copyright infringement. Design right will not help them. Under the 1988 Act, 'graphic works' such as drawings are given artistic work copyright, and the degree of artistry is immaterial—so an engineering drawing is an artistic work—and anyone who copies that drawing, in any way, infringes its copyright. But if the article depicted in the drawing is not an artistic work itself, then the copyright in that drawing is not infringed by making the article depicted. And going on from there, because the *copyright* is not infringed by copying the (non-artistic) drawing, the design right remains intact and can be enforced.

Supposing a draughtsperson draws a connecting rod for a car engine: the drawing is an artistic work—so anyone who takes a print or photocopy of the drawing infringes the copyright.

If a competitor takes either the drawing (no matter how it was acquired) or the connecting rod made to the drawing, and then makes a copy of the connecting rod, he will not infringe the copyright because the article (i.e. the connecting rod) is not in itself an artistic work.

That means, however, that the competitor will infringe the design right (providing all the other criteria of design right infringement are met).

If the drawing had been an ornamental ceramic badger or fox, that article would have been an artistic work, therefore copyright could be invoked if the design were copied and design right could not be invoked because of the exclusion of dual copyright design right protection.

It should always be remembered that there will be instances where different features of the same article will have copyright and design right protection.

A turbine rotor (Figure 4.6) is a good example of an engineering product which may have involved hundreds of hours of design work, but which receives little or possibly no protection as a design. There will be copyright in the design drawings, but no copyright in the rotor itself because it is not an artistic work. The shape of the rotor would not be registrable as a design, because the shape of the blades is dictated solely by the function they have to perform (i.e. react against the steam flow) and since the customer will be concerned solely with performance, which will be a function of the shape, it follows that the 'appearance' is immaterial and, consequently, the criteria for design registration are not met. Finally, it may not even have design right, because the shape of the blades, which is derived mathematically, may be regarded as being 'a method or principle of construction'. The rotor itself into which the blades are embedded, will be designed virtually entirely to fit into other components, or so as to be 'connected to' the rotor blades.

If the principle of the design is novel and inventive, then that principle might be protected by a patent.

Overlapping protection for aesthetic articles is illustrated by the coffee set in Figure 4.2:

1. *The shape* of the coffee jug will be registered.
2. In any event, assuming that the jug is an artistic work, its *shape* will be protected by copyright for 25 years.

Figure 4.6 The low pressure stage of a triple expansion steam turbine, under construction

3. The design on the surface of the jug and cup could be registered as a design for a 'set of articles'.
4. In any event, the surface design will have copyright as an artistic work, no matter to what it is applied, that is, it is covered by the jug, the cup and the napkin, and it would equally be covered if it were applied to curtain fabrics, tablecloths or ladies' dresses.

The interface between copyright and design right is complicated and it is certainly one where professional advice will normally be required. As a preliminary guide, however, if the article to be manufactured is primarily of an artistic nature, it will probably be necessary to look to copyright for protection, whereas if the article is not artistic it will probably be necessary to look to design right.

Summary
Registered designs cover the aesthetic design of an article and enable their proprietor to go to law to stop anyone from putting on the market articles having a shape confusingly similar to the design covered by the registration. Certain formalities must be completed and fees paid. The competitive design need not have been copied from the registered one: in other words, one is not faced with a copyright infringement situation. The courts are primarily interested in knowing that the design registration is in force, and in reaching a view on the similarity between the registered design and the 'infringing' one.

Design right covers the functional shape of an article and the proprietor is able to go to law to prevent the commercialization of articles copied from the original design. There is no registration of design right and no formalities to acquire it. The courts are primarily concerned that the design is original, that protection is not excluded (e.g. must fit) and that there has been actual copying.

5 Protection of semiconductor products

Robert J. Hart

Introduction: integrated circuits and their protection
This chapter differs from others in the book because, instead of beginning with the law and applying it to technology, the starting point is the technology itself. It begins by explaining what integrated circuits are and why they require legal protection.

What are integrated circuits?
Integrated circuits are semiconductor products, sometimes referred to as 'chips', which perform electronic and related functions. Semiconductor materials are elements or compounds that partially conduct electricity and are influenced by electrical currents applied to them. They are intermediate between conductors, which fully conduct electricity, and insulators, which do not appreciably conduct any electricity. Semiconductors in use currently include silicon, germanium and gallium arsenide.

Integrated circuits can form standard components such as micro-computers, gate arrays and memory devices; they can be semi-custom-designed chips using gate arrays and programmed logic arrays connected to meet a specific requirement; or fully custom-designed complex integrated circuit chips for use in a specialized field, for example telecommunications. Optical and electronic modulators, amplifiers and demodulators can also be readily implemented in integrated form.

Integrated circuits consist of layers of semiconductor material with insulators of various compositions that combine to form the transistors, capacitors, resistors, diodes and other components required. The semiconductor layers are 'doped' in predetermined places with traces of other elements such as boron, phosphorus and arsenic. The layers are sandwiched together with insulating and metal layers to form the component. Physically a semiconductor integrated circuit device of the order of 0.6 cm² may contain in excess of 100 000 transistors performing the functions which, if implemented in discrete component design, would require a room full of components with their associated mounting and interconnection arrangements.

The configurations of the various 'layers' of an integrated circuit are determined by directing a pattern of light on to a photosensitive surface.

The pattern may, for example, be determined by the use of 'masks' which act as a kind of stencil in the manufacturing process, although with more advanced systems a computer controlled laser may be used to expose the photosensitive surface directly.

A pure semiconductor material wafer, which is a 10cm to 17 cm diameter disk, will have hundreds of semiconductor chips photoengraved on to it so that at the end of the process the wafer will resemble a round sheet of postage stamps.

Why should integrated circuits be protected?
The semiconductor industry is an essential component of the economy of an industrialized nation. More and more electronic control functions are being implemented into integrated circuit form with the attendant increase in processing power, energy conservation, physical space saving and cost of production.

To a very large extent, the unparalleled growth achieved by the electronics industry over the past two decades has been due to the development of the semiconductor chip. The chip has made possible the creation of many of the new high technology products which have caused this growth. It has led to the development of new industries. Personal computers, word processors, video games, hand-held calculators, portable telephones and digital watches are but a few of the products which the rapid development of the chip has made possible.

Semiconductor chips have had a significant effect on other products as well. Today, motor cars, ovens, telephones, radios, television sets and washing machines all contain semiconductor chips and, as a result, are able to perform more efficiently than ever before and frequently can be sold at a lower price. By reducing production costs and increasing product quality, the semiconductor chip plays a major role in keeping a wide array of products competitive in world markets.

Continued innovation in semiconductors, however, with all its desirable effects, is threatened by the piracy, or unauthorized reproduction of semiconductor circuit layout patterns. As chips have grown more efficient and powerful, each new development has cost more in R & D investment and man-hours. Today the development of a new family of semiconductor chips can require a substantial period to complete, demand thousands of hours of engineers' and technicians' time, and may cost up to £10 million or more. These high fixed or front-end costs must be reflected in the price at which those semiconductor chips are sold, as firms seek to achieve a rate of return sufficient to cover past R & D and investments and provide for continued development of new products.

A pirate firm, on the other hand, can produce a perfect copy of another firm's main chip of a family for as little as £50 000 to £100 000. An entire family of chips can be copied for less than £1 million. As a result, pirate firms with no R & D investment to recoup can set their prices far lower than can the firms that have underwritten the development costs. The result is a reduction in the price at which the innovative firm can sell its chips. Often this means a loss in market share for the innovative firm.

Protection is required to prevent the direct unauthorized copying of an integrated circuit chip product as well as against the infringement of the rights in patentable inventions embodied in the chip product.

How are chips pirated?
The technology for copying chips is well developed and relatively inexpensive in comparison with the cost of designing the chip and initially preparing masks for chip manufacture. The copyist simply removes the plastic or ceramic casing, photographs the top metal connection layer, dissolves the metal away with acid in order to photograph the semiconductor material in the next layer, and then photographs underlying translucent semiconductor layers by varying the depth of focus of the camera. The photographs can then be used, either solely for purposes of analysis (which, as 'reverse engineering', should be legitimate in itself) or simply to reproduce unauthorized copies of the masks that were used to make copies of the original chip (which is piracy).

What type of protection is required?
The type of protection required for the vast majority of integrated circuits is against an unauthorized third party copying either the masks or the laser control 'plots' which can be used to produce an integrated circuit product. These are the vulnerable items which are easily reproduced but require substantial inventment to design in the first place. The protection provided must also be obtained quickly since the 'lead time' for a new product may be only one or two years. Protection against the unauthorized reproduction of substantial parts of a semiconductor chip product is also required to prevent the appropriation of the design by making a minor modification, or by including it in a larger design.

While protection against copying of the mask works is very important, the protection of novel and inventive circuitry embodied on the chip by patents should not be overlooked.

Throughout the rest of this chapter reference will be made to 'topographies', 'mask works' and 'circuit layout designs'. All of these terms relate to the layout of the components formed on the semiconductor substrate of an integrated circuit and are interchangeable.

Protection in the United Kingdom
For the layout designs created on or after 1 August 1989 legal protection

subsists under the Design Right (Semiconductor Topographies) Regulations 1989. Unfortunately the Regulations are very difficult to interpret. For layout designs created before 1 August 1989, different laws and regulations apply which for brevity and simplicity are not considered here.

The 1989 Regulations give a definition for 'semiconductor product' as follows:

Semiconductor product
means an article the purpose, or one of the purposes, of which is the performance of electronic function and which consists of two or more layers, at least one of which is composed of semiconducting material and in or upon one or more of which is fixed a pattern appertaining to that or another function.

Arguably the right extends to a pattern which is non-electronic in function (i.e. optical). The definition, however, clearly removes printed circuit boards with their components mounted on them as it calls for two or more layers, at least one of which is a semiconductor material.

The Regulation is cross-referenced with the 1988 Act, under which layouts for semiconductor products are protected by the design right (see Chapter 4) but with many special features. The design right protects:

1. the pattern fixed, or intended to be fixed, in or upon:
   (a) a layer of semiconductor product, or
   (b) a layer of material in the course of and for the purpose of the manufacture of a semiconductor product, or
2. the arrangement of the patterns fixed, or intended to be fixed, in or upon the layers of a semiconductor product in relation to one another.

A single layer topography is included in the definition, therefore the metallized layer of a customized or semi-customized chip can be considered as a topography in its own right.

Registration or deposit of the layout design is *not* a prerequisite to the entitlement to protection in the United Kingdom. All topographies which are original and not commonplace are protected once they are expressed in a form from which they can be reproduced, whether in the form of a drawing, a written description, a photograph, data stored in a computer or otherwise. Even a list of functional requirements of a complex ASIC (Application Specific Integrated Circuit) held in a computer operating on a chip design program could be protected.

To be original a topography must not be commonplace in the semiconductor industry at the time of its creation. However, if the topography consists of a combination of commonplace elements, it will be considered original if the combination is not itself commonplace. Computer-created topographies using silicon compilers are protected, because computer-generated designs are protected under the design right.

Term
The period of protection for an original topography is either (a) 10 years from the end of the year in which a topography was first commercially exploited anywhere in the world or (b) 15 years from its creation, if no commercial exploitation occurs within that period. This means that it is possible for a topography, which is first exploited just before the end of the fifteenth year from its creation, to be protected for some 25 years, but in most cases protection will last for 10 years from first marketing of the chip.

The definition of commercial exploitation is important with respect to the term. Commercial exploitation is the sale or hire or offer or exposure for sale or hire, of a reproduction of the protected topography or a semiconductor incorporating such a reproduction by or with the licence or consent of the owner of the right in the topography. However, no account is to be taken of any prior offer for sale or hire which is 'merely colourable' and not intended to satisfy the reasonable requirements of the public; this qualification prevents the premature starting of the period of protection in the case of advance notification of a semiconductor product, which is often used in the industry where a product is offered for sale before it has actually been implemented into silicon.

Ownership
The law in the United Kingdom gives the right in a topography design produced by an employee automatically to the employer, and to the commissioner of the design in the absence of a contract to the contrary. This is a very important point for an independent topography design house to note. If the design house wants to retain the rights to a design produced for a client it will have to ensure that the commissioning contract overrides the statutory provision. Similarly, employers may want their contracts of employment to confirm that their employees recognize that the rights in topography designs belong to the employer, although it is not essential to do so.

For computer-generated designs, the owner is the person by whom the arrangements necessary for the creation of the design were undertaken. This is an important point to note since the vast majority of chips, particularly application-specific chips (ASICs) have their topographies created using computer-aided design techniques, commonly referred to as silicon compilers. Chip designers do not directly create the topography for the chips they design, rather they instruct the silicon compiler what functions and operational performances are required from the final chip design.

Exclusive rights
The owner of the rights in the topography of a semiconductor product

has the exclusive right to make a reproduction of the whole (or a substantial part) of the topography or to deal in such a reproduction or deal with a semiconductor product incorporating such a reproduction of the topography. A person deals in a reproduction by selling or hiring it, offering or exposing it for sale or hire, or importing it into the country for the purpose of selling or hiring it. The qualification of a 'substantial part' on the right of reproduction and dealing has been included, I believe, to prevent an infringer taking the important part of a topography while leaving out, or modifying, unimportant sections. The term 'substantial part' means substantial from a qualitative rather than a quantitative aspect.

There are some exceptions to the owner's rights. The first permits reproduction of a topography for private non-commercial purposes but may well be of no real significance from an industrial point of view. The second exception permits reproduction for both commercial and non-commercial research purposes as well as in teaching (and see below for a separate section on so-called reverse engineering). The third exception relates to the European exhaustion of rights doctrine; effectively, once a copy of a topography or a semiconductor product incorporating a protected topography has been sold or hired in Europe, the rights in that copy or product have been exhausted so that further sale or hire of *that* copy or product cannot be controlled by the holder of the rights in the topography.

Infringement
The rights in a topography are infringed by any person who reproduces the whole or a substantial part of the protected topography or deals in such a reproduction or authorizes any other person to do such acts. The extension to a person who authorizes infringement may have important implications for silicon fabrication houses who allow customers to use their cell libraries to design their own customized chips. Such fabrication houses may be held liable if a design produced by customer B is an infringement of the topography right of customer A. It is important for these points to be taken into account when conducting negotiations for custom and semi-custom chip designs. These and related issues are considered below under the heading 'Chip design contractual issues'. The remedies available to a right holder involve relief by way of damages, injunction and accounts of profit.

Reverse engineering
The reverse engineering exception is effectively in two parts. Under the first part it is an exception to the topography rightful owner's exclusive right to reproduce the topography for the purpose of analysing or evaluating the topography or analysing, evaluating or teaching the concepts,

processes, systems or techniques embodied in the topography. Under the second part it is not an infringement to create another topography as a result of the analysis or evaluation permitted in the first part. At the date of writing it is too early to decide if the reverse engineering exception will allow a competitor, without authorization, to copy from the topography of a first chip into the topography of a second chip as long as the second chip is original compared to the first chip, that is, includes additional material which is not copied from the first chip.

It is to be hoped that the reverse engineering exception will be interpreted to exclude copying from the topography of one chip into another, otherwise it will be open for a pirate to, say, combine in a single topography the important parts of two or more topographies to produce an 'original' composite chip. It seems to the writer that reverse engineering should be considered in two separate parts with the permitted reproduction stopping at the analysis stage. However, the only US case which has so far gone to court seems to condone copying from one chip to another as long as the second chip includes additional material to make it original.

Chip design contractual issues
When considering custom and semi-custom design contracts it is important to consider not only the normal issues of design responsibility (product functional and product performance specifications, warranties and liabilities, and second sourcing for example) but also the intellectual property rights issues which will include topography rights in the chips' design.

Typically, for cell-based custom designs (that is the chip manufacturer allows its customers to design their own circuit using the chip manufacturer's standard 'cells' selected and connected together to give the required circuit using a computer-aided design system) the manufacturer will seek to retain all intellectual property rights to the individual cells contained in the final chip, including the right to incorporate them into products sold to other customers (except cells created specifically for the chip at the expense of the customer and agreed to be proprietary to the customer). However, the customer may acquire the rights, or an exclusive licence to use them, in the new complete semiconductor product ('the ensemble'). In any event the manufacturer should be made to agree not to use the same topographies (or the pattern generation tapes for them) to make some other customer's products.

Chip manufacturers frequently require the customer to indemnify the manufacturer from any liability based upon complying with the customer's design or based upon the manufacturer's liability to contributory infringement. This is not unreasonable because the final electronic circuit design produced by the customer may be an infringement of a third party held patent. Alternatively, the customer may have reverse engineered a competitor's chip or may have incorporated a read-only memory (ROM) which may contain a third party copyright computer program. Since the customer is the one who selects the electronic circuit or ROM, the manufacturer is unlikely to be willing to assume liability for the choice. Also, should the customer infringe a third party's patent on a device by using the newly designed chip as a material part of the device, or infringe a third party method patent by operating the chip in a particular way, the chip supplier will require to be held harmless.

Protection outside the United Kingdom
Although this chapter is about the legal protection for semiconductor products in the United Kingdom it is important to know, in outline, the position in other countries.

President Reagan signed the US Semiconductor Chip Protection Act of 1984 on 9 November 1984 and this marked the first introduction of a new type of intellectual property law in the United States for over 100 years. It also marks the first intellectual property legislation directed to a new kind of technology. The new law is neither a copyright law nor a patent law, but a hybrid form of industrial property legislation that combines aspects of copyright law, patent law and new elements found in neither copyright nor patent law.

The Act, which came into force on 8 January 1985, creates a new form of legal protection in the United States for 'mask works' and the semiconductor chip products in which they are embodied. The essential features of the Act are that protection extends to mask works which are the three-dimensional images or patterns formed on or in and fixed in a semiconductor chip product. This is a narrower concept than applies in the United Kingdom, where a mask work is protected even if it is not incorporated in a product.

The protection does not extend to ideas and concepts, and a mask work must be original to be protected. Registration is mandatory within two years after the date on which the mask work was first commercially exploited, and protection lasts for 10 years to the end of the year from the date of registration or first commercial exploitation, whichever occurs first.

Exclusive rights of the owner are:

1. To reproduce the mask work.
2. To import or distribute semiconductor chip products embodying the mask work.
3. To induce the reproduction or import or distribution of the mask work or semiconductor chip product incorporating the mask work.

Reverse engineering permits the reproduction of a mask work for the purpose of teaching, analysing or evaluating the concepts embodied in the work and also permits the results to be incorporated in another original mask work.

Marking of mask works and products is optional; if a mark is required it should be the symbol Ⓜ and the name of the owner of the mask work.

There is also a law in Japan similar to the US law, and the Council of the European Communities has published a Directive on the Legal Protection of the Topographies of Semiconductor Products, with the aim of harmonizing protection in Europe. The position at the date of writing is summarized in Table 5.1. It is to be noted that, where a country has a registration requirement, a topography must be registered in that country within two years of first commercialization in any country, otherwise it will not be protected.

Summary

Original semiconductor topographies are protected automatically against unauthorized reproduction as such or incorporation in a semiconductor product in the United Kingdom under the design right. An original topography is one which is not commonplace in the industry at the time of its creation, however, combinations of commonplace topography elements are protected.

The protection starts at creation and exists for a maximum of 10 years from the end of the year of first commercial exploitation of the topography anywhere in the world. If no commercial exploitation occurs within 15 years from creation, the protection ceases at the end of that year.

Topographies created by computer-aided design systems, such as silicon compilers, are protected. Employee-created topographies belong to the employer, and those commissioned by a third party belong to the commissioner, in the absence of a contract to the contrary.

A so-called 'reverse engineering' right permits the reproduction of a topography for the purpose of analysing or evaluating the concepts, processes, systems or techniques embodied in it and the creation of another original topography as a result of that analysis or evaluation.

Protection in many overseas countries (a) only applies to topographies which have been implemented into a product and (b) requires registration of the topography with governmental authority and may also require deposit of actual semiconductor products with the registration application.

Table 5.1 Implementation of the EEC Directive on legal protection of topographies of semiconductor products

	Belgium	Denmark	France	Germany	Greece	Ireland	Italy	Luxembourg	Netherlands	Portugal	Spain	UK
Date implementing legislation enacted	10 Jan 90	9 Dec 87	4 Nov 87	22 Oct 87	Note [1]	13 May 88	21 Feb 89	29 Dec 88	28 Oct 87	30 Jun 89	3 May 88	1 Aug 89[2]
Date implementing legislation in force	5 Feb 90	3 Mar 88	6 Nov 87	1 Nov 87		13 May 88	21 Feb 89	30 Dec 88	7 Nov 87	30 Jun 89	5 Sep 88	7 Nov 87
Employer owns employee works?	YES	YES	YES	YES		YES	YES	YES	YES	YES	YES [3]	YES
Commissioner owns commissioned works?	YES	YES	YES	YES		YES	YES	YES	NO	YES	YES	YES
Registration requirements?	NO	YES	YES[4]	YES		NO	YES	YES	YES	YES	YES	NO
Deposit requirements?	NO	NO	YES[4]	YES		NO	YES	YES	YES	YES	YES	NO
Fees payable on registration/deposit?	NO	YES	YES[4]	YES		NO	YES	YES	YES	YES	YES	NO
Provision as to use of topography notice?	NO	NO	YES[4]	NO		NO	YES	YES	NO	YES	YES	NO
Procedure for compulsory licensing?	NO	YES	NO	NO		NO	NO	YES	NO	YES	YES	NO

NOTES

[1] No legislation or draft published
[2] Replaced 7 Nov 1987 Regulations
[3] Subject to Title 4, 1986 Patents Law
[4] Governed by 2 Nov 1989 Regulations

Table prepared by Christopher Millard, Clifford Chance, London, based on information available as at 1 March 1989. © Clifford Chance, 1990. All rights reserved.

6 Patents

Jacqueline Needle

Introduction

Patents are all too often ignored by business in the United Kingdom. This disregard is justified on the grounds that patents are complex and expensive, and that 'my competitor will easily be able to get round the patent by making minor changes'. The general public perceives patents as being much more powerful. Apocryphal stories abound in which patents are used by the unscrupulous to keep fundamental inventions such as the everlasting lightbulb and the reusable match from the people.

The truth, as is often the case, is somewhere between these common misconceptions. Patents can be extremely powerful business tools, or even weapons. The basis of patent law is simple and logical. The cost of obtaining a patent in the United Kingdom to acquire an absolute monopoly for 20 years can be less than the insertion cost for one quarter-page advertisement in a national newspaper. In addition, it is not necessary to push back the frontiers of science to come up with an invention which can be protected. Toothbrushes with integral toothpaste tubes, an apparatus for playing a board game, a method of making a chocolate bar, animal feeding troughs, and domestic appliances can be found, together with new drugs and integrated circuits for computers in lists of patents granted.

In this chapter we shall look at what can and cannot be protected by way of a patent. The application procedure by which patents are obtained will be briefly described, and the use and usefulness of patents will also be examined.

What can be protected by a patent?

There is no absolute right to be granted a patent. To obtain a patent one goes through an application process during which it is necessary to demonstrate that certain criteria have been met. These are illustrated in Figure 6.1 and are:

- that there is an 'invention';
- that the invention is not excluded;
- that the invention is new; and
- that the invention is not obvious.

In considering what constitutes an invention, and is therefore

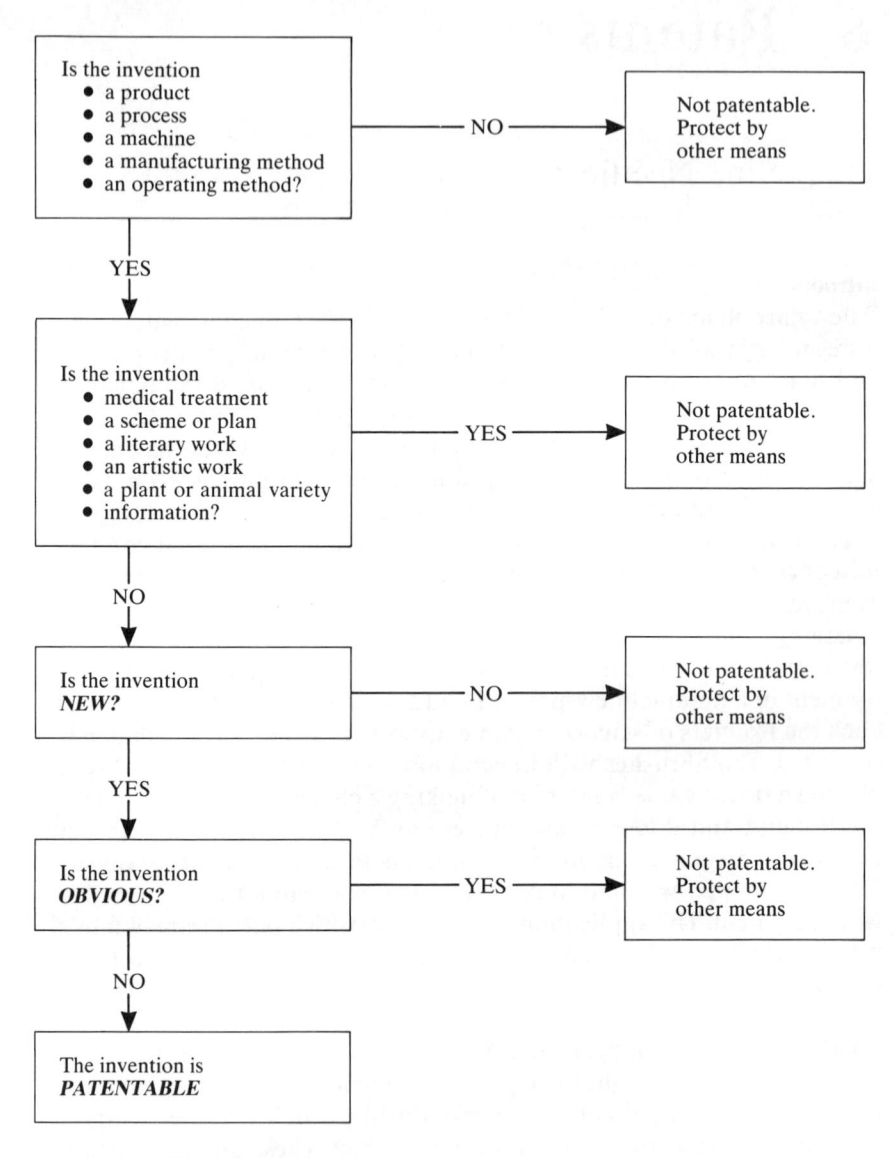

```
┌─────────────────────────────┐
│ Is the invention            │
│  • a product                │          ┌──────────────┐
│  • a process                │          │ Not patentable.│
│  • a machine                │── NO ──▶│ Protect by    │
│  • a manufacturing method   │          │ other means   │
│  • an operating method?     │          └──────────────┘
└─────────────┬───────────────┘
              │ YES
              ▼
┌─────────────────────────────┐
│ Is the invention            │
│  • medical treatment        │          ┌──────────────┐
│  • a scheme or plan         │          │ Not patentable.│
│  • a literary work          │── YES ──▶│ Protect by    │
│  • an artistic work         │          │ other means   │
│  • a plant or animal variety│          └──────────────┘
│  • information?             │
└─────────────┬───────────────┘
              │ NO
              ▼
┌─────────────────────────────┐          ┌──────────────┐
│ Is the invention            │          │ Not patentable.│
│ NEW?                        │── NO ──▶│ Protect by    │
│                             │          │ other means   │
└─────────────┬───────────────┘          └──────────────┘
              │ YES
              ▼
┌─────────────────────────────┐          ┌──────────────┐
│ Is the invention            │          │ Not patentable.│
│ OBVIOUS?                    │── YES ──▶│ Protect by    │
│                             │          │ other means   │
└─────────────┬───────────────┘          └──────────────┘
              │ NO
              ▼
┌─────────────────────────────┐
│ The invention is            │
│ PATENTABLE                  │
└─────────────────────────────┘
```

Figure 6.1 Can this be protected by a patent?

'patentable', neither the current law, the Patents Act 1977, nor the earlier statutes have been particularly helpful. The present Act does not attempt to define an 'invention', although it does require that an invention 'has to be made or used in any kind of industry'.

What can and cannot be considered to be an invention has been the subject of many cases over the years as industry has sought patent protection for an ever changing range of goods and processes. These cases show that, in general terms, patents protect the tangible rather than the intangible, and the technical rather than the artistic. To quote the judge in a case from 1819, an invention is 'something of a corporeal and substantial nature, something that can be made by man from the matters subjected to his art and skill, or at least some mode of employing practically his art and skill . . .'. So the appearance, size, colour or other visual features of an article will not be patentable, but the article itself, the manner in which it operates, or the method by which it was manufactured should be patentable. A product, article, material, apparatus or process will generally be considered to be an invention. Two examples of patented products, differing in size and complexity, are illustrated in Figures 6.2 and 6.3.

To understand better how an invention which can be protected by a patent differs from non-patentable things, consider the familiar cassette tape which is widely available for the recording of sound. Let us assume that a project involving the use of such a cassette tape has resulted in a new development, and let us consider the circumstances in which this development could constitute an invention and therefore be protectable by a patent.

1. *A newly composed piece of music has been recorded on to a conventional cassette tape using a conventional tape recorder.* In this case the development is the music, that is, the recorded information, and such a development does not constitute an invention. Similarly, there would be no patentable invention where the recorded information was a dramatized play or a recording of bird song and in all other respects the tape and recording process were conventional.

2. *It has been discovered that coating the magnetic tape with a particular substance improves its performance dramatically.* Here we have a coated magnetic tape with a different composition to the conventional tape and this constitutes an invention. Furthermore, if the development includes a method of applying the coating to the tape, or a method of making the coating to enable its application, these methods would also be considered to form inventions.

3. *The method by which sound is recorded on to the magnetic tape is changed to improve the quality of the recordings.* The method includes the generation and processing of electrical signals, and it is well established that systems involving the use and control of electrical signals are patentable. It will probably also be possible to protect the electrical circuits used to provide the signal processing methods.

4. *The tape recorder is redesigned to give it a modern 'look'. For example, the single speaker is replaced by two spaced speakers positioned at each end of the body.* No patent protection will be available for the aesthetic

Figure 6.2 An automatic sorting machine of Loctronic International Limited features this sorting area where defective potatoes are removed. The structure of the sorting area is the subject of European patent application No. 0 319 239. The machine uses colour television signals to detect the defects, and the scanning methods and systems are protected by a number of patents and applications including European patent applications Nos. 0 194 148 and 0 267 790.

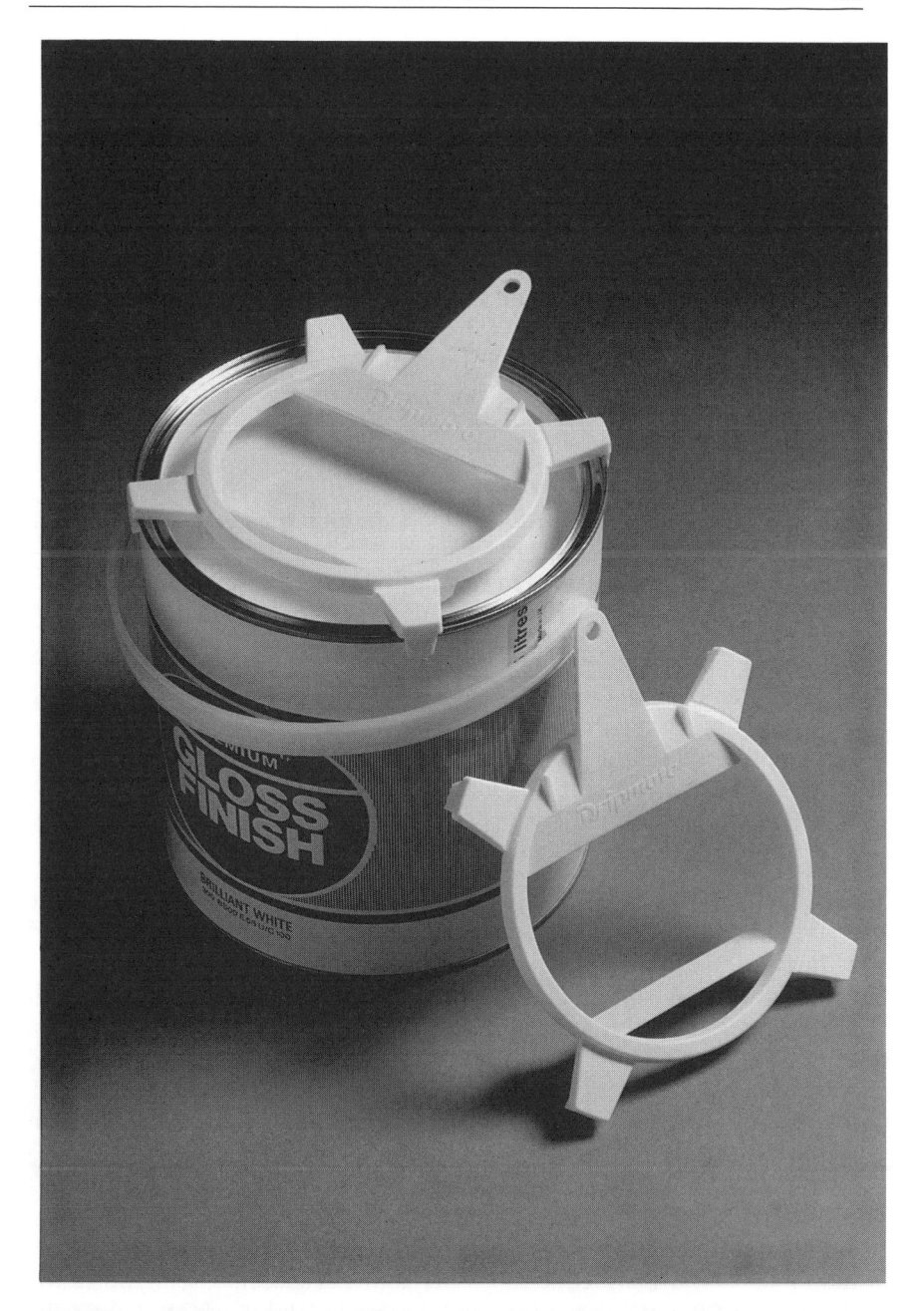

Figure 6.3 Patented brush rest for paint tin. This product of Dripmate Limited clips on to paint containers to provide a brush rest and to prevent drips. The product is protected by British design registration No. 1 059 256 and by British patent No. 2 225 309.

changes, but it may be possible to protect the appearance of the tape recorder by a registered design. However, if the decision to use two speakers requires the development of new electrical drive circuits for the speakers, these circuits may constitute inventions.

In the examples outlined above the result of the project has been compared with that which is conventional to identify what is new. This arises because of the further requirement that an invention must be new. The examples also demonstrate that a single project can lead to the development of more than one invention. Furthermore, a single product or article can be thought of as composed of a number of aspects, and more than one of these individual aspects can constitute an invention and lead to the grant of a patent.

Exclusions from patentability
Not all objects and procedures which can be characterized as 'inventions' can be protected by a patent. The Patents Act 1977 lists a number of items which are specifically excluded from protection. These are:

1. Discoveries.
2. Literary and other artistic works.
3. A method of doing business or playing a game.
4. A program for a computer.
5. The presentation of information.
6. A method of treatment of a human or animal.
7. A plant or animal variety.
8. A biological process for the production of plants and animals.

When the apple fell on Newton's head he 'discovered' gravity, but he could not obtain a patent for the principle. However, if he had developed a device, for example a pendulum clock, utilizing gravity, that device could have been protected by a patent. In this respect, it is important to remember that the things listed above are only excluded from patent protection 'as such'. Thus, the inventor of a new board game is precluded from obtaining a patent for the rules of the game. However, if the board, for example, is new in the sense that it has identifiable areas marked on it which differ from those of earlier games, it will be possible to obtain a patent for the game. The patent would protect the game apparatus, that is the board, to be played in accordance with the rules.

Figure 6.4 shows an extract from UK patent No. 2 152 391. This patent describes a board game based on the game of soccer. The figure shows the board of the game, together with the main 'claim' which defines the invention actually protected by the patent.

Three of the exclusions listed above are worth considering in more detail as they affect industries having high research and development costs and a consequent interest in protecting the fruits of this expenditure.

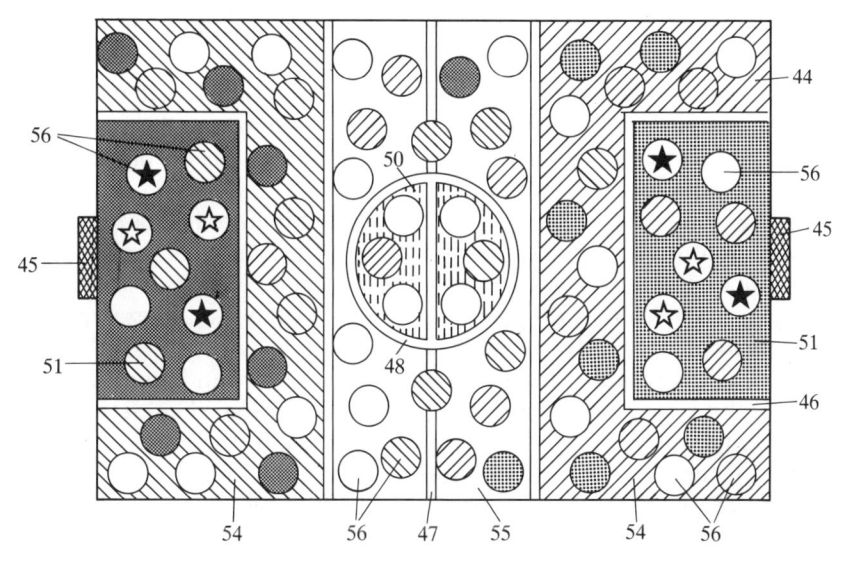

This is the 'claim' of the patent which defines its protection:

A playing board apparatus for simulating a goal-scoring contest comprising a play area divided into a plurality of zones, including a first or goal zone, a second or scoring zone and a third or scrimmage zone, a plurality of indicia spots in each of said zones except the first zone, and mask means overlying each spot and in its active condition covering the indicium of the spot, selected spots in said second zone being 'coupled' (as hereinbefore defined) to said first zone, other selected spots in said second zone being 'coupled' to the third zone, the third zone having selected spots with indicia 'coupled' to said second zone and selected spots with indicia 'coupled' to said third zone, each said mask means being capable of inactivation to expose the indicium of each respective spot.

Figure 6.4 Patenting a board game

Computer software

You would be wrong if you believed that the exclusion of 'a program for a computer' from patentability means that computer software cannot be protected by patents. The computer industry was particularly active in exploring the boundary of this exclusion in the 1960s and since then patents featuring computer programs, flowcharts and algorithms have become commonplace.

In 1962 Patrick Slee and Pauline Harris were using a computer to solve simultaneous linear equations. The method the computer was programmed to employ involved performing a first iteration on a first set of variables to produce a second set of variables, and then performing a second iterative process on that second set of variables. Slee and Harris realized that computer time could be saved by arranging for the second iteration to be commenced while the first was still proceeding and they developed a program to perform this improved method. The UK Patent Office refused to allow protection for 'A method of operating a computer to solve a linear programming problem by an iterative algorithm'. However, the Patent Office did grant a patent for 'A computer when programmed to solve a linear programming problem'. It was concluded that the programmed computer could be considered to be a temporarily modified machine and, as such, it clearly fell outside of the exclusion preventing the patenting of computer programs.

Since that time patent applications relating to programmed computers have been routinely accepted by the Patent Office. In 1969 the British Patent Office confirmed it to be official policy that no objection would be raised against applications for patents relating to methods of programming computers to operate in a particular way.

These days UK patents are also granted by the European Patent Office. Soon after this organization open its doors in 1978 it issued guidelines as to the patentability of computer related inventions. In these it was made clear that, if there is a technical effect, an invention will be patentable irrespective of whether it involves software. For example, if a new program enables a computer to operate faster, patent protection will be available both for the programmed computer and for the method of operating the computer.

The treatment of humans and animals
It is only methods of treating humans and animals which are by surgery, or therapy, or of diagnosis, which come within this exclusion. The courts have also taken the view that the types of treatment which are to be excluded from patent protection are to be strictly and narrowly confined to treatments for 'curing or preventing disease'.

Thus, in the 1960s it was established that a method of permanently waving hair could be patented. In 1971 Schering was successful in obtaining a patent for a method of contraception involving the administration of a pill, it being determined that a contraceptive method was not a treatment for curing or preventing disease. Similarly, methods of implanting hair into the human head, of the cosmetic treatment of nails and hair, and of controlling head lice have all been allowed.

The development of new drugs is expensive, and the drug companies are assiduous in obtaining patents for their new compositions. However, the considerable delays and expense in testing and obtaining approvals for entirely unknown compositions before they can reach the marketplace makes it attractive to investigate new uses for known substances. Where a composition is already known, patent protection is not available for the composition itself. It is in these circumstances that the drug company may wish to seek patent protection for the treatment method.

A substance or composition which is already known, but which has never been considered to have a therapeutic use, does not fall within the exclusion relating to treatment methods and can be protected. In such a case the substance or composition is patented, for example, for use as a medicament, or for curing disease.

Research sometimes reveals that a drug known for curing one disease or condition can unexpectedly be used with effect against a totally different condition. Such drugs are not precluded from patent protection. For example, in 1985 researchers at Wyeth Laboratories found that a compound, well known as a means to lower blood pressure, was effective to treat or prevent diarrhoea in mammals and poultry. Wyeth Laboratories were allowed protection for the use of the compound in the preparation of an antidiarrhoeal agent in ready-to-use drug form for treating mammals and poultry. They were additionally allowed a patent for a package containing both the compound and instructions as to its use in the treatment of diarrhoea.

Biotechnology
In recent times there has been worldwide and increasing interest in the patenting of biotechnology. This science provides interesting problems for patent law because the methods use, or lead to the creation of, living material.

Of course, the industrial use of living organisms has been with us for generations, for example in the fermentation processes which give us foodstuffs such as yogurt and wine, and such processes have traditionally been protectable by way of patents. Methods of chemically treating crops to increase yield or of injecting animals before slaughter to tenderize the resultant meat have been the subject of patents.

UK patent law allows the patenting of microbiological processes, but excludes biological processes and plant and animal varieties from protection. Thus, bacteria genetically engineered to 'eat' oil, and the method of making them can be protected.

The University of Harvard has succeeded in the United States in patenting a mouse, but have so far been unable to persuade the European Patent Office to follow suit. The mouse in question has been designed to have a gene sequence which ensures that it develops cancer early on in its life cycle. It is therefore a useful tool for those researching into cures for cancer, and, as such, is a valuable commercial product for its originators.

Novelty
The patents system exists to encourage innovation. At its heart is a bargain between the Government and an inventor whereby the inventor is rewarded for revealing full details of the innovation by the grant of a patent which provides an absolute monopoly in the invention for 20 years. The country also benefits by gaining full knowledge of the innovation.

During the monopoly period the information is available to the public and may encourage and inspire others to innovate. Once the patent expires, the invention can be freely used by everyone.

Naturally, the inventor only fulfils his or her part of the bargain if the information, the invention, being offered in return for a patent is not already known. This leads logically to the requirement that the invention to be protected by a patent has to be new or novel.

To obtain a UK patent, the invention has to be absolutely new on the date when the patent application is filed. This means that on the day the patent application papers are left with the Patent Office, the invention must not have been described or shown to any member of the public, in any manner, in any part of the world.

The test for novelty is 'has this invention been *made available* to the public?', that is, has the information been given to any member of the public in a situation where that person can use it freely and without restriction? It is immaterial whether the public has availed itself of the information. A British inventor will be precluded from obtaining a patent if, before the application is filed, a company in France, for example, uses the invention in its factory yard without taking steps to prevent the use being seen by passing members of the public. This use alone is sufficient to destroy the novelty of the invention, it being unnecessary to show that the use was in fact noticed by passers by. Similarly, the description of the invention in a little known, and locally circulated, Japanese language magazine is sufficient to destroy novelty. Again, it does not matter that no one has read the publication.

There are two types of disclosure which destroy the novelty of an invention. The first results from the actions of other people and organizations. For example, others may be working on similar projects and may have published their discoveries and results in papers or in their own patent specifications. The second type of novelty destroying disclosure is that which comes from the inventor himself. Many scientists are keen to publish their work either by way of articles or at conferences and conventions. Unfortunately, it is deliberate, but unwitting, disclosures of this type which so often rob individuals and companies of the chance to protect projects on which a great deal of resources have been expended.

Many developments come from teams of people working together. Clearly it would be a nonsense to suggest that in talking to each other, these inventors are disclosing their invention in a sense which would make any subsequent patent invalid. In this situation, the inventors have an often unacknowledged duty to one another to keep the information confidential. In general, any confidential disclosure of an invention will not destroy its novelty because the recipient cannot freely use the information. Circumstances in which disclosures can be considered to be confidential are discussed in detail in Chapter 1.

It is possible to envisage situations where an invention is disclosed unlawfully or in breach of a confidence, perhaps by the activities of a bitter ex-employee, or even by an 'industrial spy'. The Patents Act includes provisions to excuse such a disclosure so long as any patent application in respect of the unlawfully released material is filed within six months of that release.

Obviousness

The final criterion an invention has to meet if a patent is to be granted is that the invention is not obvious. This has variously been described as an invention having an 'inventive step' or as displaying 'technical merit'.

Whether an invention is new or novel is a question of fact. It is new if it differs in some way from that which is already known. The question as to whether an invention is obvious is subjective, and the answer can differ for the same invention depending upon who is making the judgment. For example, an invention which appears obvious to a brilliant and experienced scientist would not so appear to a schoolchild. Because of this, it is necessary to consider who is to decide whether a particular invention is obvious. In fact, the final arbiter of obviousness is an invented person who is assumed to be 'skilled in the art' in question, but not to have an inventive or imaginative mind.

Alfred Nobel was awarded a number of patents for his work with explosives, but it is important to realize that it is not necessary to do work worthy of a Nobel prize in order to qualify for a patent. Unfortunately, many inventors do undervalue their own efforts, perhaps because they do not properly value their time and expertise. If a person has worked for some while to find the solution to a problem, for example, the chances are that the solution is not obvious and therefore that there is invention.

In deciding whether an invention is obvious, there is also the difficulty that most things can look self-evident with hindsight. Aligning reflective cats' eyes down the centre of the road appears a natural solution once someone has suggested that it would be helpful to provide road markings which are visible at night. However, an inventive step can arise not because an existing problem has been solved, but because the existence of a problem has been recognized.

The Mutoh cases decided in 1984 were about appreciating the existence of a problem, rather than proposing its solution. The inventor had sought to reduce the effects of friction in the type of drawing instruments used with drawing boards, and he did this by utilizing magnetic repulsion. It was accepted that magnetic repulsion was known, although, to quote the judge in the case, 'apart from the relatively limited fields of bearings and toys [magnetic repulsion] is perhaps not so well known as the blowing of soup to keep it cool'. The judge decided that if the inventor had sought help from someone knowledgeable about bearings, it was quite likely that the use of magnetic repulsion would have been suggested. However, until the inventor pointed it out, no one had appreciated that friction caused a problem, and that better instruments could be provided by reducing its effect. Furthermore, even if someone else had recognized the problem, it would not have been obvious for the inventor to choose a man in the bearings field for a solution. These inventions were therefore judged to be not obvious.

By contrast, in 1983 new style car registration plates introduced by Jamesigns (Leeds) Limited were found to be obvious. For very many years car number plates had been made by fixing raised numbers and figures to a metal plate. In 1972 Jamesigns invented a reflective plate, illustrated in Figure 6.5, which shows the drawings from their UK patent No. 1 403 583. The Jamesigns invention was a transparent sheet, on one surface of which black painted letters were formed. Laminated to the lettered surface was a layer of a reflective material called ballantine sheeting.

In determining whether the new reflective plates were obvious, the court had to consider what was already known before the date of the Jamesigns' invention. Figure 6.6 shows the drawings from a 1934 patent specification, UK patent No. 417 230, of Adolf Kaempfer. These drawings show a glass plate, a, having a lettered surface, b, to which a reflector, c, is laminated.

It can be argued that the Jamesigns and Kaempfer structures are substantially the same, the only difference being their use of different materials. Jamesigns went further than this, arguing that although ballantine sheeting was known, it had not been used previously in such a structure because it was generally thought that its use with a transparent layer would impair its reflective qualities. Jamesigns had discovered that impairment did not happen if the sheeting was actually bonded to the transparent layer. The court listened sympathetically, and was impressed by the commercial success of the new number plates. However, it was concluded that the number plates were obvious because the Kaempfer specification actually stated that a unitary structure would prevent impairment of the reflective qualities of a reflector.

Other intellectual property rights

It is worth noting that if there is an invention which meets the criteria set out above, then a patent can be granted for it. This is true irrespective of whether any other intellectual property rights exist for the same invention. It should also be remembered that the same project can lead to the grant of more than one patent.

As an example, consider a company which sets about developing a computer system for the home market. It may develop improvements in both hardware and software. The hardware, any new structure or manufacturing

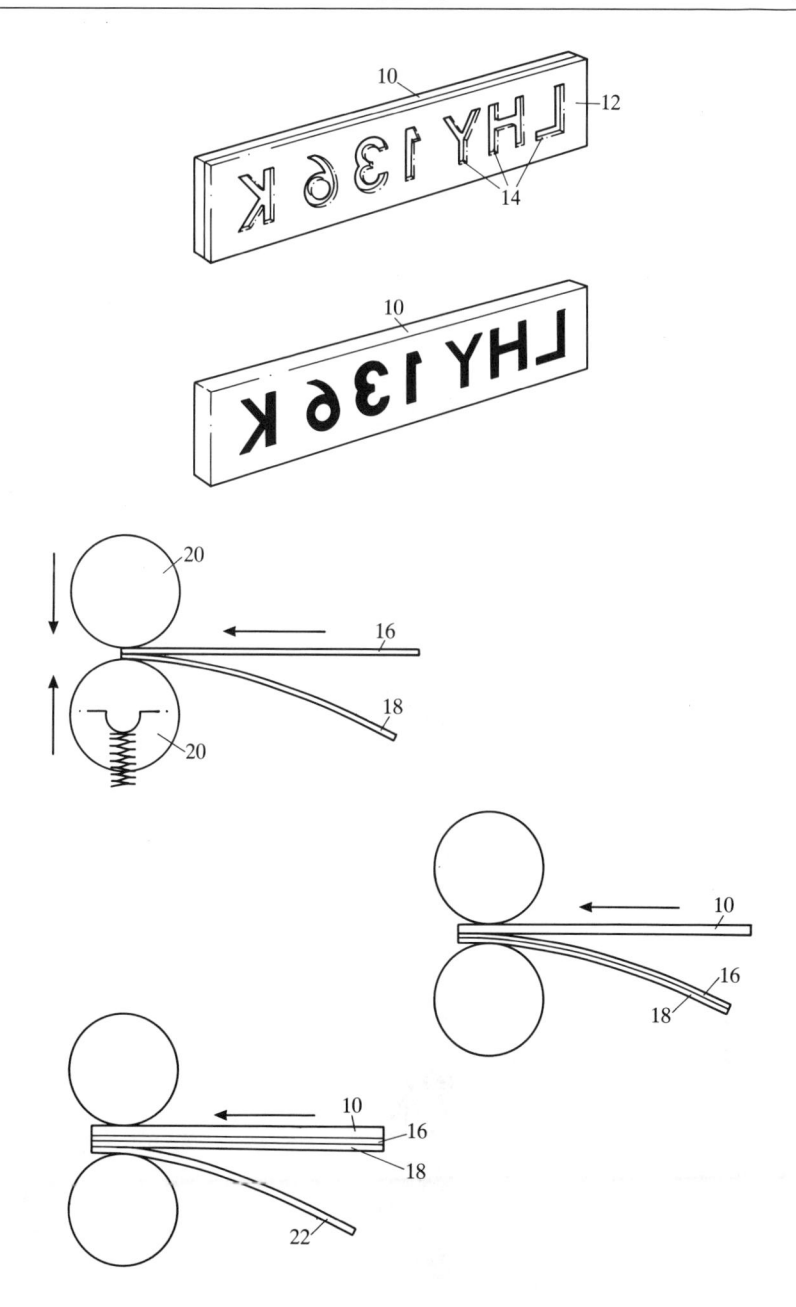

Figure 6.5 Patenting a car registration plate

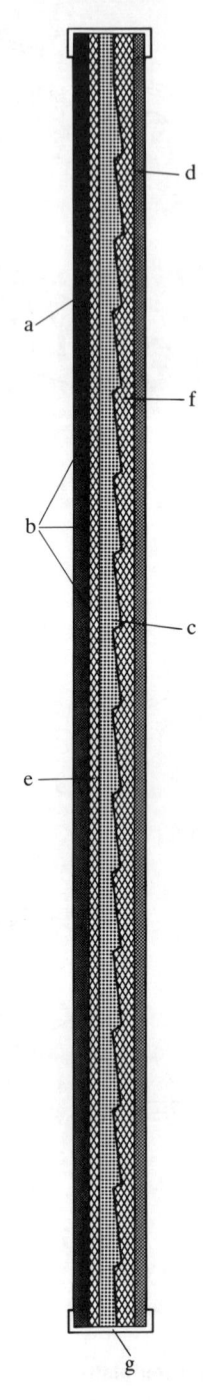

Figure 6.6 An earlier form of car registration plate

method for the chips involved, and the software procedures may all be protectable by patents. There will also be copyright protection for the software and the chip or chips may be protected by topography right. If equipment casings have a distinctive appearance they will be covered by design right, and they could also be protected by one or more registered designs.

Applying for a patent

Before an application is filed
If a project results in one or more developments which may be patentable, the individual or company needs to consider how to proceed. We shall therefore look briefly at the factors to be taken into account when dealing with this situation. A discussion of the options and strategies available will be found in Chapter 9.

Keep it confidential We have already seen that if a valid patent is to be obtained, it is absolutely essential that no disclosure or commercialization of the invention take place before any patent application is filed. Although not every development project will result in a patentable invention, and although you may not want to seek a patent for every invention which does result, the right to choose whether to protect an invention will be lost unless it is ensured that all projects undertaken within the company are kept confidential.

Be patent minded It also helps if the company can become 'patent minded' so that the question of patenting is considered on all appropriate occasions, and it is not simply assumed that 'you can't patent that', or 'this is a jolly good idea but it's not what we want'.

Firms with research departments or an ongoing commitment to development often arrange for regular visits to be made by their patent agent to review all current projects and discuss the chances of obtaining patent protection. The patent agent can also, of course, deal with any other intellectual property matters while on site and may give talks or seminars to staff. The regular appearance of the patent agent, perhaps once or twice a year, of itself raises awareness of all of these rights, and underlines the importance which is attached thereto by the company.

Is there freedom to use? When a company puts a new product or service on the market there is always the risk that it will be found to infringe the rights of others. This is true even where there is a totally new invention. It should be borne in mind that a patent protects very much more than one specific product or process. Patents are often able to protect in broad terms an underlying concept or idea. Therefore, although an invention might be new, there is still a real risk that it will infringe existing patents. This raises the question which should be asked before any new development is marketed: do we need to make any searches to find out what patents are in existence and thereby establish our freedom to use the invention?

We have already seen that it is necessary for an invention to be both new and non-obvious if a patent is to be granted. Therefore, consideration might also be given to making searches specifically to test the 'newness' of an invention, especially if freedom to use searches is thought unnecessary or is to be delayed until the project is further advanced.

Is the invention to be kept secret? There are recipes for liqueurs and chocolates which have been kept secret for years and which others have apparently not been able to discern. By seeking patent protection, all of the details of an invention are made available at an early stage and, when the patent ceases, the invention enters the public domain and everyone is free to use it. So, should inventions be patented at all? Why not just keep the details secret?

Of course, not all inventions can be kept secret. Once a mechanical invention, such as the 'Workmate' workbench or a new type of corkscrew is put on the market, its secrets are revealed for all to see. It may be that copying can be prevented, for example by copyright or design right, but such protection is not of the concept itself. In these circumstances, without a patent, the basic mechanical functioning would be there for everyone to adopt.

Let us look at the case where the secret cannot be discerned by analysis, and a company decides that no patent application is to be filed. What if a competitor comes up with, and patents, the same or similar process? The competitor's patent will not be invalid because the original invention was kept secret. The company will now be manufacturing and selling products which will infringe the patent. Can it be stopped in its tracks? The answer is no. The earlier secret use of the patented process or product gives the company a continued right to keep doing what it has been doing. Of course, because the secret has been breached the first company no longer has a monopoly in the market, and in fact has effectively lost control of the situation. The first company will also be prevented from expanding its operation by licensing or sub-contracting as its right to continued use is personal. The first company may also have to go to the time and trouble of proving to the patent owners that it does indeed have an existing right to use the invention. Clearly, there are risks in deciding to keep an invention 'under your hat'.

The application procedure
A flowchart of the step-by-step application procedure to obtain a patent is shown in Figure 6.7. It is possible to choose to take some of the steps either consecutively or simultaneously, and therefore a variety of slightly different routes to a granted patent are possible.

A patent application has to identify for the Patent Office the applicant, who will become the owner of the patent, and the inventors, in the sense of the actual devisors, of the invention. If the inventors and applicants are not one and the same, it is also necessary to explain how the applicant came to own the rights to the invention. Who is entitled to own an invention, and the patent protecting it, is discussed in Chapter 7. The patent application also has to include a written description of the invention, referred to as the patent specification.

When a patent application is filed, the Patent Office issues a receipt giving the application a number and recording the actual date it was received in the Office. This date, known as the 'priority date', is very important; it sets the timetable for the further stages of the application process, it is the date at which the 'newness' or novelty of the invention is judged, and it gives the application priority over all applications filed later.

Within 12 months of the priority date, the applicant, by paying a search fee, asks the Patent Office to conduct a search to investigate the novelty of the proposal. In response, a Patent Office examiner searches through earlier documents looking for any which describe the same or a similar invention. Generally, the examiner will search through the collection of earlier British patents and may also search patents from other countries and non-patent literature.

The examiner provides a written search report identifying any documents which have been located which may be material. However, no comment is made at this stage on the relevance of the documents found, and neither is any indication given if other objections might be made to the application.

Shortly after 18 months from the priority date, the application is published. This publication is to alert the public to the content of the application. The 18-month term is a balance between the secrecy the patent applicant may wish to preserve as the innovation is developed and prepared for launch, and the public interest which requires new ideas to be immediately available to stimulate innovation.

Within six months of its publication it is necessary to request examination of the application. During the examination process, the examiner uses the results of the search to determine if the invention is new, and also considers if the case meets all of the other criteria for the grant of a patent. At this stage there is a dialogue between the examiner and the applicant's agent. Hopefully, the agent's amendments and arguments will overcome any objections the examiner has raised so that the patent can be issued.

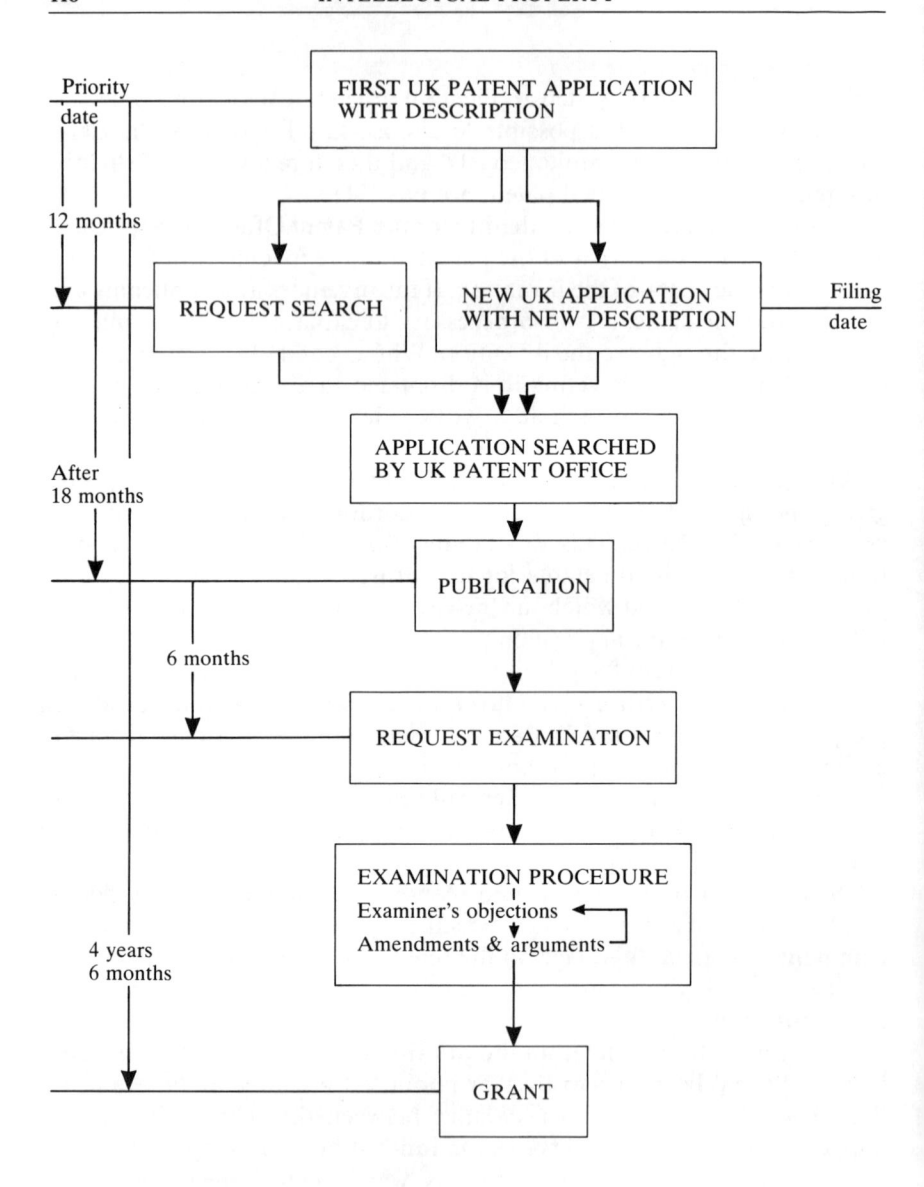

```
                    ┌─────────────────────────────┐
  Priority          │ FIRST UK PATENT APPLICATION │
  date              │ WITH DESCRIPTION            │
                    └─────────────────────────────┘
                           │            │
  12 months                ▼            ▼
                  ┌──────────────┐  ┌──────────────────────┐
                  │ REQUEST      │  │ NEW UK APPLICATION   │  Filing
                  │ SEARCH       │  │ WITH NEW DESCRIPTION │  date
                  └──────────────┘  └──────────────────────┘
                           │            │
                           ▼            ▼
                        ┌─────────────────────────┐
                        │ APPLICATION SEARCHED    │
                        │ BY UK PATENT OFFICE     │
                        └─────────────────────────┘
                                   │
  After                            ▼
  18 months              ┌──────────────────┐
                         │ PUBLICATION      │
                         └──────────────────┘
                                   │
         6 months                  ▼
                         ┌──────────────────────┐
                         │ REQUEST EXAMINATION  │
                         └──────────────────────┘
                                   │
                                   ▼
                         ┌──────────────────────────┐
                         │ EXAMINATION PROCEDURE    │
                         │  Examiner's objections ◄┐│
  4 years                │         ▼               ││
  6 months               │  Amendments & arguments─┘│
                         └──────────────────────────┘
                                   │
                                   ▼
                              ┌────────┐
                              │ GRANT  │
                              └────────┘
```

Figure 6.7 Patent application procedure

The patent specification   At the heart of the patent application is the patent specification, a specialized document which has to perform two very important functions:

1. It has to describe at least one implementation of the invention in

sufficient detail to enable someone 'skilled in the art' to put the invention into practice.
2. It has to define the scope of protection the applicant requires.

It will be apparent that there could be a conflict between the requirement to provide in a patent specification sufficient information to enable someone actually to make the invention, and the need to ensure absolute secrecy before a patent application is filed, or to get the earliest possible priority date. Fortunately, it is possible to be given a priority date for an application even though the specification is less than complete. Additional data can be incorporated into the case so long as this extra information is filed in the Patent Office within 12 months of the priority date.

There is no need to have a working model or prototype of the invention. The Patent Office works from the written description given in the patent specification. The only inventions which require more than words are those relating to micro-organisms, where appropriate samples have to be deposited with specified agencies.

To define the protection sought, the patent specification is provided with a number of 'claims' which specify the monopoly being requested. These claims are the legal heart of the document and seek to obtain the broadest possible protection. It is the existence of skilfully written claims which ensures that infringement of a patent cannot be avoided by making changes of a minor or trivial nature. For example, if a patent protects a new kind of door, one would expect it to be claimed in a manner which would protect the door irrespective of whether it has a lever handle or a door knob. Where the invention is an electrical power source, it would be protected without limitation to the machinery it would be used to power. The active ingredients of a new drug would be claimed so that it would be protected whatever the size, shape, colour and dosage of the pills into which it is made.

The patent system is very unforgiving of mistakes, or of lack of skill or knowledge. Any information which is not included in the patent specification within the first 12 months from the priority date cannot subsequently be added to the application. Similarly, if the protection claimed is less than that to which the invention would be entitled, the broader protection is lost forever. As with Oliver Twist, it is absolutely forbidden to ask for more. It is for these reasons that the majority of patent applications are written and filed by patent agents.

The status of the pending patent   It can take several years to obtain the grant of a patent. In the United Kingdom, for example, a period of four years six months is allowed from the priority date to have the application accepted. In other countries it can take even longer to be granted a patent. Although the contents of the application are published after the first 18 months, if someone begins to use the invention, it is not possible to force that person to stop by suing until a patent has been granted.

However, as soon as a patent application is published, the applicant becomes entitled to damages. Therefore, a competitor who employs the information in a published application, but takes care to stop using the invention just as the patent is granted, can still be made to pay damages. In practice this does not happen. It simply is not worth while to set up a production line, and to undertake the marketing of a new product, knowing that as soon as the patent is granted not only will all production have to cease but also that back damages will have to be paid.

When a patent application is published, it is put into the libraries of Patent Offices around the world. If someone subsequently applies for a patent, whether in the United Kingdom or abroad, the search made by the local examiner will locate the publication. In this way, a pending patent application directly prevents others from obtaining patents for similar inventions.

Protection in other countries

Patents respect international boundaries, and every industrialized country has its own Patent Office. If patent protection is required in several countries, it has traditionally been necessary to file a separate application in each country.

Fortunately, although most countries now have the same stringent requirement that there is no disclosure of an invention before the application is filed, it is not necessary to commit expenditure on a foreign filing programme at the time the very first UK application is filed. An International Convention which dates from before the turn of the century allows a 12-month 'priority period' for the filing of foreign applications. This means that, where a foreign country is a signatory to the Convention, an application filed in that country within 12 months of the priority date of a British application will be given the same priority date. The majority of countries which have a patent system are now signatories to the Convention, including the European countries, the United States, the USSR, and the People's Republic of China. Currently, the only significant exceptions are India, which has a reciprocal arrangement with the United Kingdom, and Taiwan.

Until the 1970s, the International Convention was the only assistance given to those who needed patent protection in more than one country. Not only was a separate application in each country required, but the law and procedure were different everywhere. For example, the term of a patent varied from country to country, and generally was anything from 15 to 20 years.

In recent years the patent laws of a number of European countries, including the United Kingdom, have been brought more into line. Talks have been initiated, under the auspices of GATT (General Agreement on Tariffs and Trade), to discuss ways of bringing about even more harmonization to patent laws, particularly those of the United States, Europe and Japan.

European patent applications

In 1978 a fundamental change occurred in the British system when an extraterritorial organization, the European Patent Office, was given the power to grant national British patents. The European Patent Office, whose main base is in Munich, can now grant patents for any of the 14 countries listed in Table 6.1.

The European system is simplicity itself. Instead of filing an individual application in each European country where protection is required, a single European application is filed. The documents and proceedings are in one of three official languages, namely English, French or German. A UK company, for example, would normally file the application, in English, with the UK Patent Office. The application then goes through a step-by-step application procedure which is almost identical to the UK process described above.

When the European Patent Office says that the application has been successful, and that a European patent is to be granted, it then becomes

Table 6.1 European patents: countries for which they may be granted

Austria
Belgium *
Denmark *
France *
Germany *
Greece *
Italy *
Liechtenstein
Luxembourg *
Netherlands *
Spain *
Sweden
Switzerland
United Kingdom *

Countries marked * are members of the European Community (EC).
It will be noted that EC countries Ireland and Portugal are not included.
Information correct at 1 October 1990.

necessary to register the European patent as a national patent in each of the countries. This is an administrative procedure which involves translating the specification into the language of each country. The individual countries do not have any rights to refuse to register the granted patent.

Although the fees charged by the European Patent Office are considerably in excess of those charged by any single national Patent Office, there is generally an overall saving in patenting costs where protection is required in two or more European countries. Additionally, the filing of a European application delays the expense of translating an application into the languages of several European countries, and clearly it is much simpler to deal with a single European application in English than to cope with a number of concurrent applications in a variety of European languages.

It should be noted that the countries which are parties to the European system are not synonymous with the member states of the EC. There is a proposal to establish a Community patent, but to date it has failed to get the support of all of the EC members. The proposal would require the setting up of a Community Patent Office (which could be the European Patent Office), and in this scheme a single patent application would lead to the grant of a single Community-wide patent.

International patent applications

There is no such thing as the 'world patent', beloved of popular mythology. However, since 1978 there has been an international system, known as the PCT (Patent Cooperation Treaty), which seeks to simplify the filing of foreign applications worldwide. Currently there are 44 member countries, which are listed in Table 6.2, but it is hoped that more countries will sign up in due course.

The PCT system is somewhere in between the historical approach of 'one country—one application', and the European system of 'one application—a set of granted patents'.

With the PCT, a single application is made in a company's national Patent Office, the application is in the national language, and lists all of the signatory countries where protection is needed. The first steps of the application procedure, for example search and publication, are carried out by the PCT authorities. However, it is the individual countries which grant any patents, so that examination is dealt with in each country individually. This means that during the application procedure it is necessary to request the Patent Office of each country involved to take over dealing with the application, and to provide them with a translation of the case into their own language.

The PCT system is invaluable where a company decides to look for foreign patent protection at the eleventh hour. If a company decides on

Table 6.2 International Patent Cooperation Treaty applications: member countries

EUROPE	AFRICA
Austria *	Benin
Belgium *	Burkino Faso #
Bulgaria	Cameroon #
Denmark *	Central African Republic #
Finland	Chad #
France *	Congo #
Germany *	Gabon #
Greece	Madagascar #
Hungary	Malawi
Italy *	Mali #
Liechtenstein *	Mauritania #
Luxembourg *	Senegal #
Monaco	Sudan
Netherlands *	Togo #
Norway	
Romania	
Soviet Union	
Spain *	
Sweden *	
Switzerland *	
United Kingdom *	# indicates a member of OAPI— African Intellectual Property
* indicates a member of EPC— the European patent system	Organization—an African regional patent system akin to the EPC
AMERICAS	SE ASIA AND AUSTRALASIA
Barbados	Australia
Brazil	Japan
Canada	Korea, North
USA	Korea, South
	Sri Lanka

Information correct at 9 October 1990.

the very last day of the 12-month priority period that a Japanese patent application is required, for example, it would be virtually impossible to file the application in Japan in the traditional manner. In this respect, although modern facsimile transmission provides a means to physically put the specification in Tokyo, it cannot provide an instantaneous translation into Japanese, and neither can it cope with the fact that it is already the next day in Japan when the documents are sent!

The PCT system is not a way of saving money on a foreign filing programme. In fact, because it adds an extra stage, it may be found to increase slightly the overall cost. However, it is a useful way of deferring the major expense of filing foreign applications for between 8 and 18 months, and it does provide a way of overcoming crisis situations of the type outlined above.

Registration of a UK patent
The International Convention which provides the 12-month priority period dates from Victorian times. The Victorians' other legacy is the ability to obtain patent protection in countries where there is no patent system by registering a granted UK patent.

Commercially, probably the most important countries where patent protection is obtained by registration of the UK patent are Singapore and Hong Kong. The countries which register UK patents are set out in Table 6.3.

Towards a foreign filing strategy
While the cost of obtaining one patent in one country is not high, particularly when compared with development and promotion costs, if that cost is multiplied by 5, 10, 20 or even 100 countries it begins to be very significant. In deciding whether to file abroad, and if so in which countries, the factors to take into account include:

1. The nature of the invention and where it can be made or used.
2. The location of actual or potential competitors.
3. The ease of obtaining a patent or similar protection.
4. The cost.

The float glass process owned by Pilkington Brothers Limited, was protected in over 60 countries. The invention was concerned with the manufacture of glass for construction, and therefore had universal applicability.

Pilkington's was able to recoup its investment in patents either by licensing existing local glass makers to use the process, as was done in the United States, or by setting up joint venture companies to exploit the invention, as was done in Mexico.

Such widespread coverage would not be required for an invention where the sophistication of the manufacturing techniques, or the need for special plant and equipment, means that, in practice, the invention could only be made in a handful of countries.

Consideration should always be given to where protection is actually needed. Is there a particular competitor, and if so should a patent be obtained in the country where the competitor is based? Are there countries where there will never be a market for the product, or are there

Table 6.3 Countries in which UK patents can be registered

CARIBBEAN and CENTRAL AMERICA	AFRICA
Anguilla	Botswana
Antigua	Gambia
Barbados	Ghana
Belize	Sierra Leone
Bermuda	Swaziland
Cayman Islands	Somali Republic
Dominica	Tanzania
Grenada	Uganda
Guyana	
Montserrat	
St Christopher and Nevis	
St Helena	
St Vincent	
Trinidad & Tobago	
Virgin Isles	

EUROPE	SE ASIA AND THE PACIFIC	OTHERS
Cyprus	Brunei	Bahrain
Gibraltar	Fiji	Falkland Islands
Guernsey	Hong Kong	Seychelles
Jersey	Kiribati	Southern Yemen
	Singapore	
	Solomon Islands	
	Tuvalu	
	Vanuatu	
	Western Samoa	

Information correct at 1 October 1990.

markets which will be particularly important? Where are the companies based who may be potential licensees?

Generally, it is easier to obtain national patents in Belgium, France and the United Kingdom than it is to get a European patent, or a patent in the Netherlands. Irrespective of the cost advantage of the European patent route, if all of the European countries where patent protection is required are ones where it is relatively simple to get a patent, you may choose to obtain patent protection by way of several individual national applications rather than a European application.

In some countries, such as Italy, West Germany, Portugal, Japan and Spain, there is provision to protect devices and apparatus by way of a 'utility model' or 'petty patent'. Although these protect inventions and theoretically require the same criteria to be fulfilled as patents, utility models do not have to undergo the same examination as patents and are generally easier to obtain. Particular inventions might be better protected by such means where they are available.

Keeping and using patents

The use of patents
To understand how patents can be used, it is important to appreciate what a patent *cannot* do. First of all, you cannot become the owner of an invention by obtaining a patent for it. For example, consider the situation where you find in a foreign country a new product, which is not available in the United Kingdom, but which has the potential for commercial success. You might be tempted not only to market the product here, but also to apply for a UK patent. However, as explained in Chapter 7, the owner of an invention is either its inventor, or a person or company which has obtained rights from the inventor. As you have, in this example, received no rights to the invention from the inventor any patent granted to you can be transferred to the rightful owner.

Neither does a patent confer a right to use an invention. A new drug can only be put on the market if it complies with the Government regulations for pharmaceuticals. It is immaterial that the drug company has a patent for the product. Similarly, a new, improved product which infringes an existing patent can be kept off the market even though it is itself patented.

What the patent does confer is the right to control an invention. Thus, a patent enables its proprietor to enforce a total monopoly in the invention, or alternatively, to allow others, under such conditions as the proprietor sets, to enter the market.

In the pharmaceutical industry, for example, patents are frequently used to keep an absolute monopoly on a new drug so that the high development costs are recouped. Thus, the owner of the patent ensures that no one else puts on the market the drug protected by the patent. As there is no competition, the sale price can be as high as the market will allow and the proprietor has full freedom to promote the product and develop the market. In this situation the patent owner will probably make it clear on the packaging of the goods, and on any advertising leaflets and the like, that there are patents in existence. This serves to warn competitors to 'keep off the grass'.

The main alternative way of using a patent is to license others to use the protected invention and to take a fee or royalty. This could be done, for example, where the patent proprietor believes the potential market is bigger than can be supplied directly. There may be important markets in countries where it is easier for a local company to trade than for an outsider, or where the patent owner does not have the resources. If the invention is in a field away from the patentee's normal business, it may be preferable to license another company to use the invention. In this case, the patentee may choose to give up all rights to use the invention, by making the licence exclusive. By this means, the exclusive licensee is put into much the same position as a patent proprietor who monopolizes the invention.

Many fundamental inventions of the modern electronics industry, such as the transistor, were the subject of patents. The companies which did not own those patents continued to research the area and to patent their developments. This enabled them to offer improvements to the holders of the basic patents in return for licences to use the basic patents. This strategy can often work particularly well for a newcomer into a well-established industry, and was used with some success by Inmos when they were set up in the 1970s. How patents are used, and the strategies available are discussed in some detail in Chapters 8 and 9.

Infringement

We have already seen that it is the claims in a patent specification which determine the invention which the patent actually protects. UK patent No. 1 267 032 covers the workbench invented by Ron Hickman which is known by the trademark 'Workmate'. Figure 6.8 sets out claim 1 of Hickman's patent and shows a diagram of his workbench which is within the language of this claim.

Basically, a competitor's product will be an infringement of a patent if it can be fairly described by the words of one of its claims. For example, if the claim specifies that a device has a helical spring, it will not be infringed by a similar device which omits that spring. Similarly, if a claim says a drug has three active ingredients, it will not be infringed by a compound having only two of those ingredients, even if those two are identified in the patent as being the most important.

In general terms, it is an infringement of a UK patent to make, use or sell something in the United Kingdom which is covered by the patent. It is important to note again that patents respect national boundaries and that a UK patent only enables control of the invention within the United Kingdom. This means that a competitor may make the invention in France, for example, quite legally (if there is no French patent) and export those goods to any other country where there is no patent. However, if there is a UK patent, those goods cannot be imported into the United Kingdom.

It is a civil, rather than a criminal, offence to infringe a patent. Traditionally, all infringement actions were heard in the Patents Court, which is part of the Chancery Division of the High Court. However, a Patents

CLAIM 1

A workbench including a pair of elongate vice members disposed in side by side relationship and having their upper surfaces lying in substantially the same horizontal plane to form a working surface, the members being supported from below by a supporting structure and means being provided to prevent movement of each member upwardly away from the supporting structure, at least one of the vice members being capable of movement towards and away from the other vice member, the said movement being caused by actuation of either one or both of a pair of spaced, independently operable, vice operating devices which are operatively coupled to at least one of the members by means which enable the gap between the vice members at one end thereof to be greater than the gap at the other end thereof.

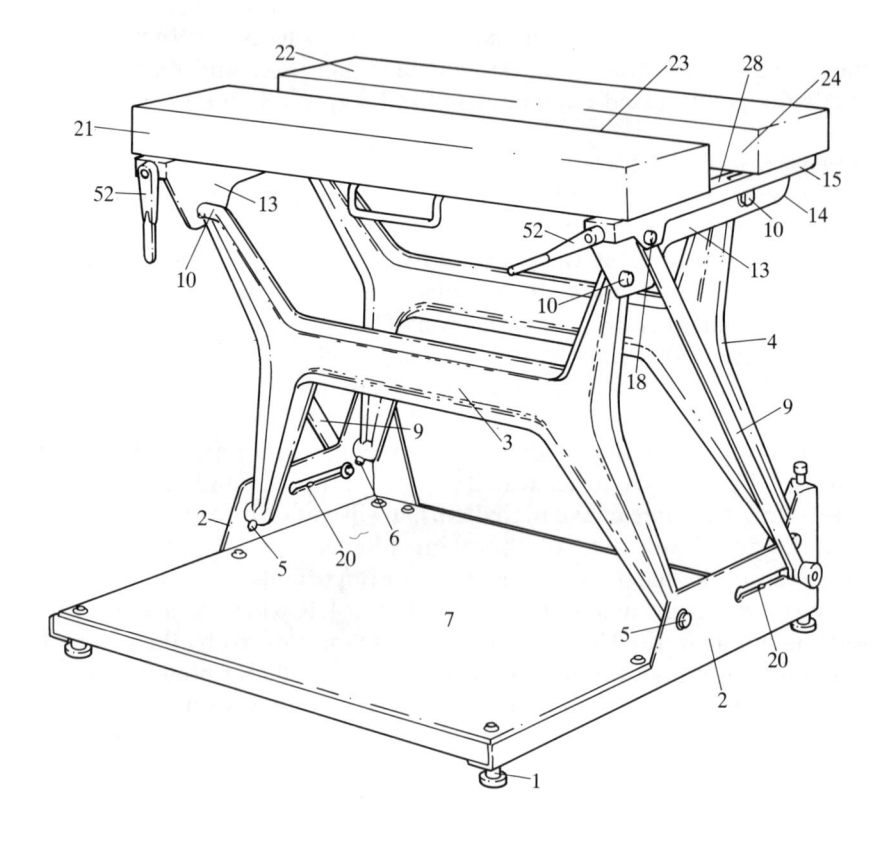

Figure 6.8 Hickman's 'Workmate' workbench

County Court was set up by the Copyright, Designs and Patents Act 1988, and can also hear patent infringement cases. It is expected that the costs of proceeding in the Patents County Court will be considerably lower than the costs of a High Court action.

When a patent owner finds that goods which infringe a patent are being made or sold in the United Kingdom, the usual first step is for the patent agent to bring the existence of the patent to the attention of the infringer. This safeguards the patent owner's right both to damages for any continuing infringement and to legal costs. More importantly, an exchange of correspondence is often all that is necessary to persuade the infringer either to remove the infringing goods from the market or to take a licence. This is especially true if action is taken immediately the infringing articles appear on the market.

If correspondence does not resolve the matter, the next step is to issue and serve a writ so that the infringement proceedings are commenced. If the proceedings are to be contested, a defence has to be entered. The usual response in a defended action is twofold: 'we do not infringe, and anyway the patent is invalid'. It is a rare, and important, patent case which, in the United Kingdom, proceeds to trial. Frequently, actions are settled during the preliminary stages and at a time when substantial costs have not been incurred. In any event, it is now possible to insure patents against infringement so that the insurers will finance an infringement action if necessary.

If a patent protects a tangible product, marking the product with the patent number acts as a warning to potential infringers.

Maintaining a patent

Renewal fees

In the United Kingdom a patent can last for 20 years from its filing date. Where the very first application filed led to the grant of the patent, the filing date is the priority date. In the alternative case, where a second specification, incorporating additional information, was filed within 12 months of the priority date, the filing date is the date on which that second specification was filed.

To keep a patent in force it has to be renewed annually by paying a fee to the Patent Office. These renewal fees, which have to be paid by the anniversary of the filing date, are on a sliding scale so that the amount payable increases with the age of the patent. If a fee is not paid in time, it can still be paid within six months of the anniversary date except that fines also have to be paid. Therefore, if a company wants to use an invention covered by a patent, and finds that an annual renewal fee has not been paid, the company should wait until the end of the six-month grace period before proceeding. Not only is earlier action premature, it might also alert a patentee to the fact that a patent on the point of being dropped still has value and so cause the patentee to renew it.

If the renewal fee remains unpaid at the end of the six-month grace period, the patent ceases and the information it contains is available for everyone to use.

It is not unknown for the payment of a renewal fee to be missed by accident. If this happens it is possible to apply for restoration of the patent, but only if the mistake is discovered in time. Restoration has to be applied for within 19 months of the anniversary date when the missed renewal fee should normally have been paid. Restoration will never be granted where the proprietor has deliberately chosen not to pay a renewal fee but subsequently changes his mind.

Clearly, if a patent ceases and then is restored, competitors may have already begun to use the invention. In this situation, the competitor cannot thereafter be stopped from continuing to use the invention, although this person is precluded from licensing others to do the same.

It is important to consider the matter very carefully before deciding to allow a patent to lapse. The reasons for wanting to have a patent initially should be reviewed to see if they are still valid. It is easy to imagine that because a product has developed, the original patent will no longer cover the existing product. Frequently, this is very far from the truth, and it will be found that the updated product, although superficially very different from the first prototype, is actually based on the same principles and protected by the patent.

Even if the new product is not covered, it could still be that a competitor is being kept out of the market because the original patent is more the thing they want to do than the new product.

Of course, some patents do come to the end of their useful life before the end of their 20-year period. However, one final consideration to make before it is abandoned for all time is: 'Will this be of interest or use to anyone else?' If it is, the patent could be sold outright. Where no obvious buyer can be brought to mind, licences could be offered by suitable advertisements in the trade press and other media.

Maintaining validity
Keeping a patent in force is straightforward, it is simply a matter of ensuring that the annual renewal fees are paid in time. However, it is possible to lose the right to enforce a patent by the actions and inactions of the patentee.

The grant of a patent is a privilege and does not follow automatically even if an invention meets all the necessary criteria. In this respect it is essential that all dealings with the Patent Office are honest and open and without fraud. Similarly, there is a duty to deal with a patent in good faith.

Autoliv Developments AB had a UK patent application. Before it was granted, the company discovered that the main claim was not novel. But it did not bring this fact to the attention of the UK Patent Office and nor did it seek to amend the patent. Some time after the patent was granted, the company decided to commence infringement proceedings, but knowing that the main claim could not stand up to court scrutiny, it applied to amend the patent as a prelude to proceeding. Permission to amend was refused. The court decided that, in allowing the patent to be granted knowing that its main claim was invalid, Autoliv had not demonstrated the necessary good faith. As it could not amend the patent, the main claim remained invalid and therefore the patent became unenforceable.

Once a patent is granted it should not be forgotten and simply renewed on an automatic basis. It is important to keep the situation under review, and to be aware of a need to take action if information located subsequently suggests that the patent is flawed in some way.

It is also possible to lose some control over a patented invention by not working the invention in the United Kingdom, that is, by not making and selling a product here, or by importing the product. In these circumstances it is possible for someone wishing to make and sell the invention in the United Kingdom to ask for a compulsory licence under the patent. Although the patentee is then forced to grant a licence, royalty payments will still be due.

Summary

Patents are powerful and can be extremely valuable. Managers should:

1. Ensure there are procedures preventing the publication of information before a decision on patenting has been made.
2. Be 'patent minded', and consider for each project if patent protection would be useful.
3. Ensure that other managerial level staff are aware of the value of patents and of the basic concepts of patent protection.
4. Beware of assuming that something cannot be patented. Seek advice from a patent agent if protection for a particular project would be useful.
5. Have proper procedures for determining if patents are to be renewed. Beware of the 'this product has developed, the patent must have been superseded' trap.
6. Ensure that the company's patents are paying their way. Seek licensing or sale opportunities for any which are not being actively exploited within the company.
7. Monitor the marketplace and react quickly if any infringing products appear.

8. Consider if insurance against the cost of an infringement action would help the company obtain the best benefit from its patents.

Case study—The 'Screwpull' corkscrew

In November and December 1988, the Patents Court, which is part of the Chancery Division of the High Court, was concerning itself with the merits of corkscrews. The corkscrew at the centre of a patent infringement action was the brainchild of a Mr Allen and is known by the trademark 'Screwpull'.

Mr Allen had invented the 'Screwpull' corkscrew in 1978 and, on 17 July 1978, filed a patent application for it at the US Patent Office. On 9 July 1979 a British patent application was filed. Because the UK application was filed within 12 months of the US case, it was able to claim priority from the US application. The UK patent No. 2 027 681, which was eventually granted, had the priority date of 17 July 1978.

UK patent No. 2 027 681 claimed a corkscrew having a helix coated with a friction reducing material known as PTFE. The claim also specified the corkscrew to be of the self-pulling type, that is, to be one where, when the helix is first rotated it moves into the cork, and then its continued rotation moves the cork up the helix to extract it. Figures 1 and 2 of the patent are shown in Figure 6.9. The patent had more limited claims requiring the corkscrew additionally to include an arrangement for the control and centring of the helix.

Two more UK patents, Nos. 2 101 571 and 2 101 572, claimed different aspects and features of the same corkscrew. One protected the provision of arrangements to grip the bottle, while the other concentrated on the shape of the tip of the helix. A later European patent covered a development of the same corkscrew in which ribs were provided in the main body to grip the cork as it is extracted.

In October 1985 a Dutch company called Brabantia (UK) Limited launched its new corkscrew at an exhibition. Although this was very different in construction to the 'Screwpull' corkscrew, it was a self-puller and it did have a PTFE coated helix. Accordingly, the Brabantia corkscrew was covered by the language of at least the main claims of UK patent No. 2 027 681. Therefore, a letter was sent to Brabantia telling the company that its corkscrew infringed the patent and inviting the company to remove it from the market.

Nothing further happened until February 1987 when Brabantia began to sell its corkscrew. Presumably, in the interim, Brabantia had investigated the patent situation in some detail with its patent agents and had been advised either that it did not infringe, or that the patent could not be enforced against Brabantia. Immediately the Brabantia corkscrew appeared again on the market, Hallen Co., a company set up by Mr Allen to make and sell the 'Screwpull' corkscrew, took action. Hallen Co. issued and served a writ against Brabantia for infringement of patent No. 2 027 681 and also asked the court for an interlocutory injunction to prevent Brabantia sellling the corkscrew pending trial. The injunction was granted. It is important to note that the Brabantia corkscrew was put on the market in February 1987, and that Hallen commenced proceedings on 12 March 1987. It is essential to act this quickly in order to have any chance of obtaining an immediate injunction.

PATENTS 131

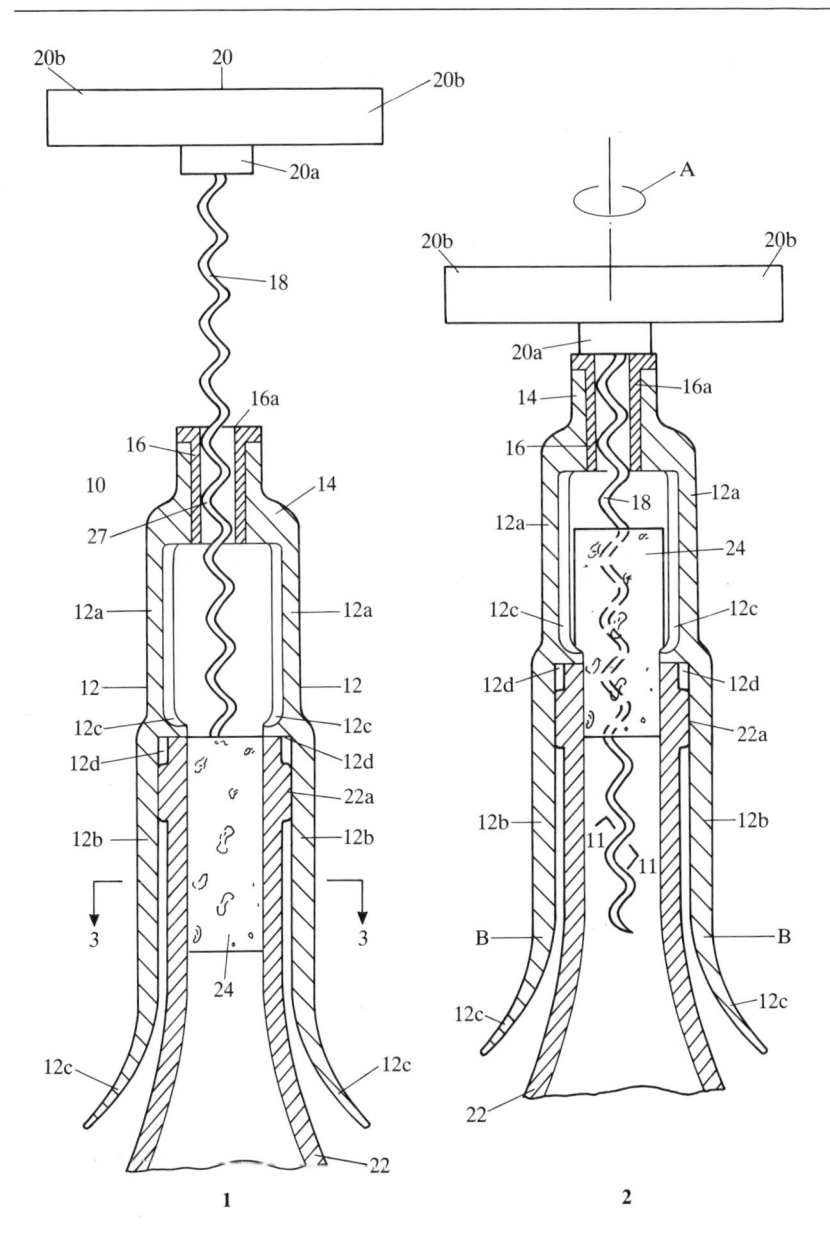

Figure 6.9 The 'Screwpull' corkscrew

The trial of the infringement action was heard over a six day period in November and December 1988. At that trial it was established that although the Brabantia corkscrew was a very different design to the 'Screwpull' type, it was a self-puller and it did have a helix coated with PTFE. Brabantia did not argue that it did not infringe the patent. The defence was that the Hallen patent was invalid because it claimed an invention which was obvious. Brabantia could not argue that the invention was not new. It did not have any examples of self-pulling corkscrews dated earlier than the priority date of the patent. However, Brabantia was able to produce documents, all dated before the priority date of the patent, to show that self-puller corkscrews were well known before 17 July 1978 when the first US patent application had been filed. Indeed, one example of a self-puller which was produced in court was dated 1862. Evidence was also given to show that, before the priority date of the patent, corkscrew helices had been coated with PTFE to improve their penetration into the cork.

The court heard a large volume of evidence as to how good the 'Screwpull' corkscrew was, and 'personalities' such as the TV wine presenter Jancis Robinson were among those who gave evidence. Hallen's submission was basically that until 'Screwpull' corkscrew there was just no market for self-pullers, and that the PTFE coating had caused unexpected and dramatic improvements.

The judge did not agree. He decided that it had been obvious to coat the helix of a self-puller corkscrew with a PTFE coating, given that other types of corkscrew used the same coating. He concluded that the main claims of the patent were invalid and therefore not enforceable against Brabantia.

Hallen had the last laugh. The judge had no criticism of Hallen's more restricted claims to a PTFE coated corkscrew with control and centring arrangements and found that these claims were also infringed by Brabantia. Further, there was no suggestion that the more limited claims were obvious. Therefore, although Brabantia had succeeded in part, it had not managed to escape the patent. The Brabantia corkscrew remains off the market, and that situation will continue until at least 1999 when the Hallen patent will cease.

7 Ownership of intellectual property

Tibor Gold

Introduction: the terminology

Intellectual Property (IP) sounds rather grand but it is the terminology that is daunting: in principle, it is no different from any other kind of property. Ownership of it may be transferred, that is, bought and sold, and that is called 'assigning'; the document of transfer is an 'assigment', the seller is called the 'assignor' and the buyer is called the 'assignee'. Permission may be given by the owner to another person to use the property and that is then called 'licensing'; by 'person' is meant a natural person or a legal person, such as a company. IP can also be mortgaged or a charge created over it, rather like a bank loan being secured by the bank creating a charge over the stock of the business. As we shall see, some formality is involved in its transfer.

Like all property IP may be worthless or it may be valuable. Very often at the time of acquiring it no exact value can be put on it and it is, therefore, best always to think of it as potentially valuable. As with any other kind of valuable or potentially valuable property the circumstances of its acquisition should be well documented.

The general rule

In previous chapters the various kinds of IP have been explained in greater detail. Although there are differences in the fine detail of ownership rules of the various branches of IP, essentially it all starts from one basic proposition: the creator or originator of the IP is its first owner, unless... The major common 'unless' is where the ownership is regulated by a contract which will overrule the statutory rules of ownership. The contract may have existed before the actual creation of the IP or it may have been made after it but, broadly, so long as the contract is not grossly unfair, the law will enforce it. A second 'unless' applies to IP created by employees. Both exceptions will be amplified below.

What can often affect the question of determining ownership is that fresh legislation can change the rules so that two sets of rules can coexist. In Chapter 6 it was seen that the maximum life of a patent is 20 years. Thus, until 1998, we will have patents in force which were granted under the Patents Act 1949. While the *general* rules for determining ownership under that Act and the common law have not been changed by the entry into force of the Patents Act 1977 on 1 June 1978 as far as *employees* are concerned, the latter introduced a wholly new law concerning employee inventions made on or after 1 June 1978.

Similarly with copyright. It was seen in Chapter 3 that in most cases the duration of copyright protection for artistic or literary work is 50 years from the end of the year in which the death of the author occurs. In this century we have had major copyright legislation in 1911, 1956, 1968 and 1988. The position with regard to ownership has subtly changed each time. Accordingly, in determining ownership care must be taken to establish accurately the date when the work was originated, to be sure which statute applies to it.

For instance, the position with regard to computer-generated works was quite obscure. The Copyright, Designs and Patents Act of 1988, which is now in force, clarified the law; the new rule for the ownership of IP in computer-generated works is that the owner will be presumed to be the person who made the arrangements necessary for the creation of the work or design. With regard to registered designs and design right, the Act of 1988 clarifies the law concerning commissioned works: the person giving the commission is treated as the original proprietor. Curiously, the Act is silent on ownership of commissioned copyright works.

Formalities

Although it was stated in the introduction to this chapter that essentially the same rules apply to IP as to any other kind of property, the law generally insists on more formality in the buying and selling of IP than that for ordinary chattels such as a car. Both the patent and the copyright legislation stipulate that an assignment is valid only if it is in writing and signed by the assignor; in the case of a patent both parties to the assignment must sign. Although a court in its equitable jurisdiction might enforce an assignment made verbally or a patent assignment signed by only one party, without a court decision its legal validity would remain in doubt.

There is a Register of Patents available for public inspection and the Patents Act has provisions for voluntarily registering assignments. One major incentive to record patent assignments in the Register is that if the owner wins an infringement action under the patent, the court will not award damages for post-assignment infringements if the assignment was not recorded in the Register. The lesson is clear: put the assignment into writing and proper form, and record it at the Patent Office!

In order for an assignment of a registered design to be recorded, the document must also state that the corresponding design right is also assigned. Where a design is protected by design right and by a registered design, an assignment of the design right will be taken automatically to assign the registered design as well.

Trade marks

The general rule does not sit well with the special case of trade marks. Of course, many trade marks include, or consist wholly of, a graphical design, sometimes referred to as a logo. Such a design is almost certainly a *copyright* artistic work. The person commissioning the design, who is the prospective owner of the trade mark, should put issues beyond doubt by ensuring that the commission fee includes full assignment of the copyright in the design. There is, however, unlikely to be any copyright complication in word marks, as a single word or short slogan will not qualify as a literary work.

In general, however, trade mark ownership rights arise either by the owner being the first to make an application for registration at the Trade Marks Registry, or by being the first to use the trade mark in the course of trade, whichever happens earlier. It is inherent in making an application for registration of a trade mark that the applicant declares himself or herself to be the owner of it. If that declaration is not made in good faith, then the application is invalid from the beginning and can be struck off the Register at the initiative of someone aggrieved.

Co-ownership

In the treatment of ownership of IP above it has been assumed that there is only one owner. As with 'ordinary' property, there is in principle no reason why there should not be more than one owner of IP. Common sense would imply that, where there are, for example, two owners, each owns 50 per cent of the rights.

However, patents are once again 'different'. The Patents Act 1977 has an unexpected provision relating to joint ownership. It provides that where two persons jointly own a patent, they each have 100 per cent! Put more rigorously, the law says that in the case of joint ownership each person has an equal and *undivided* share in the patent. That is, each is free to deal with it totally independently of the other as if the other did not exist. In the case of a patented product they can each make and sell it; in the case of a patented process, they can each use it. The only inhibition on this freedom is that neither person can assign or license the patent without the consent of the other. This can work out all right between co-owners who are each manufacturers and are of comparable 'muscle' but can work out very unfairly in other situations. Take the example of a development contract between a university and a manufacturing company which provides for co-ownership of patents resulting from the development. The effect of the provision is that the company can exploit the invention very much as it likes and is in practice quite unhindered. Conversely, the university has lost out totally: not being itself able to manufacture (one assumes) it cannot derive any benefit from the patent because the only realistic use it can make of the patent—licensing or sale—is wholly at the mercy of the company.

Consultants, R & D contracts

Where IP is generated as a result of a contract with or commission to an independent outside person or company, statute law gives ownership of any registered design or design right to the commissioner, but leaves copyright and patent ownership with the author or inventor. For all types of IP a contract between the parties can regulate the ownership position but, sadly, too often the contract is merely verbal and not written down; or, even if written, remains wholly silent about ownership of the IP rights. This can give rise to completely avoidable disputes, in which the commissioner or hirer of a consultant (wrongly) assumes that the fee paid to the outsider automatically covers transfer of copyright and patent ownership. That is simply not so. It is therefore strongly recommended that (a) there should always be a written contract between the parties, (b) the contract puts wholly beyond doubt ownership of *all* IP aspects of any work done by the outsider, and (c) the outsider/consultant undertakes to execute all necessary IP assignments. The commissioner or hirer of a consultant should remorselessly enforce the undertaking in (c).

The best advice is thus always to put everything in writing at once! Many firms and companies incorporate all the necessary assignments into their standard contract forms.

Directors

It is well established in company law that a company director is akin to a trustee so that he or she owes the company a special duty of loyalty known in legal jargon as a fiduciary duty. Thus a director must disclose to the company any information, which he or she may obtain in any manner whatever, which affects the company and must not put himself or herself in a position where there is a conflict between the fiduciary duty and personal interests. This is so even where the director's actions are open and information has not been withheld from the company or the director's actions benefited the company. Generally, a director, as originator of IP, owes the company at common law a fiduciary duty which includes transfer of the ownership of IP to the company. Interestingly, if the director is also an employee by virtue of a contract of service, the Patents Act 1977 puts this duty more narrowly because it states that any invention made by a director-employee will belong to the company only if it was made in the course of the director's duties. In reality, even in the event of a director making an invention outside his or her duties, the courts are very likely to hold that the invention nevertheless belongs to the company because of the wide scope of the fiduciary duty to the company.

Any attempt by a director to keep the IP in his or her own name would result in the court declaring a type of trust known as a 'constructive trust' in which the director would be held to be a constructive trustee of the company to which he or she must fully account.

Employees and IP
As nowadays most IP is created by employees, the treatment of employees' rights will be more detailed.

Employees and industrial relations
The author recommends that the management of employee inventions and other forms of employee-generated IP should be seen in the context of industrial relations. It is treated as axiomatic that employers would wish to create a framework in which employees are loyal, and fully disclose to the employer any IP that they generate. Employers should have adequate procedures to resolve ownership disputes speedily and justly. Some companies have IP committees to deal with questions of this nature and, where they keep personnel aspects before their eyes or liaise with the personnel department, things go more smoothly.

A warning should perhaps be sounded here: where the treatment by the employer of employee inventions is unfair, an employee may resign and claim constructive unfair dismissal. This is because it is an implied term of a fundamental nature in every contract of employment that there is a two-way flow of mutual trust and confidence between employer and employee. An unfair or unduly protracted arbitration system over entitlement matters could be evidence of a breach of this implied term by the employer.

Employees and inventions
The legal situation applying to inventions made up to 31 May 1978 is different from that applicable to inventions made on and since 1 June 1978. But before plunging in, it is worth considering the meaning of the two words 'employee' and 'invention'.

Who is an Employee?
We have already seen that directors are treated in a special way even if they are also employees. For the rest, it might at first seem that in the majority of cases there is no great doubt as to who is an employee and who is not. There is in fact a surprisingly large amount of past litigation on the matter. With the increasing use of 'home' workers connected to a

place of employment only by means of communication ranging from post to computer terminals and modems ('teleworking'), the determination of the status of someone as employee, or not, is assuming an increasing importance.

In the law the status of 'employee' is treated as a mixed question of fact and law, and is not necessarily determined by the label the parties choose to put on their relationship. There have been cases where employees obtained a consent of their employers to be treated as self-employed with the obvious tax advantages, but subsequently it was established that in law they were employees with the consequent advantages to them of employment protection rights and disadvantages *vis-à-vis* the Inland Revenue.

In disputed cases the courts 'lift the veil' and look at the realities, balancing the factors involved, such as whether the claimant has other sources of work, whether he or she is entirely under the control of the employer, whose plant or tools are used in the course of the work, or check which party bears all financial risk. The courts also look at the agreement made by the parties between themselves, whether the 'employee' received holiday pay, whether income tax was paid under Schedule D, whether National Insurance was paid on the employed or self-employed basis and the like. The courts have recognized that no single test is adequate for all circumstances and so proceed in a pragmatic way. In its simplest form, they ask whether the person doing the work is doing business on his or her own account or not. If 'yes', then he or she is performing a contract for services and is not an employee.

An illustrative example of how the courts go about balancing these factors may be found in Case Study 1 at the end of this chapter.

'Invention'

It is easy to slip into the assumption that section 39 of the Patents Act 1977 dealing with the ownership of inventions can only apply to things which have been patented. But that would be wrong. It is perfectly clear from this and other sections of the Act that the word 'invention' is to be taken much more widely. It is not, however, a term that is defined in the statute.

What other kinds of 'invention' exist? Firstly, there are inventions that do not meet one or more criteria of patentability. We saw in Chapter 6 that these are novelty, inventive step and industrial applicability. Secondly, some inventions are simply excluded from the scope of the Patents Act, for example those concerning medical treatment of human beings. Thirdly, there are inventions which their owners decide not to protect by way of a patent even though they could do so but instead keep secret, relying on secrecy and/or confidentiality (see Chapter 1) to secure a lead over their competitors. The ownership of these sorts of unpatented inventions is still governed by the Patents Act.

It should also be noted that an 'invention' may, additionally to patent aspects, have design or copyright aspects. Since, as will be seen, the employee's position is much better under the Patents Act than under the corresponding registered design, unregistered design and copyright statutes, the Patents Act now makes it clear that in cases where the ownership of the IP relating to an 'invention' is split, in the sense that the non-patent aspects belong to the employer, the employee owning the patent aspects of the invention has, in effect, immunity from infringement of the employer's rights if the invention is put into practice by or on behalf of the employee.

Inventions made before 1 June 1978
Patents for this category of cases will expire in 1998. Since it would be rare for ownership disputes to raise their ugly heads at this late stage, the treatment will be brief. Essentially, the Patents Act 1949 had virtually nothing to say on the subject. The matter was left to common law under which the inventor was the owner unless a contract with a third party specified otherwise. Disputes turned very largely on the written and unwritten but implied terms of the contract between the disputing parties. Where one party was an employee, he or she was in a highly disadvantageous situation. In the absence of any explicit term it was held to be an implied term in a contract of employment that anything that the employee produced 'in the course of his employment' or which was within 'the duty of fidelity' belonged to the employer. 'In the course of employment' became a technical and much litigated term, but broadly speaking applied to anything which was authorized by the employer irrespective of the actual job duties of the employee, while the 'duty of fidelity' made it inconsistent with the employee's duty of trust and good faith towards the employer to hold the invention against the company.

Most employers, however, did not rely on the implied term, but instead inserted extremely wide, explicit clauses in contracts of employment laying claim to virtually all IP originated during the existence of the contract of employment, even if generated outside the scope of the actual job duties of the employee. The only limit on excessively one-sided contract terms was the common law doctrine of restraint of trade. This doctrine required that the employer should be able to show that the contract term in question is 'no wider than is reasonably necessary for the proper protection of himself and his business, and is not injurious to the public as a whole'.

An example of the application of the doctrine of restraint of trade is given in Case Study 2 at the end of this chapter. It should be noted that despite the advent of section 39 of the Patent Act 1977, dealt with next, the doctrine is alive and may in suitable cases be invoked in parallel with that section, for post-June 1978 inventions.

Inventions made on or after 1 June 1978
Section 39 of the Patents Act 1977 sets out a self-contained code for determining ownership of 'inventions' in respect of employees whose work is wholly or mainly in the United Kingdom. The wording of the section makes it clear that all the rules that the common law developed in the previous 100 years or so have been swept aside and old precedents are at best merely persuasive. What the new law states is that inventions will belong to the *employee* unless the employer can bring its generation within one of two factual situations. Joint ownership between employer and employee is not contemplated.

Each of these situations centres attention on the *duties* that the employee was employed to perform. Of course, the primary source for determining what the duties were at the time of making the relevant invention will be the contract of employment and the ancillary documents such as pre-engagement correspondence, letter of appointment, handbooks and work rules. But the courts will focus on the *actual* duties at the time the invention was made and if these deviate from what is in the contract, the actual situation will prevail.

The first factual situation applies basically to all employees except those in the higher echelons of the organization. There is a twofold test for 'normal' employees. The first stage is to determine the normal duties of the employee or duties which were specifically assigned to and accepted by the employee. Once the parameters of such duties have been determined, one then proceeds to the second stage and asks the question as to whether the circumstances were such that an invention might reasonably be expected to result from the employee's performance of those duties. This is where the greatest departure from the pre-1978 situation occurs. The 'old' contracts of employment included clauses which simply appropriated the invention to the employer, irrespective of what the employee's duties were and also irrespective of whether the performance of those duties was expected to result in inventions. So if a researcher employed by a paint company, with the duty of improving the company's paints, makes inventions relating to paints, those inventions will belong to the company. But if the invention is something to do with pharmaceuticals completely outside the researcher's duties, that invention will be his or hers even if the company actually also makes pharmaceuticals. Should the researcher's employment contract stipulate otherwise, it will to that extent be void.

The wording of the statute makes it clear that the reasonableness of the expectation is an objective test and not subjective: it is not the employee's or the employer's expectations that are decisive. The court would no doubt take into consideration factors such as whether the employee in question made other inventions and, if so, whether those inventions were recent and similar in technical field, whether other employees with similar duties and/or in similar grades habitually made inventions and the like.

In the case of employees of higher status, section 39 provides a second gateway. It still requires as a first step that the invention must have resulted from the performance of the employee's duties, but then one asks whether the employee had responsibilities of a nature which would render it inconsistent for him or her to hold the invention for himself or herself. The statutory words actually say a 'special obligation' to further the interests of the employer's business.

There has been one case decided by the court since the new regime of determining entitlement to inventions came into force. This case is very instructive of the court's new approach. Details are at the end of this chapter in Case Study 3.

The flowchart in Figure 7.1 shows how the ownership rules operate.

Procedure for dealing with disputes about ownership of inventions
When any two parties (of which an employee and an employer are merely a subset) are unable to resolve their dispute as to entitlement to an invention they have two choices. They can go to the High Court or to the Patents County Court for a declaration or they can make use of an elaborate mechanism set up in the Patents Act for the determination to be made in the Patent Office. The Patent Office decisions to date have involved inventions for which no application for a patent had been made, cases where an application for a UK or foreign patent had been made but was still pending, as well as granted patents.

The choice between the forums, the Patent Office, the Patents County Court, and the High Court, will centre on the questions of legal costs, professional respresentation, the amount that may be awarded and the strict applications of formal rules of evidence. Registered patent agents usually represent parties in the Patent Office. They may do so also in the Patents County Court, and they may also appear on appeal from the Patent Office in the Patents Court which is part of the High Court.

Legal aid
Thresholds of civil legal aid are set at a very low figure. The usual employees who might generate IP are unlikely to qualify. Normally, therefore, an employee in dispute with his or her employer is likely to choose the Patent Office because it is cheaper. Also, legal aid is unavailable for Patent Office proceedings. But employers should be aware of the possibility of an impecunious employee being able to sustain litigation in the High Court or the Patents County Court through qualification for legal aid.

INTELLECTUAL PROPERTY

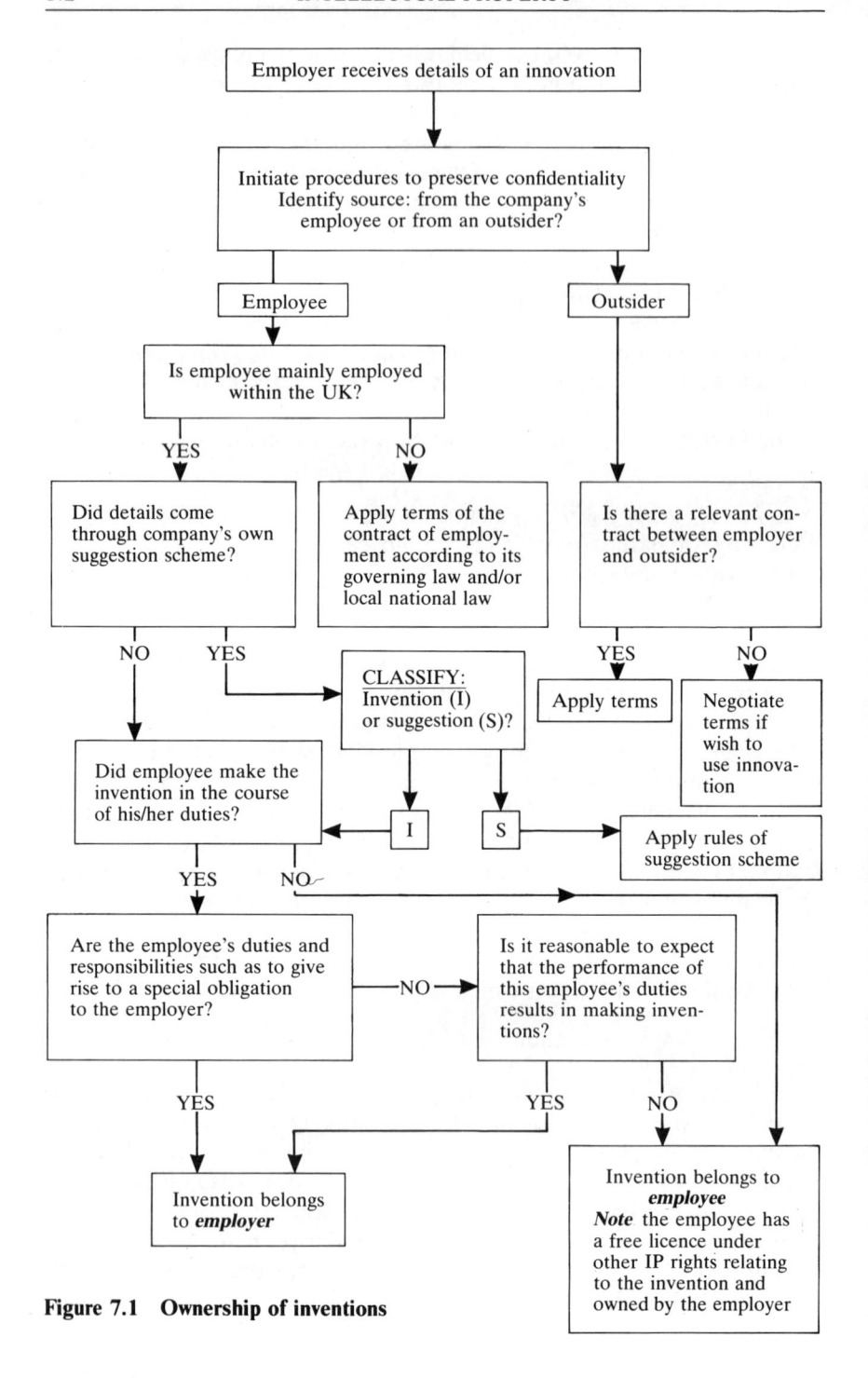

```
┌─────────────────────────────────────────┐
│ Employer receives details of an innovation │
└─────────────────────────────────────────┘
                    │
                    ▼
┌─────────────────────────────────────────┐
│ Initiate procedures to preserve confidentiality │
│ Identify source: from the company's     │
│ employee or from an outsider?           │
└─────────────────────────────────────────┘
          │                    │
       Employee              Outsider
```

(Flow chart continues with branches:)

- **Employee** → Is employee mainly employed within the UK?
  - **YES** → Did details come through company's own suggestion scheme?
    - **NO** → Did employee make the invention in the course of his/her duties?
      - **YES** → Are the employee's duties and responsibilities such as to give rise to a special obligation to the employer?
        - **YES** → Invention belongs to *employer*
        - **NO** → Is it reasonable to expect that the performance of this employee's duties results in making inventions?
          - **YES** → Invention belongs to *employer*
          - **NO** → Invention belongs to *employee*. *Note* the employee has a free licence under other IP rights relating to the invention and owned by the employer
      - **NO** → (to Is it reasonable to expect...)
    - **YES** → CLASSIFY: Invention (I) or suggestion (S)?
      - **I** → (to Did employee make the invention...)
      - **S** → Apply rules of suggestion scheme
  - **NO** → Apply terms of the contract of employment according to its governing law and/or local national law → CLASSIFY: Invention (I) or suggestion (S)?

- **Outsider** → Is there a relevant contract between employer and outsider?
  - **YES** → Apply terms
  - **NO** → Negotiate terms if wish to use innovation

Figure 7.1 Ownership of inventions

Time bar
The Patents Act lays down a time limit for making a claim of ownership. This time limit applies only to inventions which have been patented and it is two years from the date of grant of the patent. The only exception to this time limit is where it can be shown by the claimant that the wrongful owner knew that he or she was not truly entitled to the patent—an obviously difficult thing to prove.

Employee's rights to payments for patented inventions
Whichever of the two, the employee or the employer, is found to be the owner of an employee invention, the employee has certain additional rights which come into existence only if a patent has been granted for the employee's invention and the patent has been of benefit to the employer. This patent may be a British patent or a foreign patent. It may indeed be a form of legal protection less than the full patent, for instance, in Germany there is a form of protection known as a *utility model* or petty patent. 'Benefit' here means money or money's worth.

In such a case, the employee may apply either to the Patent Office or to the court within *one year* of the patent ceasing to have effect, either because it has run its full 20 years or because it was dropped earlier by the employer.

How can the patent be of benefit to the employer? Self-evidently, when it protects the patented product and keeps the competitors or potential competitors away from the marketplace. Alternatively, or additionally, if the patent is licensed so that the product is manufactured by another person, then the royalty income from the licence is attributable to the legal monopoly created by the patent. There may also be a third kind of benefit, the intangible benefit of having a 'blocking patent' which hinders competitors even where it is not used by the patent owner.

Where the employee's invention has always belonged to the company, that is, where the performance of the employee's duties led naturally to the making of the invention, as discussed above (in relation to section 39 of the Patent Acts 1977), the employee is entitled to money, rather quaintly called 'compensation' in the Act, only if the benefit conferred by the patent proved to be 'outstanding'.

Although in assessing the amount of benefit to the employer a careful separation must be made between factors due only to the legal monopoly right and other factors which are not relevant in this context, such as promotion, advertising, price, etc., where a product is protected by a patent there is a presumption that the patent is of benefit. As to 'outstanding' we have few guidelines so far, but the benefit must be something beyond normal expectations both by the employer and by the general standards of the industry concerned. The size of the employer's business is taken into account; what is 'outstanding' to a small enterprise employing a few employees can be a great deal smaller than that involving a huge international conglomerate. The court would weigh up factors such as what benefit the employer has previously had from other patents and from similar products which were not patented. In a recent case a company secured a multi-million pound contract for the patented product but nevertheless the employee's case failed (even though the company was not very large) simply because that same company obtained a similar-sized contract for a similar product which was not patented: hence, it could not be said in that case that the benefit attributable to the *patent* was 'outstanding'.

It may well be that the true effect of the 'outstanding benefit' provisions of the Patents Act will not be found in contested cases, first because procedurally it is difficult for an employee to get the appropriate information as to the size of the benefit the company derived, and secondly because, one assumes, employers may well prefer to make private settlements with the kind of employee who has come up with a patent of outstanding benefit in the first place and who may, therefore, come up with further valuable inventions in the future.

The other limb of the employee compensation scheme of the Patents Act concerns patented inventions which were initially owned by the employee who subsequently sold (assigned) or exclusively licensed the patent to the employer to exploit. Note straightaway that the statutory scheme does not cater for situations where the licence agreement between employee and employer is non-exclusive. (These terms are explained in Chapter 8.) In this situation the question of whether the employee is entitled to money additional to that obtained under the original assignment or exclusive licence boils down to examining the relative benefits of the patent to the employer and to the employee and then adjusting the ratio in such a way that the employee gets what the Act calls 'a fair share of the benefit'.

The compensation schemes outlined above can be overruled by collective agreement between the employee's trade union and the employers. The possibilities of contracting out of the compensation scheme by other means are limited: see below under 'Contract terms and their enforceability'. The forum for determining entitlement to compensation and its amount is the Patent Office or the High Court, at the choice of the employee. In the event of an application for compensation being unsuccessful, or where an award had been made but has turned out to have been inadequate, the employee is at liberty to apply again.

Guidelines as to the amount of compensation
Section 41 of the Patents Act provides some guidelines for the tribunal determining the amount of compensation. The guidelines differ accord-

ing to whether the invention was originally owned by the employer or the employee, but have the common factors of the contribution of any co-inventor and the contribution of the employer to the invention. There has not so far been any judicial interpretation of this section.

Contract terms and their enforceability
We saw earlier that under common law it was perfectly legal and indeed common for employers to include in contracts of employment terms regulating the rights of an employee in an invention even before the invention was actually made. Such terms have been rendered void by virtue of section 42(2) of the Patents Act. This says that any term in a contract dated before a given invention is made, which diminishes the employee's rights in that invention, is unenforceable. However, the law has not changed in relation to the duty imposed on an employee to keep information belonging to the company confidential if such information has the appropriate quality of secrecy or confidentiality. As to information which has that quality, please refer to Chapter 1 on confidential information, especially the passage discussing the case of *Faccenda Chicken* v. *Fowler*.

There is no consensus as to what constitutes a diminution of an employee's rights in inventions. In particular, there is controversy whether the very common requirement in contracts for employees to disclose all inventions to the employer is such a diminution, in cases where the invention turns out to belong to the employee. It may be wise to ensure that employee disclosures are kept confidential by the employer and that a small reward is paid for all disclosures even before ownership is fully determined.

Section 42 (2) does not render unenforceable an agreement between an employer and an employee concerning an employee's invention where the agreement was entered into *after* the invention was made and where the invention always belonged to the employer. In contrast, where the invention initially belonged to the employee and was subsequently sold or exclusively licensed to the employer, any agreement ousting the employee's rights to apply for compensation, whether made before or after the invention was made, cannot be enforced against the employee.

Suggestion schemes
Many companies have suggestion schemes which have the aim of encouraging the flow of ideas raising efficiency and productivity in the company by improvement of manufacturing processes and the like. The dividing line between suggestions which are no more than that and those which may involve an 'invention' may often be very difficult to draw. Clearly, methods that aim to save money, material or energy or which suggest an improved layout of machinery might well remain suggestions

pure and simple. On the other hand, a suggestion concerning an improvement in a manufacturing method or in the functioning of a product may well amount to an invention. Therefore, it is very important for the rules of suggestion schemes to take due account of provisions relating to ownership in the Patents Act. It should not, for instance, be assumed that the submitted suggestion automatically becomes the employer's property.

What then is the position with regard to suggestions which are not also inventions? The position is determined by contract law which requires an offer and an acceptance. A lot depends on the wording of the rules of the scheme and the notices affixed to or around the box itself. It is usual in law to treat the suggestion scheme and notices as an 'offer' by the employer to give *bona fide* consideration to a suggestion and to pay a reasonable amount for any use made of it; a suggestion placed in the box would then be treated by the law as an 'acceptance' by the employee of the employer's 'offer'. It would seem that in the case of suggestions which are not caught by the Patents Act, that is, those that are not inventions, the employer has the option of claiming a licence to use the suggestion.

Another problem of assuming ownership over all suggestions lies in the difficulty of satisfying contract law which requires adequate 'consideration' (=money) to the employee. This is because the adequacy of the consideration will depend on the usefulness of the suggestion to the company, which cannot really be determined until after it has been used.

Hence it is recommended that any suggestions scheme should be drafted so that every suggestion used should be rewarded on a sliding scale depending on the degree of use and benefit to the company. This could avoid problems in two ways: firstly, it would enable the company to take steps with more confidence against an employee, who having received an appreciable sum of money still tried to sell his or her idea elsewhere. Secondly, if an employee tries to license an invention to a third party, it would be easier for the company to argue that the significant purchase price of the suggestion from the employee was adequate to support a valid contract assigning all rights to the company, therefore the employee could be stopped from licensing the invention to others.

Record keeping
We have already seen that an employee may make a claim to ownership of a patent up to two years after its grant. For a British patent this can mean up to seven years from the date when an invention is made, because some considerable time may elapse between the making of the invention and the filing of a patent application for it, and it may take a further four to four-and-a-half years between the application date and the date of grant. That is quite a long time during which employees may leave the employment of the company, as indeed may their immediate superiors

or co-inventors. It is clear, therefore, that good records should be made from the outset before memories fade or diverge.

Worse, the patent may be a foreign patent filed in a country where it takes longer to get a patent than in the United Kingdom. For instance, in Japan in certain circumstances it could take 12 years to obtain a patent!

Worse still, we have seen how in the case of employee inventions a claim for 'compensation' may be made up to one year after the patent has expired or ceased to have effect. Given that the maximum term of a patent is 20 years from its date of application, which itself may be perhaps as much as a year after the making of the invention, the employee's application for compensation may in theory come up to 22 years after the making of the invention: a real Methuselah! In other words, the establishment of the true facts of the situation surrounding the making of the invention, the employee's role in it and the relevant job duties from contemporary documents may indeed involve research in dusty archives—if they exist.

Whatever the position of ownership may be, it is recommended that an express assignment of inventions is taken from the employee even in clear-cut cases. Such assignment is in any event necessary for patent applications in certain foreign jurisdictions such as the United States. Despite the apparent bureaucracy involved, it is recommended that good paperwork and good office systems are established for channelling inventions from employees through to the company's personnel and patent departments so that records are kept about inventions as soon as they are made, and these records are updated as patent applications are filed, prosecuted and patents granted. There should be a committee to settle employee ownership questions.

Employees and ownership of IP other than patents
The decisive question is whether the copyright work or the design (registered or unregistered) was, or was not, made 'in the course of employment'. What falls within the scope of 'in the course of employment' will depend on the actual circumstances of the job and the relation of the design or work to it.

Perhaps the most famous IP case interpreting this phrase involved the well-known journalist Nora Beloff and the magazine *Private Eye*. For details please see Case Study 4 at the end of this chapter.

Copyright and moral rights
For the sake of completeness it is mentioned that the entry into force of the new copyright law on 1 August 1989 introduced a wholly new right for authors of copyright works, known as 'moral rights', familiar on the Continent but not recognized in the United Kingdom until now.

The first right is the right to be identified as the author, sometimes known as the 'paternity right'; the second one is the right to object to derogatory treatment of the work.

Moral rights are unlike property rights because they cannot be assigned (sold) but they can be transmitted on the author's death by will or through his or her estate.

However, authors can consent to waive these rights and copyright assignments should cover this topic. In the case of employees, there is no moral right if the copyright work belongs to the employer because the work was done in the course of employment. Moreover, if the employer has not identified the employee-author (as is expected to be the usual case), the latter cannot object to the employer's subsequent derogatory treatment of the work.

Summary
IP is in principle like all other property. It is owned by its originator, who may by contract of employment or by contract of transfer (=assignment) pass ownership to someone else. Patent transfers must be in writing, signed by the seller and by the buyer. For the transfer of other types of IP, the transaction should still be in writing but it suffices if the assignor, that is, the seller, signs the document.

For patents, there are special rules on co-ownership. There is also a special regime of ownership rights of employees' inventions. The focus here is the relation between the invention and the duties of the employee-inventor at the time of making the invention.

Furthermore, for inventions that have been patented a 'compensation' scheme exists for making money awards in certain situations where the benefit derived by the employer from the patent is disproportionately larger than the benefit derived by the employee. Because of the long time that may elapse between acquisition of ownership and a dispute, the acquirer (especially if an employer) should keep good records of all the circumstances of the acquisition.

Case study 1—Who is an employee?
This was a case heard by an Industrial Tribunal concerning two gentlemen, Messrs Cherrie & Harwood, who brought a case against the Spiritualist Association of Great Britain for unfair dismissal. The two gentlemen were spirit mediums who had done sessional work for this Association. The Association informed them that they were not wanted any more. The two mediums brought a claim for unfair dismissal. Of course, only employees can make a claim for unfair dismissal and so first their status as employees had to be decided. When the court examined all the circumstances it was found that the principal task of the two mediums was

to give evidence of survival after death. Members of the public could go along to the Association's building for sessions which were advertised and for which they paid the Association a fee. For that fee they were then provided with an appointment with a medium who helped them get in touch with their dear departed. The mediums were paid hourly and, as was done in those days, paid their own National Insurance stamps. They got paid whether anyone from the public turned up or not. The sessions were held on the Association's premises. It was found that they were subject to the direction of the Association not to leave the building without permission on days when they had agreed to attend and not to tell fortunes. The Tribunal found that it was the Association which provided the 'plant and tools', that is, the building, reception staff, canteen, cloakroom facilities, and so on. The members of the public paid not the mediums but the Association. Thus the Association took all the financial risk and chance of profit. All of the foregoing factors favoured employee status. On the other hand, the parties' own agreement was that the mediums should be self-employed and they certainly did not receive holiday pay or sick pay. They paid income tax under Schedule D and paid their own National Insurance contributions. Balancing all these factors the Tribunal came to the view that the mediums were in fact employees and consequently could claim to have been unfairly dismissed.

Case study 2—Restraint of trade

Perhaps the most famous restraint of trade case was *Electrolux Limited* v. *Hudson*. Here a storekeeper working for Electrolux had a contract of employment which provided that he was to assign to Electrolux all rights in any inventions whatsoever that he might make. At home one day he with his wife invented an improved adaptor for the dustbags of vacuum cleaners. The court held that, despite the relevance of the invention to the employer's business and despite the notion that the contract of employment was freely entered into and willingly accepted by the storekeeper, the clause went far beyond what was, in effect, equitable between a storekeeper and his employer; a storekeeper was not the type of employee who was expected to make inventions. Accordingly, Mr Hudson was entitled to ownership of the invention. See 1977 *Fleet Street Reports* page 312.

Case study 3—The 'Manager' who was neither a manager nor paid to invent

Mr Harris had the job title of 'Sales Manager'. His company, Reiss Engineering, manufactured and sold a special kind of valve under a patent licence from a Swiss company. Mr Harris came up with an improvement on this valve and patented it in his own name. This patent formed the basis of the ownership dispute.

The court examined the reality of Mr Harris's actual job duties. He was found to have been employed mainly to sell the valves and to keep existing customers happy by visiting them, conveying comments and criticisms back to the company and dealing in what is nowadays known as customer after-care. Evidence showed that on a previous occasion when he made a suggestion for technical improvement of the company's products he was firmly told by management senior to him not to concern himself with such matters. It was also established that whenever there was a serious technical problem with the valves the problem was referred to the Swiss company for solution.

The company put its case on two alternative grounds. Firstly, it was said that Mr Harris had normal duties the performance of which was expected to result in the invention in question. On the basis of the facts given above the court had no hesitation in finding that Mr Harris's performance of his duties could not be expected to result in making inventions.

The company then argued that by virtue of being a 'Sales Manager' Mr Harris owed a 'special obligation' to the company. As we have already seen, even for this category of employee one must start by examining the duties of the employee. When the court looked at the reality of Mr Harris's status, it found that 'Sales Manager' was a bit of a bogus pretentious title. Mr Harris was not any kind of manager. For instance, he had no right to 'hire or fire', he was not even entitled to agree holiday dates with his subordinates, he did not have a reserved place in the company car park and never attended board meetings unless specifically invited. Accordingly, the court held that Mr Harris was not an employee who had a 'special obligation' to the company. So Reiss Engineering's case failed under both heads and Mr Harris was held entitled to own the invention in question (*Harris v Reiss Engineering* 1985 *Reports of Patent Cases* page 19).

Case study 4—The journalist who did not own copyright in the memo

Miss Nora Beloff was employed by *The Observer* and wrote a note to one of her colleagues which fell into the hands of *Private Eye* which published it. When she sued *Private Eye* for infringement of copyright, *Private Eye* challenged her ownership of it by alleging that she wrote the note in the course of her employment and, therefore, the copyright in the work belonged not to her but to *The Observer* and thus she was not entitled to sue. Despite the absence of a written assignment from Miss Beloff to *The Observer* the court held that the note was made in the course of her employment, so Miss Beloff's action failed (*Beloff* v. *Pressdram* 1973 *Reports of Patent Cases* page 765).

8 Licensing and other exploitation

Harry Shipley

Introduction
Even if the concepts of intellectual property and its details are new to a manager, he or she is likely to realize fairly soon that the process of simply securing intellectual property protection is unlikely to meet managerial objectives. The manager will have gathered that intellectual property can be used to enable achievement of a commercial or financial advantage from proprietary technological developments. However, there is a gap between the securing of intellectual property protection for these developments and the practical realization of their potential advantages; to close it requires a knowledge and understanding of the ways in which intellectual property can be exploited. This chapter, which in some senses is at the heart of the book, looks at this subject, particularly the question of licensing, applying a less detailed but broader perspective than some of the treatment elsewhere in the book.

Indeed, this less detailed approach is to be expected, because exploitation of intellectual property is a field to which the manager can relate previous experience and expertise. We are looking at intellectual property in the marketplace, not only as the subject of trading in its own right but also influencing the trading of other things. Although what is being traded may in some cases be less than familiar, the process of exploitation is little different in principle from the commercial process that is the everyday activity of many managers.

Nature of rights and litigation
In fact, for the manager unused to intellectual property, some confusion can be created by the use of the word 'right'. In general, the only right given by an intellectual property right is the right to prevent someone else doing something which infringes your monopoly. This has been expressed crudely but effectively as only giving you the right to sue; no positive right to exploit one's intellectual property exists.

A useful way to think of this is to take the example of a compact disk; no one person owns the copyright in the disk and indeed there is no unitary copyright in it at all. The various copyrights in the disk are rights to control copying, performance and so on, not rights to play the disk. What does exist are overlying rights each of which enables someone to prevent performance or copying: the composer in respect of the music, the librettist in respect of the words, the arranger in respect of the orchestral arrangement, and so on.

Nevertheless, it can be a convenient shorthand, as we shall see, to regard intellectual property rights as if they were positive rights to exploit, but it is a very common source of misunderstanding to apply that idea in the wrong circumstances.

Assignment and licensing

There are two classic legal techniques used in exploitation of intellectual property: assignment and licensing. Assignment is dealt with in Chapter 7, but the difference between the two methods needs to be clearly understood.

The idea of selling something is widely and commonly understood, so as an assignment is basically a sale this process is fairly readily understood. The concept of licensing can be a little more difficult. In principle the parties agree a contract between them whereby the owner of the intellectual property rights agrees not to enforce those rights against the licensee, so long as the licensee does not undertake activity outside the scope permitted by the contract, and pays the stated consideration, most often money.

A particular feature of licensing is that both parties—and indeed the public—can be better off as a result. This is because the licensor is getting exploitation of the technology without using limited resources; the licensee is getting access to technology not otherwise available; and the public may well be getting better products more cheaply through the application of the licensor's technology to the licensee's products. This touches on a very important point—that exploitation of intellectual property can be exploitation of someone else's intellectual property, through a licence inward from the owner. Although it is obvious that for every licensor there must be a licensee, the benefits of licensing in, enabling one to have access to technology otherwise unavailable, are rarely mentioned. But, by taking a licence in, some companies have used it as a very successful springboard to expand their business. All that is said about licensing out applies to licensing in, but, of course, from the opposite point of view.

Choosing the exploitation path

A very significant decision the intellectual property owner has to make is who is going to exploit the technology. This is part of the strategic consideration, of course, and the owner will have to decide whether the resources are available, as in manufacturing capacity, customer support ability or marketing base to exploit the intellectual property fully (or even, in some cases, at all) and whether someone else needs to be brought in. There is an infinite number of ways in which other parties can be involved, and a manager will need to form a clear view of the parties' potential relationship. This can range from an arm's length situation, to one where the one party acts as agent for the other. The questions that need to be asked are succinctly and accurately summarized as:

1. Who does what?
2. Who pays what?
3. Who takes what risk?

These decisions are, of course, the same ones as a manager would be taking in setting up any relationship with one or more other parties for any sort of trading purpose. The scope for inventive arrangements that satisfy all parties is very great in licensing, but paradoxically this freedom can leave a manager without guidance from precedent and in uncharted waters. So this freedom in practice often turns out simply to be the freedom to get things wrong. The bold manager who seeks good advice early is at a distinct advantage.

Once the role of partner (in the non-legal sense) has been settled and the basic decision that a licence is required taken, the terms can begin to be addressed. In any real situation, there will probably be several distinct pieces of intellectual property—for example, in a software licence there will be the copyright in the software documentation as well as the copyright in the software itself, which may need different handling. Further, a particular piece of intellectual property may have application in several different technical fields, for different customers and in different places. Given the ability to word satisfactorily licence grants of the appropriate scope, different licences can be set in place for any combination of different sectors, and the owner needs to consider how to get the best advantage from this division. To take a hypothetical case, a new chemical may have a market in domestic aerosol dispensers for cleaning glass and windows while being a new and useful feedstock for the chemical industry. An assignment cannot be so readily split, but where the intellectual property is inherently split between different jurisdictions—US and UK patents for example—an assignment of one without the other is possible.

Sole and exclusive licences

Many managers will be aware, if not confident of the exact meaning of the terms, of exclusivity. An accurate usage of the terms *exclusive, sole* and *non-exclusive* is crucial in licensing, because it is vital to understand exactly what is being agreed. The terms have definite legal meanings in English law: non-exclusivity is fairly obvious, meaning that other licences to the same intellectual property may be granted. An exclusive licence is one in which the licensor agrees neither to grant other licences to the intellectual property in question nor to exploit that intellectual property personally. Exclusivity, however, causes problems in this area because the licence has to define not only the permitted activities but also the activities not permitted to the licensor. Licence grants in conventional terms are often deficient in this area, because for many purposes a rather open-ended grant can be used.

A sole licence is one in which the licensor agrees with the licensee to grant no more licences, but the licensor is free to exploit directly. It is worth noting in passing that the agreements between licensor and licensee that create exclusive and sole licences are matters of contract between them and not matters of intellectual property law as such. An approach to the wording of sole and exclusive licences that can be recommended is always to spell out specifically the precise scope and nature of any exclusivity, avoiding jargon. This is especially so where the contract is international, because the interpretation of the terms in other countries and jurisdictions is variable and uncertain.

Compensation

This subject appears to give much unnecessary difficulty. However, if a little imagination is applied, construction of the right compensation profile can make the difference between success or failure of a deal. A common misapprehension is that the format of any payments is predetermined. Though there are indeed certain generally observed conventions, these are but starting points and, subject to agreement, most payment profiles are possible.

There are two standard sorts of payment. They are *lump sum payments* (usually initial or at fixed times) and continuing *royalties* based on a payment of some part of sales revenue. Very often both types of payment are found in the same agreement.

Payment profiles are, as was said above, infinite in their possibilities, but some common variations are more frequently used than others.

Minimum royalties

The licensee may agree to pay a minimum amount to the licensor in a particular accounting period, whenever the amount payable calculated from sales is less than that figure. The licensee is obviously given an incentive to maximize sales. The technique has also been used to encourage a licensee to give up a licence that is bringing in little revenue but is costing money to service; a minimum royalty is set at something like £100 per reporting period.

The terms of minimum royalty provision must be clearly stated, including the effect of failure to pay. Does default in paying the minimum mean the end of the agreement? Will the licensee have the right to make up the deficiency or be obliged (as opposed to merely being permitted) to do so? Very often a minimum royalty clause is linked to exclusivity and failure to perform to the required level leads to loss of exclusivity.

Periodic lump sums
A lump sum payment at the start of a licence, seen as an access fee and defraying some of the costs of setting up the agreement, is common. But lump sums can be paid at any time, and under various conditions. For example, the lump sums may be non-refundable prepayments of royalties: for software this can become a situation where either licensed copy serial numbers or even copies themselves are released against payment of lump sums as the agreement continues.

Reducing or increasing percentage royalty rates
Royalty rates do not have to remain fixed during the course of an agreement, and can be arranged to go up or down either on a time scale or on sales or royalties paid. Equally, a licensee can be offered options at various stages during the agreement of paying further lump sums and getting a lower royalty rate. Such arrangements need to be set out in detail at the start.

Flat rate per item
Most managers know that royalty rates are very commonly set as percentages, but a flat monetary rate per item is also possible. It is important then to clarify exactly what an item is, since it is then the basis for royalty calculations. This method may be used where the licensor views the licensee's approach as entrepreneurial, and therefore as too great a risk to the licensor's income if royalties were aligned to the sales price. The licensee can, with a flat monetary rate, be given considerable freedom to fix prices according to market conditions. A refinement of this is to set a minimum flat rate per item but still retain a percentage royalty rate. So, if the sale price rises, the monetary value of the percentage rate can become more than the flat rate and so the actual amount of the royalty paid rises in line with the rise in sales price.

Single royalty rate over a range of items
It is inadvisable to have complicated royalty arrangements: they usually lead to difficulties in payment. The best practice is to have a definite rate, and a base figure to which it is applied that is easily determined by the accounts department. Therefore, it is sometimes desirable to construct a single royalty rate compounded over several different products sold.

For royalties, it is important not only to set the percentage or flat monetary rate per item but also the base on which the royalty is calculated—which products sold will count if several items are included in the agreement and what the selling price is defined as with or without carriage, insurance, tax, etc.

Inevitably to most managers the main concern will be the actual royalty rate. This varies considerably, and there is never a right or wrong amount: too high a royalty rate has probably more severe consequences than too low a rate, in that the project will carry a higher risk of failure. One can only extract from the market what it will bear, and this return must be shared between licensor and licensee.

There are traditional ranges of royalty rates for various industries, and these will be difficult to vary. As a guide, for a royalty based on the invoice price less tax, carriage, etc., five per cent is a good starting point. This moves up or down, to a large extent on the basis of the contribution of the value of the intellectual property to the overall value of the product. There is also a weighting, although not as large as might be expected, with the quality of the invention.

Looking at specific types of product we can start with hand tools, and other mechanical apparatus with a high cost of manufacture. These will generally bear a lower rate, down to one per cent or lower in extreme cases, while rates of up to ten per cent or higher for electrical and electronic equipment with a fairly important invention will be found. Software, because it has an almost negligible cost of manufacture, will have rates of between 10 per cent and 50 per cent or even higher. These figures are influenced by the total agreement, with services such as training that are to be provided being an important factor as well as the initial lump sum, if any.

Discussion of lump sum payments is even harder, and the rates need to be in proportion to the royalties and to take account of any unusual rate of royalty. But a lump sum is a useful token of a company's commitment to the deal and should be pressed for in most cases. In some cases the notional amount of a lump sum can be applied, for example to advertising or other promotional or start-up activity. Suitable safeguards to ensure that it is used as has been agreed will be needed in the agreement.

Special types of licence
Certain types of licence agreement have developed a special sort of existence.

Registered user agreements
Registered user agreements are used in dealing with registered trade marks. The licensing of any trade marks needs to be approached with

great caution, and expert advice should be sought from a trade mark specialist. The subject is discussed at greater length in Chapter 2.

Franchising agreements
From registered user agreements have developed franchising agreements, which have a strong element of trade mark licensing in them. The full range of franchising possibilities is very great and cannot be dealt with in any detail here. They can vary in style from the car showroom or petrol station in which the car manufacturer's or oil company's house style and trade marks dominate the business, to businesses which at first sight appear to be a branch of the licensor's company. The well-known modern franchises such as Tandy (electronic goods), Computerland (computer hardware and services), Pronuptia (wedding wear) and Dynorod (drain clearance) tend to be of this latter sort. A further variant is the manufacturing franchise such as Coca-Cola, where the right to manufacture (rather than sell), while looking like the licensor's company, is granted.

Patent licences
Patent licences are often regarded as a significant part of licensing because they derive from the centrepiece of the intellectual property system: patents themselves. In practice, they are almost always found as part of a mixed licence with some know-how, show-how, or other intellectual property. 'Bare' patent licences do arise, and one common circumstance is international standards situations. Licences to patents on fair and reasonable terms are required if a patented technique is adopted for a standard. Another situation is where infringement has taken place unwittingly, and a forced licence has to be accepted.

Although bare licences are rare, a patent can still be a very useful peg around which to draft a licence.

Know-how and show-how
Together with copyright, know-how and show-how are very widely licensed intellectual property; most licences contain some, and many contain only these three. Some explanation of know-how and show-how is called for: the distinction is quite important in licensing especially for taxation purposes. As intellectual property they are characterized as not being a statutory right and largely (in the United Kingdom at least) depend on contract to enforce them. Various definitions of know-how and show-how have been produced but they tend to be specific to a particular area. One way of looking at the difference between the two is to take the hypothetical case of a new computer manufacturer. The information required to design the printed wiring boards so that they operate satisfactorily at a high clock speed might be know-how; information

necessary to set up a production line to turn out boards to that design might be show-how. The former concerns knowledge that is not generally available, and the latter concerns knowledge that is available but which the recipient needs to be taught. Not being registered rights, they can be easily overlooked but they often are the reality of what is being licensed and are a vital element of the deal.

Software and copyright licensing
Copyright licensing covers a vast scope, including the sale of the works of book authors, and thus much of it is outside the scope of this chapter, and indeed this book. The background to software and copyright can be found in Chapter 3, and all that needs to be done here is to emphasize that software is licensed and not sold. In other countries legal frameworks other than copyright have been used to protect software. In the United States, for example, trade secret law was already well established when the need to market software came about and so it was also used. Trade secret law continues as a strong influence in US law, therefore it features strongly in US licensing.

In Europe, the scope of copyright protection outside the United Kingdom is not as wide as within. In West Germany the law on unfair competition is used in some circumstances. The situation in Europe is changing as the proposed EC Directive on computer software is currently being discussed. Changes are being suggested that may lead to the modification of the original idea of a UK style of protection; hopefully in the future there will be fewer problems with the differing scopes of copyright protection for software across Europe.

Distribution and marketing agreements
Distribution and marketing agreements may well have intellectual property aspects, especially if software is involved. Such agreements for software need to be clearly distinguished from those relating to hardware, otherwise there can be some very unclear and uncertain provisions. A further aspect of these agreements is the nature of the rights they sometimes purport to grant, for example some may say they grant a right to market. The term 'marketing' (whatever it might mean) is being used to cover a basket of intellectual property right usages that are not spelt out, for example trade mark use. This avoidance of intellectual property terms is particularly unwise.

Nature of rights being licensed
The question of the existence of a marketing right is one example of a wider pitfall in licensing—that the licensor must have the right to stop an activity before being able to grant effective licences to others to perform it.

Several classic legal cases have centred on and illustrated the problem of the right being licensed not being one to which the licensor had a monopoly. In the 'Uncle Mac' case, the question was whether a radio personality had any exclusive rights in his radio name when used outside the radio environment. The answer was no. The principle arose as well in the Wombles skip case, where a firm hiring rubbish skips in Wimbledon could not be prevented from using the Wombles name, and in the Kojakpops case a firm selling lollipops as sucked by the TV detective Kojak was able to do so even without a licence. These cases and more have all failed because there was no right to prevent the activity in question.

Licensing agreement formats
A typical licensing agreement will have several standard features. Some of these are discussed in this section.

Style
Agreements rapidly become unmanageable unless control on style is imposed. Each subject must be treated properly once, and then left alone for the rest of the agreement. Unless it is possible to see clearly how a particular topic is dealt with there is a grave danger that redrafts during negotiation will produce contradictory and ambiguous additions. Precision of wording is essential, and lack of agreement must not be covered up with fuzzy language. Unless an agreement is truly agreed it is rarely worth having.

Preamble
Often simply and directly referred to as the 'whereas clauses', some agreements leave them out. There is no requirement to have such clauses, but they can make drafting very much easier and 'set the scene' very effectively. The preamble makes an ideal place to set out any historical facts that may assist in interpretation, or any facts that were in dispute but have been agreed during negotiation. What each party is bringing to the agreement can also be recited here, and some minor definitions can be made.

Parties
Although it seems obvious, it is essential to consider who the parties to the agreement actually are and whether they are acting for and including the rest of the company group. It is customary to give warranties about the power of each party to enter into the agreement, but in the case of groups of companies this may not be strictly accurate where the intellectual property in question is technically owned by another member of the group. Great caution needs to be exercised.

Definitions
Most agreements have definitions sections, and these are useful in reducing the complexity of drafting. But meaningless definitions can easily creep in, and the temptation to start writing conditions in the definitions section should be resisted. In construing an agreement, it is important to remember that a definition in isolation means nothing, but everything as used in the body of the agreement. Conventionally, initial capital letters are used for defined terms in the agreement.

Licence grant
The heart of any agreement is the licence grant. Drafting it has been compared to the drafting of patent claims and comparable skills are needed. The grant must define the boundary between what the licensee may and may not do. Divisions by technical field, geography, purpose, time and product are but a few of the divisions that can and are made, and may of course be interlinked. Thus exclusivity may be provided for a period in a geographical area and in respect of a certain class of product, while outside of this range the licence is non-exclusive.

Also the intellectual property that is being licensed needs to be identified, and different portions may need treating in varying ways. Some parts of the licensed technology can be peripheral, albeit useful, in carrying out the main subject matter. This peripheral part might already be licensed to another party, or might be being used by the licensor as part of normal business. An exclusive licence for this part would be impossible, but exclusivity might be possible for another part of the technology and might satisfy the licensee's needs. Copyright in documentation is often overlooked, but should be treated if an agreement is going to be trouble-free in its operation.

Termination
This is a subject that sounds simple but often in practice becomes very complicated. Once an agreement has come into operation it becomes impossible to wind back the clock and return to the state before the agreement was signed. Some parts of the agreement (e.g. confidentiality) will need to continue in force despite the agreement being terminated. In other cases licences need to continue, albeit on a paid-up basis. Where the agreement is for software distribution end users will expect to be able to continue to use the software and get maintenance services. The reason for termination may make appropriate a different set of provisions: where termination takes place as the ultimate sanction for breach by the other side some harsher terms than otherwise can be justified.

Escrow

Escrow clauses, whereby access to the source code of software is given, are dealt with in Chapter 1, but are common in software licences. It should be remembered that such a clause only gives access to the source code and that the licence to use it as required is a further matter. Care should be taken to ensure that a new licence does not have to be granted at the time the release from escrow operates because of the avoidability of some contracts with a company in receivership. This licence should be provided for in the original licence document.

Risk

The risks in any deal are basically threefold:

1. Intellectual property infringement.
2. Product liability.
3. Contractual warranty.

These are very important points which must be addressed in an agreement, and the balance of the risks between the parties may be influenced by the country. In the United States one will find a greater tendency to assume that the licensee will bear more risk than in the United Kingdom.

Intellectual property infringement is the risk that in exploiting the licensed intellectual property another party's intellectual property will be infringed. As will be recalled, intellectual property is a negative right, here this becomes important; assurances about the non-infringement of a third party's intellectual property must not be assumed because of the existence of the licence. Even where explicit reassurance in the agreement is given, this can only be to ameliorate the position should such infringement occur.

One special exception is copyright. Copyright infringement requires actual copying, and this should be something that is within the knowledge of the licensor. A fairly secure copyright indemnity should, therefore, be easily obtained. The final balance on other intellectual property infringement risks in an agreement varies considerably; many organizations have policies on agreements which try to avoid liability. The party that accepts the risk will expect to find provisions to enable it to control the progress of any litigation, and to be free to modify its product so that it does not infringe.

A further matter is the question of the pursuit of infringers of the rights being licensed. A common-sense approach is vital, for an obligation to pursue infringers at all costs, by either side, is unrealistic.

Product liability comes in two varieties. That for personal injury and death is largely constrained by statute, at least in the United Kingdom, and little can be done to avoid liability if an end user chooses to sue one for damage caused. Large companies will always expect to be sued as a much more substantial target than smaller entities in the licensing chain by which the product came to the market. Nevertheless, indemnities may be sought to offset the cost of a claim, and consideration to requiring the small licensor to take out insurance to cover the indemnity should be given.

Second is the reliable working of the product, which may give rise to claims. Such claims can be direct or consequential and acceptance of liability may distinguish between them and place a limit on the amount of compensation. Such a limit can be expressed in terms of amounts paid under the agreement. Here again software is a special case, since it is a product usually known to be faulty—with bugs in it—when 'sold'. The need to think about consequential damage is important, for example the use of a spreadsheet software program which produced faulty design of an aircraft. Some licences for software disclaim its suitability for critical applications such as avionics and nuclear engineering.

The compromise reached between the parties in the end is a reflection of their respective strengths and commercial positions.

The licensor should always be expected to give a warranty in respect of the right to grant the licences and enter into the undertakings of the agreement.

Developments, modifications and grant back

This is a further contentious subject. It is fairly certain that over the course of an agreement the technology will advance. The question is whether the licensee has the right to modify and develop the product, and if this should happen who will own the resultant modifications, and have the right to exploit them. Obviously, the licensor would like to own all the intellectual property in the modified product at no personal cost; opinion is beginning to turn against this as being anti-competitive. Also, especially for software where the licensee does not have full knowledge of the technology being licensed (specifically he often does not have the source code), the licensee has an interest as to whether the software/product will be developed by the licensor, on what terms access to it will be granted and what support the licensor can offer in the event that a problem with the product emerges.

The acquisition of intellectual property implies that it will be exploited in some form and the active form of exploitation is most frequently some form of licensing. Successful licensing needs the setting of clear objectives, a practical knowledge of contract law and an understanding of intellectual property matters, especially outside the area of registered and statutory rights. It is a field where success may well depend on the creativity of the manager, and as such can be a very satisfying occupation. Software licensing can further require a basic understanding of computing and information technology for success.

Anti-trust and EC restrictions
This book cannot do more than provide a very brief outline. Anti-trust legislation exists in many countries and its aim may be broadly stated as the exposure of companies to competition.

The European Community (EC) is generally the source of greatest worry for a UK manager; the powers of the Commission are considerable, as are the levels of fines that may be imposed. The upper limit is 10 per cent of the turnover of the economic group involved in the preceding financial year, which is usually a fairly substantial sum. To take one example, in the polypropylene case 15 companies were fined a total of 57.85 million ECUs (£42.60 million).

The level of fines is now no longer influenced by the plea of ignorance, at least as far as the principles are concerned; the Commission takes the view that the basic jurisprudence on competition law is now so well established that no excuse for non-compliance is acceptable.

Within the United Kingdom there is still domestic legislation. Currently this is formalistic, little enforced and subject to political policy in its operation. At the time of writing changes are proposed in a White Paper. In it the financial penalties proposed for managers and directors are potentially a serious change.

Articles 85 and 86 of the Treaty establishing the EC are the source, and are reproduced at the end of this chapter. Some points to note are:

- Article 85 is concerned with agreements; Article 86 is concerned with dominant position.
- Article 85 is split into three: Section 1 prohibits certain agreements; Section 2 declares such agreements to be void; and Section 3 applies 'the rule of reason'—that where there are public advantages flowing from an otherwise prohibited agreement it should be allowed.
- Article 86 is about abuse of a dominant position and has no 'rule of reason' clause.
- There is no requirement to have a *significant* effect on inter-state trade.
- The meaning of 'agreement' or 'undertaking' is unlikely to give much scope for argument.
- The effect of Article 85(2)—agreements become automatically void— is likely to extend to the whole economic transaction. The views expressed that only the specific clause itself will be 'blue-pencilled' seem optimistic. Clauses declaring an agreement not to have an

anti-competitive effect seem similarly overoptimistic. Ones providing for renegotiation, in the event that part is declared illegal, do nothing of course to ameliorate any such illegality and may provide evidence that the parties thought that the agreement was anti-competitive.

A brief selection of some of the more important topics in EC competition law is:

1. *Price fixing* This is by now well established as an unacceptable practice in very many parts of the world. Care must be taken to make any agreement 'squeaky-clean' in this respect. Because price fixing is so easy to arrange, so difficult to detect and so universally unacceptable any hint in an agreement that it is taking place must be avoided. For example, even agreeing to exchange marketing information, if there is no overt and legitimate reason for doing so, may come under suspicion.

2. *Exclusive arrangements* Exclusivity is a difficult subject. At its worst it is impossible to justify; at its best it is to everyone's advantage. Often if there is a good reason for exclusivity that benefits the world at large and not just the parties it will be found to be acceptable. The perceived danger of exclusive arrangements between parties at the same horizontal level in the distribution chain is greater than ones between parties that are vertically related.

3. *Market sharing* It is also fairly widely accepted that efforts to share markets by agreement between companies is not to be allowed. The same sort of remarks as applied to price fixing apply, for the same sort of reasons, to market sharing. Agreements need to be kept free of any suspicion.

4. *Non-objective discounting* A thread that runs through EC anti-trust policy is that of objectivity rather than subjectivity. This applies particularly to discounting, and terms of trading must be on the basis of the transaction, not the person being traded with. This extends to having to disregard previous transactions with the same company, so fidelity discounts are prohibited.

5. *Contractual extension of intellectual property* One may not extend an intellectual property right by writing additional protection into the contract to license it. So payment of royalties must not extend beyond the life of the intellectual property right being licensed, and the rights of the licensee to challenge the validity of the right must not be circumscribed.

6. *Passive and active selling* A concept that has been built up in competition law is the distinction between marketing and selling. The exclusivity of marketing—the setting up of a marketing organization and support operation—may be justified while exclusivity of actual

selling may not. Thus exclusivity for marketing may be justifiable in a particular country, but not exclusivity of selling in that country.

Block exemptions

The Commission, for some types of agreement such as patent licences, distribution agreements and know-how licences has provided Regulations that allow the benefit of the exemption in Article 85(3), provided that certain conditions apply. There have traditionally come to be names applied to three different types of agreement clauses, as set out in these various block exemptions.

1. *White clauses*   Provisions that are acceptable because they do not fall within the scope of Article 85(1). Thus the agreement may contain them and no exemption is needed.
2. *Black clauses*   Provisions that are unacceptable in any circumstances. They will always fall within the scope of Article 85(1) and cannot gain any exemption because they do not meet, and are intrinisically incapable of meeting, the provisions of Article 85(3). Article 85(3), it will be recalled from above, applies the 'rule of reason', that where there are general advantages to be had from what would otherwise be a breach of Article 85(1) they may be permitted.
3. *Grey clauses*   Provisions that are acceptable, for although they fall within Article 85(1), they also come within Article 85(3) and can therefore be exempted.

Block exemptions are useful for two reasons: first, if an agreement can be drafted to keep within the exemption it can save a great deal of time and trouble; and, secondly, they give an insight into the thinking of the Commission.

If the benefit of general exemptions cannot be obtained there are two procedures by which various levels of assurance can be obtained. One can notify agreements and apply for negative clearance, depending whether the agreement is one falling within the limits of Article 85(1) or is allowable under Article 85(3). Detailed advice is needed if this is intended.

Anti-trust law is mainly, in practice, a matter of EC provisions, but in the United Kingdom and other countries may become important as political climates change. The basic jurisprudence is now well established and every manager concluding agreements, in Europe in particular, should have a working knowledge of the provisions and know how to get detailed and expert advice and opinion when needed. The penalties can seem high to UK eyes, and to avoid unpleasant surprises an effort to understand something of the wider European perspective is essential.

Financial aspects of licensing
The importance of a strategy linking the acquisition and maintenance of intellectual property rights (IPRs) and their exploitation cannot be overemphasized. The expense and resources employed in securing protection need to be related to the advantage anticipated for a particular piece of technology. Chapter 9 treats strategy in some detail, therefore it is only necessary here to point out that intellectual property rights are assets in exactly the same way as more conventional assets. Their acquisition, maintenance, use and disposal need consideration in just the same way as with any other asset. The taxation of intellectual property also needs consideration. Intellectual property is taxed, especially when being traded, and a manager needs to have a working appreciation of the process. To complicate matters, different sorts of intellectual property are taxed in different ways and, of course, taxation varies between countries. This is a further reason for clearly identifying the types of intellectual property in any agreement.

Taxation occurs in at least five ways:

1. The agreement may be taxed *per se*.
2. The money paid under the agreement may be subject to withholding tax and any withholding tax paid can in some circumstances be credited against tax actually payable.
3. Tax may be payable on payments received and payments made may be tax deductible.
4. Materials transmitted between countries under agreements that involve the supply of technical information and help—especially software—are subject to customs duty and value added tax (VAT).
5. VAT is payable.

Withholding taxes are probably the best known taxes in licensing, but also are misunderstood. They are not true taxes, in the sense that they are largely administrative provisions, paralleling pay-as-you-earn (PAYE) income tax. They enable the taxation authorities to ensure that they collect money, but most often they can be credited to the taxation bill for the company. In many cases withholding taxes can be reduced or eliminated by proper handling.

For UK taxation, withholding taxes are payable on patent royalties to incorporated licensees and on copyright and patent royalties payable overseas. The position of unincorporated licensees is that royalties may be paid after deduction of tax—the payee is entitled to pay net—and no basic rate relief on the payment will be given unless it is deducted. In the United Kingdom withholding tax is at the basic rate of income tax. Similar provisions apply to most other countries.

Double taxation treaties are linked to withholding taxes. It is accepted that it is wrong for withholding tax to be deducted by one country and for the same money to be taxed in the country of receipt. So a variety of treaties, each having individual wording which must be checked for the detail, enable payment to be made, having complied with the necessary administrative provisions, either without deduction of tax or at a reduced rate of tax, and for any tax deducted to be credited to the licensor's domestic tax liability. In some cases, and with some restrictions, tax deducted where no application to pay gross has been made can also be credited.

Payments made and payments received affect the taxation position of a company or individual. From the intellectual property point of view the major consideration must be to ensure that the intellectual property involved is correctly identified and amounts payable in respect of each sort are clear. For if one's objective is to reduce liability to tax, then ambiguity is highly undesirable.

The division between capital and income is a vital one; to confuse and complicate matters not only do the normal accounting divisions apply, but judicial decisions and special statutory provisions make some capital payments income for tax purposes. Particularly affected are patents and know-how. For taxation purposes the distinction between know-how and show-how, discussed above, is a vital one, since show-how is taxable only as a normal business expense.

Allowance of expenses is permitted under the normal rules, so that it is important to know what case and schedule receipts are taxed under. Royalty payments made are made out of profits, and so generating a tax loss may be less easy.

The problems of importing goods are outside the scope of this book, except to say that the technical support to licensing agreements is often in the form of software and the import of this can require care. Customs duties are not payable on software, but are payable on the medium on which it is carried. VAT is chargeable on the total value, but is reclaimable under normal procedures.

Most licensing payments are subject to VAT, with fairly exact rules as to the date of supply.

Exchange controls and export restrictions on money in some countries mean that the ability of the licensor to have the money remitted to the UK or elsewhere can be in doubt. Government approval of licence agreements is also a requirement in some countries, and can make a mockery of the negotiated rates and conditions, with the approval being offered late in the day at a reduced rate. Also, obligations to transfer the technology, so that after a limited agreement life it can be freely used in the overseas country, even to compete with one's own operations, are found in some places.

The purpose of all intellectual property is, in the end, the improved financial performance of the organization and the twin aspects of intellectual property as an asset and the taxation of the transactions must be taken into account. All the sophistication that may be applied to the handling of intellectual property can be effectively negated if one finds that a transaction is taxed when no allowance has been made. The need to make use of an organization's assets is well appreciated; that intellectual property is such an asset, even if underemphasized in conventional accounts, needs to be equally appreciated by the manager.

Summary
The acquisition and ownership of intellectual property have many purposes including active exploitation particularly by licensing. In licensing there are many strategic decisions to be taken, both of a commercial and intellectual property nature, including the licensing partner, scope of the licence and financial arrangements. A wide range of lump sum and royalty profiles can be used to suit the circumstances of both parties.

Certain special types of licensing agreements have appeared, including registered user agreements for trade marks and franchising agreements, and, of extreme importance today, software licensing. Nevertheless, licensing agreements of whatever sort have certain features in common which all need to be considered and careful attention to which will add to the certainty of any deal. Product liability is of considerable importance for software licensing where the product is usually faulty because it contains bugs.

Anti-trust law has been familiar to licensors and licensees in the United States for a considerable time, but this dimension to licensing is being added to licences concluded in Europe by the anti-trust and competition laws of the European Community. Considerable jurisprudence has been built up in matters such as exclusive licences, price fixing and restriction of the country of licensee's activity. Block exemptions setting out acceptable terms of licences and other transactions of specific sorts have been published, and Commission clearance for others can be obtained.

The taxation of intellectual property is increasing in importance and matters such as withholding taxes, the taxation of royalties, and allowances claimable need attention.

The Treaty of Rome

ARTICLE 85

1. The following shall be prohibited as incompatible with the common market: all agreements between undertakings, decisions by associations of undertakings and concerted practices which may affect trade between Member States and which have as their object or effect the prevention, restriction or distortion of competition within the common market, and in particular those which:

    (a) directly or indirectly fix purchase or selling prices or any other trading conditions;
    (b) limit or control production, markets, technical development, or investment;
    (c) share markets or sources of supply;
    (d) apply dissimilar conditions to equivalent transactions with other trading parties, thereby placing them at a competitive disadvantage;
    (e) make the conclusion of contracts subject to acceptance by the other parties of supplementary obligations which, by their nature or according to commercial usage, have no connection with the subject of such contracts.

2. Any agreements or decisions prohibited pursuant to this Article shall be automatically void.

3. The provisions of paragraph 1 may, however, be declared inapplicable in the case of:

    - any agreement or category of agreements between undertakings;
    - any decision or category of decisions by associations of undertakings;
    - any concerted practice or category of concerted practices;

    which contributes to improving the production or distribution of goods or to promoting technical or economic progress, while allowing consumers a fair share of the resulting benefit, and which does not:

    (a) impose on the undertakings concerned restrictions which are not indispensable to the attainment of these objectives;
    (b) afford such undertakings the possibility of eliminating competition in respect of a substantial part of the products in question.

ARTICLE 86

Any abuse by one or more undertakings of a dominant position within the common market or in a substantial part of it shall be prohibited as incompatible with the common market in so far as it may affect trade between Member States. Such abuse may, in particular, consist in:

(a) directly or indirectly imposing unfair purchase or selling prices or other unfair trading conditions;

(b) limiting production, markets or technical development to the prejudice of consumers;
(c) applying dissimilar conditions to equivalent transactions with other trading parties, thereby placing them at a competitive disadvantage;
(d) making the conclusion of contracts subject to acceptance by the other parties of supplementary obligations which, by their nature or according to commercial usage, have no connection with the subject of such contracts.

9 Strategy and litigation

Alan Burrington

Introduction

In the previous chapters there has been a discussion of the various intellectual property rights which exist in law, the way in which they are created, the various commercial activities to which they relate, the question of ownership and how they can be exploited together with some of the legal constraints on their exploitation including those which apply within the European Community.

The present chapter is concerned essentially with managerial questions involved in the utilization of intellectual property rights. It will be dealing with this question from the viewpoint of a manager in industry although some of the issues also apply to the individual who is concerned with the protection and exploitation of an innovation or the protection of a product identity.

The chapter will be divided into two sections: the first is concerned with the general strategies that can be employed in connection with intellectual property and the second is specifically concerned with litigation.

IP STRATEGY

From previous chapters it will be apparent that the different types of intellectual property right have different characteristics and therefore are likely to relate to different types of industry and commerce. For example, patents undoubtedly relate to the technical research world of ideas but they also extend along the development and engineering spectrum to the point where they overlap with registered designs, design right and to some extent copyright. In its turn copyright is most closely associated with literary and musical works as those terms are generally understood. Registered designs, design right and copyright to some extent overlap in that they all relate to the form of an article and not to the idea underlying it.

In a separate compartment, as it were, lie registered trade marks and the associated common law right enforceable by a 'passing-off' action. These relate to what one might term 'product identity'. In many ways the legal basis of these 'product identity' rights is completely different from that relating particularly to patents and to a lesser extent registered designs.

It is clear from the above that a particular type of intellectual property right may be critical in a certain type of industry/commerce but completely irrelevant in another. It is useful for a manager to have some broad feel for these relationships.

Clearly there are industries (and one might in fact say all industries) where all forms of intellectual property right can be relevant at some time or another. However, the purpose of this section is to give an impressionistic view of the relative importance of the different types of intellectual property right to different types of industry and commerce.

In technologically based industries patents are generally the dominant intellectual property right with copyright augmenting them in the software field. In contrast, in consumer product based industries, particularly those involving consumable products such as food, trade marks and the associated common law right of 'passing off' are the dominant rights. In the publishing world, whether literary or musical, copyright is the dominant intellectual property right.

Registered trade marks and the common law remedy of passing off generally have immediate and direct commercial relevance because companies usually do not obtain registered trade marks for purely speculative reasons. The legal protection closely follows and mirrors the commercial reality.

Similarly, copyright, because of its automatic creation, inevitably correlates with the actual commercial reality. Similar comments could be made concerning design right.

When it comes to registered designs, although they have some legal similarity to patents, commercially they are usually obtained only in relation to a product that is actually to be marketed.

In contrast with these intellectual property rights just described it is in the area of patents that there is probably the widest variety of uses or strategies.

Whatever the nature of the intellectual property right that is relevant to a particular type of industry/commerce, there are striking differences in the way that intellectual property rights are used from industry to industry.

For the purpose of illustrating this last statement there will now follow an oversimplified outline of the different ways patents can be and are in fact used.

These uses can conveniently be classified under the following three headings:

1. To achieve a monopoly position in a product.
2. To generate an income from licensing.
3. As a form of insurance policy.

It is probably true to say that 1 above is the layman's view as to how patents are in fact used with probably some appreciation of 2. A large proportion of industry uses patents to achieve 3.

At one end of the spectrum lies the pharmaceutical industry which, because of the nature of the product, places great reliance on patents and endeavours to use them to achieve an effective monopoly in the product wherever possible. In contrast, in the mechanical engineering industries, it is very common for companies to use patent portfolios simply as a form of insurance policy against their competitors alleging infringement of that competitor's patents.

In order to give the reader some appreciation of the differing ways in which patents are in fact used from industry to industry, some specific industries will now be considered in a little more detail.

Three different industries

Pharmaceutical industry
This is primarily a research based industry in which considerable sums are spent in trying to create effective new drugs. Because of the nature of the product the research is probably more of a hit and miss exercise than in many other industries. It appears to be the case that in the pharmaceutical industry it is a question of backing many horses and hoping that one of them will turn out to be a winner. This results in a lot of wasted effort. However, once a new effective drug has been identified the costs of putting it into production are probably relatively low compared with the cost of putting products into production in some other industries.

It follows that the cost to a competitor of entering the market in competition with the originator of a new drug is relatively low. As a consequence the object of the innovating company is to prevent the drug being copied and not to license it.

Motor industry
This can be divided into two sectors: the vehicle manufacturers/assemblers and the component/sub-assembly manufacturers who act as the former's suppliers. The way in which patents are used is completely different as between these two groups.

The vehicle manufacturers/assemblers do relatively little technical research and most of their front-end technical effort is directed to engineering and development of the product, and to some extent the means for manufacturing it. Compared with the pharmaceutical industry the ratio of the cost of research to the cost of engineering and development is much lower. However, in contrast, the capital investment required to launch a new vehicle is relatively considerably higher than for a pharmaceutical product.

As a consequence there is a very high price to a competitor who wishes to enter the market. Whether a company is successful and profitable centres around the basic efficiency of the company and its marketing and distribution skills and not its research ability.

Therefore, the motor manufacturers/assemblers do not use patents to attempt to obtain a monopoly in the marketplace but instead use them mainly to neutralize their competitors' patents, that is, as a form of insurance policy. As a secondary objective and possible spin-off from holding patent rights they may also grant licences to third parties. However, this is usually done on a passive basis, that is, they grant them if requested to do so but do not devote any significant resource to exploiting their patents actively by way of licensing.

In contrast, the component/sub-assembly suppliers to the vehicle manufacturers/assemblers tend to be much more aggressive and positive in their use of patents. These suppliers are, of course, competing with each other for the business of supplying the vehicle manufacturers/assemblers. Therefore, if a supplier can create an obstacle to its competitor(s) in terms of being able to supply a particular component, that supplier then has an advantage over the competitor in obtaining that particular order.

As a consequence component suppliers tend to be very active in protecting their new designs and relatively aggressive in trying to enforce them against their supplier competitors.

There is a conflict here because it is in the vehicle manufacturers'/assemblers' interest to have suppliers competing for their business on an equal basis, thus driving down the price. The vehicle manufacturer therefore has an interest in 'neutralizing' the patents held by its suppliers. There are a number of ways this can be done.

One way to achieve this objective is for the vehicle manufacturer/assembler to obtain patents itself before the supplier does so, it being very common for the technical people of both the supplier and the vehicle manufacturer to work together on the evolution and final design of the component. Another way is for the vehicle manufacturer to use his economic muscle to impose an order-sharing arrangement between two selected suppliers. Included in such arrangements would be one in which in exchange for placing a guaranteed volume of business with a first supplier, that supplier would grant the vehicle manufacturer a paid-up licence with the right to license third parties, that is, another competitor supplier.

Electronics industry
In some ways this industry works in a very similar manner to mechanical engineering based industries, such as the motor industry, in that it consists of a pyramid of companies at the apex of which are the manufacturers

and assemblers of products and equipment for the end customer. Such companies are supported by several layers of suppliers, each layer of supplier in the pyramid generally supplying companies in the layer immediately above it. The lower a company's position in the pyramid the more aggressive it is likely to be in relation to obtaining patents and trying to enforce them. This is because as you move down the pyramid from the final manufacturer/assembler, the capital cost involved in producing the product is reducing and therefore the risk of copying is increasing.

The classic case of ease of copying in the electronics industry is software. It is an irony of the patent systems of the world, including that of the United Kingdom, that generally speaking they ostensibly specifically exclude computer programs from patent protection. However, in practice it is possible to protect computer programs and software by patents.

This brief view of the relationship of patents to different kinds of industry is of necessity superficial and only covers a very narrow part of the total spectrum. However, it is hoped that it will give the reader some feel for the differing ways in which patents are used in different sectors of industry, the way in which they are used being dictated by the economic realities of a particular industry.

What policy for patents?
When a company's patent policy is being considered it is often the case that the alternatives to patenting, of simply publishing or keeping the innovation secret, are considered.

These three possibilities in many ways encapsulate the issues involved in deciding what policy a company should adopt towards patents. These key issues are inextricably bound up with the type of business the company is in and whether it is already a major 'player' in that business or is moving in that direction or is a start-up company. Patents should be looked at as a management tool, therefore their relevance and how they can and should be used depends on the company's particular commercial position.

Clearly there is a wide spectrum of company situations that can arise in practice, but this subsection will endeavour to highlight the key issues in relation to specific situations so that the reader can then hopefully relate them to a particular situation.

These questions are going to be examined in relation to a UK company with a sizeable research operation, which is the major source of patentable technical innovation within that company. It will also be assumed that the company is, or wishes to be, active in the US market.

In order to obtain a patent it is generally necessary to make a sufficiently detailed technical disclosure in the patent specification to enable a knowledgeable person to put the invention into practice. The exact level of disclosure required varies from country to country. For example, in Germany the level is relatively low because the German system assumes that the patent specification is being read by a highly skilled technical person (Germany is a technocracy where it is common to find engineers and other technical people running large companies). In contrast the level of detail of disclosure required in a US patent specification is much higher than in Germany because it is assumed that the patent specification will be read by persons having a relatively low level of technical knowledge. (The United States is a country where lawyers probably have a more dominant position in industry than in most, if not all, other countries.) The philosophy in the United Kingdom used to fall somewhere between that in Germany and the United States. However, since 1978 when the European Patent Convention came into effect, there has been a significant harmonization of patent laws in Europe and to a significant extent the level of technical disclosure required in a UK patent and a European patent is substantially the same, but still considerably lower than that required in the United States.

The relevance of these differences in level of technical disclosure required is brought into sharp focus when one looks at a UK based research operation and asks the question 'At what point in the evolution of a piece of research should the first patent application be filed?'

This question involves a basic conflict. If matters are delayed until there is sufficient detailed technical information to support a US patent application, there is the risk that another company will in the meantime file a patent application on the same or similar innovation. However, if a UK patent application is filed immediately the general idea underlying the innovation has arisen, then it is quite likely that there will be insufficient technical information in the patent specification to support a US patent application or even possibly a UK application.

However, if the company were only concerned with the UK market, or even with other markets excluding the United States, the conflict and resulting operational problem would probably not arise.

There is also another associated problem where research operations are concerned and this is related to the fact that a researcher's reputation is judged by the number of technical/professional papers that he or she publishes. There is thus pressure to publish early rather than late and, furthermore, because of the nature of the research the material published will very often be in the form of a theoretical analysis or broad concept rather than a detailed realization. For a patent to be valid it must be filed at the relevant Patent Office before the invention is disclosed to the public. Therefore, the researcher's desire to publish early tends to mean that any patent application must be filed even earlier, with the likely consequence that it does not contain enough technical detail of the practical realization of the invention to support a US patent application. In fact, as indicated earlier, the level of detail may not even be sufficient to support a valid UK patent application.

How is this dilemma to be resolved? Should publication take precedence over patenting? It is a conflict which has to be resolved by the company's management by balancing the possible adverse effect on the standing (and feelings) of its research staff against the importance of the US market, or indeed of obtaining patents in general.

The same problem can also occur, but less often, when filing in the United Kingdom and other countries because, although their legal requirements for level of technical details are less stringent than those of the United States, there is nevertheless a minimum level of technical disclosure required—a minimum level that may not be present at the time a research paper is to be published.

If a company does not have a research operation but is basically designing products, that is, the activities are engineering and development, then the problem outlined above does not generally arise. However, even here there is still the question of when to file the patent application, that is, as soon as the broad design idea has evolved or to wait until a specific implementation has been worked out. Again the potential source of problems lies in the US legal position. You file early to beat your competitors but fail to get a US patent. You file later in order to provide a good basis for a US patent but are beaten by a competitor who files earlier in the United Kingdom.

Figure 9.1 illustrates in broad terms the decision tree involved in the tripartite question of whether to patent the technical innovation, publish it or keep it secret.

Referring to Figure 9.1, a technical innovation is made and results in a certain level of technical disclosure or information. This disclosure is then considered from three points of view: namely, its commercial relevance to the activities of the company; its technical merit in terms of providing a solution to a technical problem; and its inventive level in terms of whether it is sufficient to support a valid patent in the light of the known prior art.

A decision is then made on the basis of these three inputs, either to file a patent application or not to file a patent application. In the former case, the technical innovation will normally be published by way of publication of the patent application (although publication can be prevented at the cost of abandoning the patent application). In the case of deciding not to file a patent application, a further decision has to be taken as to whether to keep the technical innovation secret or to publish it.

Let us assume that a company has decided to file patent applications on its innovations. What does it then do? Its 'innovations' may not in fact

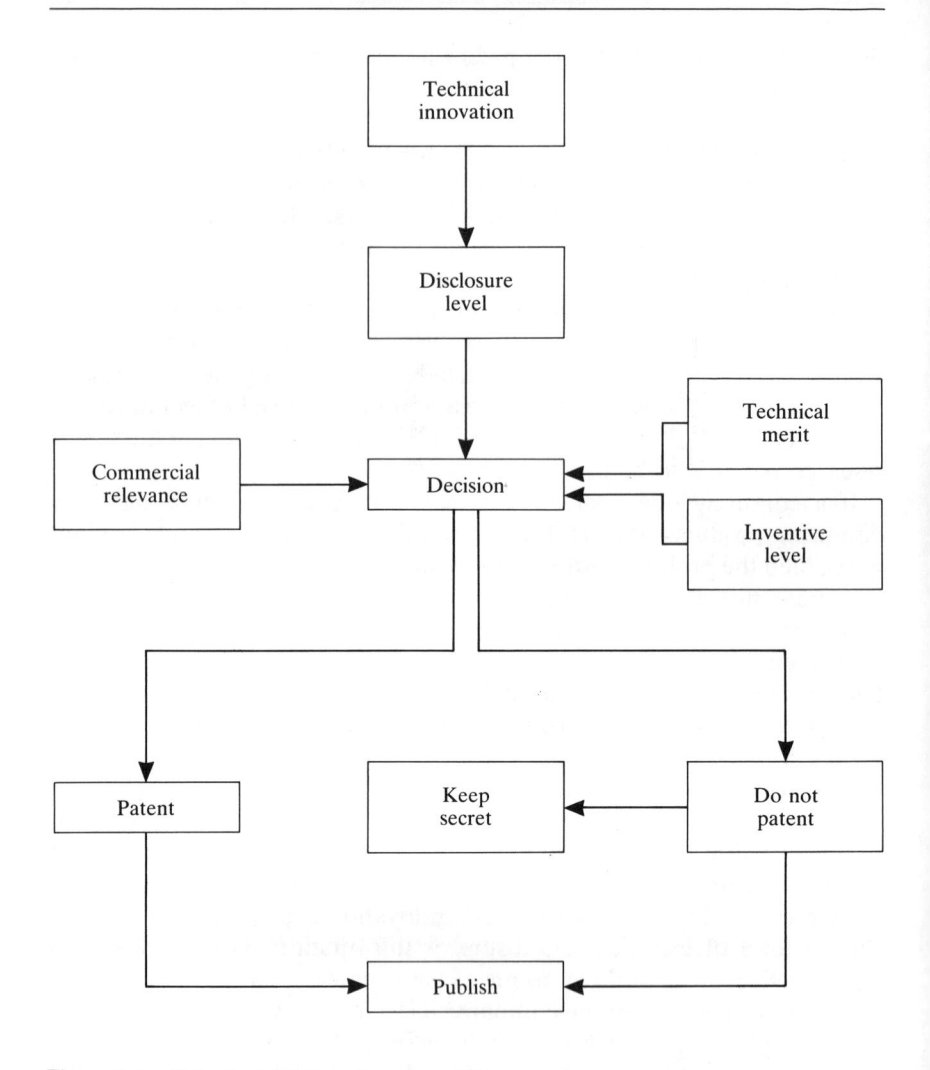

Figure 9.1 Patent, publish or keep secret?

be patentable because of what, it turns out, is already known or, worse still, it may infringe a third party patent. Therefore, we have to consider the question of patent and prior art searching.

Patents and searching
Searching through prior patents and other prior publications is carried out for two basic reasons. The first is to establish that your company is free to manufacture and sell a particular product without infringing third

party rights, and the second is to test the patentability of an innovation that your company has created. These two types of searches have two quite distinct purposes, therefore, depending on the circumstances, one might carry out one of them but not the other.

We shall first consider the question of ensuring so-called 'freedom to use' in relation to a new product. Theoretically it might sound good practice always to carry out searches through prior patents in order to identify any which might be infringed. Having identified any such patents the normal practice would then be to have a patent agent advise as to whether the new product would infringe and, if so, whether the patent is likely to be held valid if litigated, that is, does it present a real risk? If it were concluded that a patent or patents presented a real infringement risk, and therefore a financial exposure, then an assessment ought to be made as to the likelihood of the third party being willing to license the patent(s) and, if so, the likely royalty rate.

However, instead of carrying out such an exercise (which would be quite expensive and time consuming, the latter fact probably being more critical in terms of the timetable for launching a new product), it might be quite legitimate simply to launch the product and hope to deal with any third party intellectual property problems if and when they arose, for example by taking a licence.

Which of these two approaches is appropriate depends upon the size of the company business, the rate at which new products are launched and whether or not the company has a patent portfolio.

If a company is small, is about to launch its first new product and has no patents of its own then there would be a strong argument in favour of carrying out the investigation outlined earlier.

However, if, in contrast, the company is large and well established in its field, launches a steady stream of new products and has a patent portfolio because of a policy of filing patent applications, then there would be a strong argument against carrying out such investigations on a routine basis. Instead, such a company should rely on negotiating a licence, if necessary, should a third party patent exist and that third party attempt to enforce it at some future date.

Let us now consider the question of searching the prior art before filing a patent application, in order to decide whether your company in fact has a validly patentable innovation. Such a search could be carried out in order to avoid the expense of filing a UK patent application, or the even more expensive exercise of filing foreign patent applications if the innovation turns out to be unpatentable.

As stated earlier a valid patent can only be obtained if the 'invention' claimed in it is not already known to the public, that is, has been published or used before the date when the patent application was filed.

It would seem reasonable to carry out a search through the prior art before preparing and filing a patent application, in order to see whether the 'invention' is in fact novel and inventive over that prior art.

Whether it is reasonable to carry out such a search in fact depends upon the circumstances in which the 'invention' was made.

Under the 1977 Patents Act, it is now possible to file a request for an examination when filing the UK patent application and to receive the search result from the Patent Office within about six months of that filing. Therefore, one is in a position to judge the patentability of the innovation in good time before incurring the considerable expenditure involved in filing foreign patent applications.

However, what about carrying out the search before you even file the UK patent application? The cost of carrying out such a 'novelty' search can be of a similar order of magnitude to the cost of filing the patent application. Furthermore, if the company is already established in its commercial field, it will have considerable background knowledge of what has been done technically in that field in the past. In these circumstances it has been found, in practice, that the chances of a novelty search disclosing a piece of prior art which will completely anticipate the innovation is relatively low. The company will have incurred both the cost of the search and the cost of filing the UK patent application. Therefore, it is likely that on balance it is not worth while as a routine matter to carry out such 'novelty' searches.

If, in contrast, the company is entering a completely new field of activity then a patent and literature search can be a very good way of obtaining a view and feel of what has been done in the past in that field. Such searches can be carried out by a number of agencies including the UK Patent Office.

If a company is operating on a portfolio basis where patents are concerned, and is operating in its own established commercial field, then by and large it is not an effective use of funds or staff time to carry out novelty or clearance (infringement) searches as a routine matter whenever the company makes an innovation.

It is better to file a patent application, first to establish a bargaining position *vis-à-vis* any aggressive third party competitor and, secondly, to obtain the UK Patent Office's search report within about six months of the filing of the application, in order to enable a view to be taken as to the chances of obtaining valid and effective UK and foreign patent protection.

Managing an intellectual property portfolio
Although the spectrum of intellectual property rights covers patents, registered designs, registered trade marks, common law trade mark rights, copyright, unregistered design rights and arguably know-how, it is only

the rights which are registrable that are now going to be considered, that is, patents, registered designs and registered trade marks.

The purpose of this subsection is to try to highlight some of the issues that one should consider when dealing with intellectual property rights on a portfolio basis, as distinct from dealing with individual intellectual property rights. Of course, one cannot in fact entirely divorce the factors which are relevant to considering intellectual property rights individually from those which are relevant to considering them on a portfolio basis.

However, there is an essentially different approach between the two cases simply because with any portfolio, whether it be of patents or shares in companies, one is attempting to balance the risks, strengths and weaknesses so that the portfolio as a whole is effective in achieving the objective.

Let us first consider a patent portfolio. As indicated earlier in this chapter a company's patent policy is, or should be, dictated by the economic realities of the commercial field in which it operates. These economic realities will dictate whether patents are used in a passive way, as a form of insurance, or in an active way, to try and obtain either a commercial monopoly or in most cases, more realistically, a financial return on investment in research development and engineering, by way of licensing.

There can be considered to be four decision points in the life cycle of a patent application/patent and thus indirectly of a patent portfolio.

The first decision point is whether to file a UK patent application at all on a particular technical innovation/invention. The second decision point, which comes about nine to ten months later, is whether to continue with the prosecution of the UK patent application and, more importantly, whether to attempt to obtain any foreign patent protection. The third decision point is whether to continue to prosecute an already filed UK or foreign patent application in the light of objections raised by the Patent Office examiner. This prosecution phase can typically last two to three years and very often longer. The fourth decision point is whether to pay renewal fees on patents that have been granted, such renewal fees normally falling due each year.

At each of these decision points a number of factors should be considered in arriving at the decision. Essentially there are three factors: technical, legal and commercial.

The technical factor concerns assessing the technical/engineering worth of the innovation/invention. For example, is it an elegant solution to a long-standing problem? Does it offer a significant cost saving over previous designs?

The legal factor is related to forming a view as to the legal strength or value of any patent that might be obtained or has already been obtained. This strength or value is made up of two elements. The first element concerns the breadth or scope of legal cover or monopoly given by the patent, or which is anticipated will be obtained by filing a patent application. The second element concerns the validity of the patent, or patent to be obtained, in the light of the prior art as known to the company, that is, how strong is the patent?

The commercial factor relates to the immediate or potential relevance of the technical innovation/invention to the company's present or future commercial activities.

In this analysis it is assumed that the company does not engage in purely speculative or so-called 'blue sky' research and that there is in fact a direct or potential commercial objective in mind at the time the innovative work is carried out.

As a practical matter it may be very difficult to obtain the requisite commercial input to the decisions, particularly in a large company where the relevant commercial decision makers are unlikely to have decisions on patents or patent applications high on their list of priorities—even if they are on the list at all! In practice, it is often found to be much easier to obtain the technical and legal inputs than the commercial input and yet in the last analysis it is the latter which is really important and critical.

Because any potentially patentable innovation originates from the technical staff, they naturally have a direct interest in the question of patenting, although there are technical people who regard having to provide information for patenting purposes as a low priority call on their time.

Similarly, any patent adviser, whether in-house or outside the company, has a direct interest in advising on the scope and validity of any patent or potential patent.

It is common in large companies to have a relatively formal mechanism by which attempts are made to obtain the technical, legal and commercial inputs to the various decisions referred to earlier. A common mechanism is a so-called patent committee which sits at regular intervals, typically monthly, and which is ideally drawn from persons who can make the technical, legal and commercial inputs referred to. Another mechanism consists in questionnaires sent to the technical and commercial people to answer.

As suggested earlier, it is unfortunately the case that very often the quality of the commercial input is not of a sufficiently high level to render the overall decisions as valuable as they might otherwise be. It is also a fact that in the absence of the requisite quality and level of commercial input, it is only too easy for the decisions taken to be determined almost solely on the basis of the technical and legal considerations.

This can result in a patent portfolio whose characteristic is its perceived technical virtuosity and legal strength rather than its commercial relevance.

In the real world of negotiating commercial deals involving patents it is the commercial relevance of the patents and their number which count rather than the finer points of their legal status. In other words it is better to have several patents of doubtful legal strength but undoubted commercial relevance than have a single patent that one is confident could withstand a legal attack upon it but which is only of marginal commercial relevance. Of course, it would be nice to have a patent which is highly relevant commercially and legally fireproof but this is not often the case.

Let us now consider the constitution of a patent portfolio. At any given time it will be made up of patent applications, which have been filed but have not yet had a patent granted on them, together with granted patents upon which renewal fees have to be paid annually in order to keep them in force. In addition, there will be a number of innovations which are the subject of patent applications in the course of preparation, prior to filing at the Patent Office, and others which are to be the subject of a decision in the very near future as to whether or not a patent application should be filed on them.

As UK patents can last for up to 20 years (and most other countries have similar periods for the maximum life of patents) it can be seen that the age profile of a patent portfolio can span a considerable period.

The profile of a patent portfolio, particularly in the early years, can have one of two quite distinct shapes depending upon which of two policies or strategies is followed.

It is in the nature of technical innovation that the nearer one is to the beginning of the process the more difficult it is to identify those innovations/inventions which will turn out to be commercial winners. The corollary of this statement is that the longer one can delay decisions the more likely they are to turn out to be correct.

Bearing this point in mind let us now look at the first question that has to be decided—namely, whether to file a patent application at all on a particular innovation/invention. One approach is to apply a very fine filter at this stage in terms of the criteria that the innovation/invention must meet. This results in relatively few patent applications being filed but, once they are filed, they tend to maintain their own momentum and become patents unless prevented from doing so by relevant prior art cited by the Patent Office examiner.

The alternative approach is to have a relatively coarse filter at this early stage on the basis that the level of uncertainty is at its highest. Therefore, it is best on balance, initially, to back a relatively high number of innovations/inventions by at least filing a UK patent application on each of them. This has the effect of deferring a decision to a point some nine to ten months later when the question of foreign patent protection has to be considered. (Note that any foreign patent applications must generally be filed within 12 months of the filing of the basic UK patent application in order to benefit from the so-called 'convention period'.) The cost of filing foreign patent applications is an order of magnitude greater than the cost of filing the original UK patent application, therefore a decision at this point has much greater cost consequences than the earlier decision whether or not to file a UK patent application.

In this alternative approach the fine filter is applied at the foreign filing decision stage.

Of course, there is nothing in theory to stop a fine filter from being applied at both stages but experience indicates that companies tend to operate in practice in one of the two ways described.

What is meant by 'fine' and 'coarse' filters? In this context the term 'fine' filter is intended to describe a situation where an attempt is made to assess all three elements referred to earlier: namely the technical, the legal and the commercial factors.

In contrast the term 'coarse' filter is intended to describe a situation where unless there is some clear-cut reason for not filing a UK patent application, then one should be filed.

It is thus a question of emphasis and attitude. With the 'fine' filter, reasons are being sought for not filing a UK patent application whereas with the 'coarse' filter the onus is reversed.

Trade marks

Trade marks are of differing importance depending upon the type of business involved. One could say that, for example, at the capital equipment end of the spectrum they are of little or no relevance whereas at the consumer end of the spectrum of products they can be all important. At this latter end of the spectrum lie goods such as food, drink, drugs and services.

As an illustration of the importance of trade marks in certain businesses, in recent years in the field of food and drink the practice has arisen of valuing a company's trade marks and entering them as an asset on the balance sheet.

As indicated in Chapter 2 the legal protection available for trade marks consists essentially of rights obtained by registration and rights obtained by use.

A company which depends heavily on its trade marks for its success must clearly have some strategy for protecting and policing the use of those trade marks.

In this chapter it will only be possible to touch on a few of the key points that arise in practice in administering a trade mark portfolio.

Unlike patents, copyright or registered designs the continuing validity of a registered trade mark is generally dependent upon its use. Therefore, of all the intellectual property rights that we have discussed trade marks inevitably have the greatest correlation and affinity with commercial reality.

For that reason, and because they can be understood by everyone, they very often attract the most management attention.

Although there is nothing to stop a company building up a 'bank' of trade marks for future use, there is the inherent danger that at any given time a significant proportion of those registrations will be invalid because they have not been used. Whether this is so in a particular case will depend upon how long the registration has been in existence. Such an approach can also involve a company in higher trade mark filing, prosecution and renewal expenditure than would otherwise be the case.

As an alternative to registering trade marks well in advance of any possible commercial use, a company might adopt the opposite policy of only filing a trade mark application in a particular territory when it knows that it is about to launch, or has in fact just launched, the relevant product in that territory.

This alternative approach has its own attendant dangers. What are they?

The countries of the world can be divided up very crudely into those in which trade mark rights are granted on the basis of prior use of the mark by the proprietor and those in which rights are granted to the person who first registers the mark. The United Kingdom, many Commonwealth countries and the United States fall into the first category, whereas most other countries fall into the second category to a greater or lesser extent.

The danger referred to earlier arises because of the second category of countries, namely those in which rights go to the first person to register the trade mark rather than to the first person to use it.

It can be seen that if a company only applies to register its trade marks in a particular territory at or shortly before the time when it is about to launch a product in that territory it runs the considerable risk that a third party will, upon learning of the existence of the product from its earlier launch in the home market (the United Kingdom), file a trade mark application in that other territory prior to the date of launch. By filing such an application that third party then has the potential for holding the owner of the trade mark to ransom. This has happened many times.

Another aspect of this problem manifests itself in connection with very well-known trade marks, the proprietors of which have failed to register the mark in a particular territory. In fact it is not unknown for individuals to make a living by 'hijacking' well-known trade marks in this way and then in effect selling them back (through selling the registrations) to the original proprietor. One can see that there is a conflict between trying to ensure that this does not happen, but at the same time keeping the trade mark registration expenditure within acceptable limits. Like other commerical decisions it is a question of judgment in any particular circumstance as to when one incurs the expenditure of attempting to register a trade mark in a particular territory.

Let us now consider the question of the adoption of a new trade mark for a product and its subsequent protection by means of registration.

Considerable sums of money are involved in arriving at a new product identity, or corporate identity, and numerous factors are taken into consideration in arriving at the final result. The dominant factors are, and must be, marketing rather than legal factors. In practice an identity is chosen firstly on marketing factors and then checked to see whether it gives rise to any legal problems, including those in relation to trade mark rights owned by third parties.

The reality is that if legal problems do arise they have to be dealt with in the nature of a fire-fighting exercise. It is very rare for the legal filter to be applied at the beginning of the exercise to ensure that any product identification (trade mark) which is chosen is free from any legal problems.

It has been found in many situations to be virtually impossible to select a new trade mark for worldwide use which will not give rise to a legal problem somewhere in the world. It is generally not a practical solution to try to carry out comprehensive worldwide trade mark searches at a sufficiently early stage to prevent this from happening. Again it is a question of judgment and deciding which territories to search in respect of a shortlist of trade marks.

In practice, one often confines one's searching simply to the United Kingdom but even here there are limitations as to how far one can go in satisfying oneself that there are no legal problems.

As indicated earlier, in the United Kingdom there are two forms of trade mark protection. Historically the first to arise were rights resulting from use of a trade mark (so-called common law rights) and the second were rights from having registered the trade mark at the UK Patent Office. One can search the Trade Mark Register of the UK Patent Office in order to try and ascertain whether a particular new proposed trade mark is likely to infringe any third party's rights. However, there is no comprehensive way of checking on whether there are common law trade mark rights in existence which could be infringed by the adoption of the proposed new trade mark. Certain things can be done to reduce this risk, such as searching through trade directories.

Trade mark portfolio

Those companies possessing a business where product identity is critical, that is, where the product is sold to the end consumer, can find themselves holding a considerable portfolio of individual trade mark registrations.

This is because, generally speaking, each country has its own national system for registering trade marks (putting aside the mechanism under the Madrid Convention for obtaining a batch of national registrations on the basis of a single trade and application filing) and, furthermore, the Register is divided into classes and it is therefore necessary to obtain a separate registration in respect of the goods which fall into different classes. Such classification systems are for the administrative benefit of the various Patent Offices (Trade Mark Registries) but result in trade mark proprietors having to incur increased costs to protect their trade marks adequately.

Therefore, it is not unusual for some large companies to hold trade mark registration portfolios running into tens of thousands of registrations worldwide. In any event the size of a trade mark portfolio is generally at least one order of magnitude larger than a patent portfolio, assuming that the business of a particular company is such that it generates a reasonable number of innovations and its products are sold directly to the end customer/consumer.

Another characteristic of a trade mark portfolio, which distinguishes it from a patent portfolio, is the fact that trade mark registrations can last forever subject to the payment of renewal fees at intervals which generally are considerably longer than those for patents. In the United Kingdom the normal interval between trade mark renewals is 14 years whereas for patents it is one year.

These long renewal intervals bring with them problems which are peculiar to the managing of a trade mark registration portfolio, not the least of which is the likely absence of continuity among the relevant staff in the company.

Therefore, it is all too easy for registrations to remain in force long after their commercial justification has ceased to exist. Furthermore, as the validity of a trade mark registration is generally dependent upon the continued commercial use of the trade mark that it protects, it is not uncommon for a trade mark registration portfolio to contain a significant number of potentially invalid registrations. Why should this matter?

Nothing is really lost by this except for the tendency to spend management time in reviewing registrations that are no longer relevant and also even renewing such registrations with the attendant cost. It is a fact that people tend to be reluctant to abandon registrations with the result that the portfolio grows at a higher rate than is perhaps justified by the underlying commercial reality.

Therefore, it is suggested that it is good practice periodically either to attempt to review the portfolio (if it is not too large) with a view to removing dead wood or to try and ensure that renewals or registrations are only made on the basis of a high quality commercial input.

Licensing
As indicated earlier, there are three basic reasons why a company would

obtain intellectual property rights, particularly patents. The first is to attempt to obtain a monopoly in the relevant marketplace for a certain product. The second is to obtain an income by licensing the patent(s) to a third party and the third is to use a patent portfolio as a kind of insurance policy.

In the first situation the company would not willingly license its patents or other intellectual property rights, for example copyright, but may reluctantly do so as a result of having to sue an infringing third party and then coming to the conclusion in the course of the subsequent litigation, that it is unlikely to win the action. This is neither 'active' nor 'passive' but 'forced' licensing.

'Active' licensing is what happens in the second situation described. A company may, *ab initio*, conclude that in order to obtain the maximum return from its investment in technical innovation, it needs to license third parties simply because it does not itself have the capacity or capability to exploit the technology fully. A good example is where the company only has a commercial presence in a limited territory, for example the United Kingdom, but wishes to exploit the technology outside the United Kingdom.

In such a situation, the company will need to treat licensing as a well-defined and quite definite commercial activity. It follows that it will need to devote significant resources to it in order to make it commercially successful. These resources will include front-end effort to identify suitable licensees and to negotiate agreements with them, and follow-up effort devoted to servicing and technically supporting the licence agreements entered into.

By its very nature, licensing a third party can mean setting up a potential competitor to your own company's commercial activities. Because of this, the decision to enter into an active licensing policy should not be taken lightly, particularly also in view of the considerable investment and time which will be involved in negotiating and supporting any licence agreements.

For a company whose activity is devoted essentially to research and development, the decision to license is relatively simple because the company does not itself have the resources to exploit effectively the technical innovations. The choice here is not between going it alone or licensing, but between licensing or selling the technology and its associated intellectual property rights outright.

'Passive' licensing is what happens in the third situation where a company, which holds an intellectual property portfolio, is approached by a third party for a licence.

In this situation the company can take one of two views. It can take the view that anything received under a licence is a financial windfall because the intellectual property portfolio was only obtained for 'insurance' purposes. In this case, the company would agree to the request for a licence. Alternatively, it can take the view that because any licensee is a potential competitor, and the company is not in the business of helping competitors, that the answer to any request for a licence should be 'no'.

There is always a significant risk in saying 'no' because the third party is quite likely to go ahead anyway and infringe your company's intellectual property rights. You then have the problem of deciding whether or not to try and enforce those intellectual property rights by litigation. In view of the very uncertain nature of patent litigation (see later in this chapter), litigation can often be difficult to justify even where there are good positive commercial reasons. In the situation just described there really are no good commercial reasons but simply a reaction to a failure of the third party to respect your patent, which was only obtained in the first place for purely 'insurance' purposes.

Even if your company had no intention of exploiting the subject of the patent at the time of obtaining it, it is not unknown for the reaction to a request for a licence to be met by the observation that 'if a third party thinks it is worth exploiting our patent, perhaps we should do so ourselves', and therefore not agree to license the third party.

LITIGATION

Introduction
There is a view that if you get as far as contemplating litigation then you have already failed as a manager. This view is probably more prevalent in the United Kingdom than in the United States where litigation tends to be regarded by management as just another management tool.

In this section litigation is going to be looked at from the following viewpoints:

1. The reasons for litigating.
2. General comparisons between the various philosophical bases for litigation in the common law countries and the civil law countries.
3. An outline of the court structure in the United Kingdom.
4. A general outline of the procedures involved in litigation.
5. United Kingdom litigation and the European Community (EC).

Why litigate?
The basic question of 'why litigate' is tied in with the equally basic question 'why obtain intellectual property rights in the first place?' We have already seen earlier in this chapter that the reasons for obtaining intellec-

tual property rights (patents in particular) vary from industry to industry and to a large extent are driven by the economic realities of that industry.

If the company obtains patents for purely defensive/insurance reasons, then it is most unlikely that the company will (or should) ever wish to commence litigation to enforce any of its intellectual property rights.

However, if its reason for obtaining intellectual property rights (patents) is to attempt to obtain a monopoly or to generate a royalty income, then the question of litigation must be actively considered whenever a third party refuses either to respect the existence of the intellectual property right or to take a licence on terms acceptable to the company.

There is a third possible situation in which litigation may be considered and that is so-called tactical litigation.

It is probably true to say that in the United States and Japan the obtaining, use and enforcement of intellectual property rights is more likely to be regarded by the management as an integral part of its commercial activities than would be the case with a UK company. It follows from this that litigation would also be regarded as being part of an arsenal of commercial weapons or tactics open to the company's management. Therefore, situations can arise in which litigation of intellectual property rights is commenced by a company as part of an overall tactic for achieving a particular commercial objective, which is not directly concerned with the enforcement of that particular intellectual property right. In the writer's experience such tactical use of intellectual property rights is less likely where UK companies are concerned.

There are many commercial considerations which can underlie and motivate the enforcement of intellectual property rights by means of litigation. For example, the owner of an intellectual property right may not be willing to license it and may be attempting to use it in order to obtain a monopoly within a particular commercial area. In contrast, the owner of an intellectual property right may be quite willing to license it and might in fact have a policy of licensing in order to generate income as an alternative to exploiting the intellectual property right personally. In the latter situation either the failure of an 'infringer' to be willing to take any licence at all, or to be willing to take a licence but not on terms agreeable to the owner of the intellectual property right, can in effect force the owner of that right to resort to litigation in order to achieve reasonable objectives. Unfortunately, the litigation process does not provide for the plaintiff merely to have the court require the defendant to enter into a licence, the only remedies that are available to the plaintiff being an injunction to stop the defendant from infringing and/or damages or an account of profits. In this respect the court procedures do not adequately provide for what is being sought commercially and in fact result in 'overkill' in the situation just described.

Although litigation, once started, tends to acquire its own momentum, there is nothing to prevent it from being stopped at any stage as a result of an agreement being reached or while negotiations take place. In fact it is very common for negotiations to take place in parallel with the litigation proceeding. In other situations the litigation takes over from and replaces all negotiation. Which of these situations applies in any particular case depends upon the overall commercial situation and the personalities involved.

It has to be admitted that although, as stated earlier, litigation can be stopped at any stage, for many people the issuing and serving of a writ has sufficient emotional overtones to make the defendant less rather than more likely to come to the negotiating table. It is a question of making a judgment in each situation as to which tactic is appropriate in order to reach an agreement, assuming that that is the objective rather than the objective of trying to obtain an injunction to prevent the 'infringer' from continuing to infringe, that is, there is no licence on offer from the owner of the intellectual property right.

It is often said that as far as litigation in general is concerned, the cases which come to court are those which are on the borderline as far as the underlying legal position is concerned. In other words the majority do not get to court, simply because the legal position is crystal clear either one way or the other.

While this may be true in some other fields of the law it is submitted that, generally speaking, it does not apply in the field of intellectual property rights, particularly patents. This is because patent disputes have at their core the virtually unanswerable question 'Has the inventor been clever enough to justify the grant of a valid legally enforceable monopoly?' The level of 'cleverness', or inventiveness, is to be judged against the state of the prior art at the time the 'invention' was made.

Few, if any, patent actions turn on fine points of law. What they do turn on is the evidence adduced to establish, or otherwise, that the patentee has in fact reached the earlier mentioned undefined and indefinable level of 'cleverness'.

Because of the nature of the UK 'adversarial' legal system and its almost total reliance on evidence being given orally, the credibility of witnesses under cross-examination and the skill of counsel in conducting that cross-examination becomes a key if not dominating factor in how a court will decide a case. This is not true of 'inquisitorial' based legal systems e.g. elsewhere in Europe. It thus becomes most important whether a particular witness is a 'good' witness in terms of his or her ability to present evidence in the witness box and to withstand successfully cross-examination.

In some cases a patent action may appear to focus on the question of 'infringement', rather than the question of 'validity', but in view of the current tendency of the courts to give liberal interpretations to the strict wording of patent claims it is suggested that the essential question comes back to the 'cleverness' factor referred to earlier.

If it is accepted that this unanswerable question is at the root of all patent actions, it can be seen that in many disputes both parties will inevitably have grounds for feeling that they have a not insignificant chance of winning if the matter were litigated.

Therefore, while in many fields of law there is a conflict and choice between achieving justice or certainty, in the patent field the option of certainty is to a significant extent not available to the law because of the underlying question referred to earlier.

This uncertainty exists in all patent actions irrespective of the commercial stakes or the technical complexity/simplicity of the 'invention' involved. It follows that the amount of time and cost that can be involved in adducing evidence on this key issue is largely independent of the nature of the individual dispute. It is submitted that what drives patent litigation, and therefore determines its cost and complexity, is to a significant extent the value of what is at stake commercially.

To some extent similar comments could be made about so-called 'passing-off' actions in that, given enough time, both parties could produce voluminous evidence to support or counter the view that one party's goods have been 'passed off' as those of the other party.

Common law systems v. civil law systems
In order to appreciate and to put into context some of the more detailed information which will be given later in this subsection, it is useful at this point to outline the philosophical bases for the two broad legal systems which one finds around the world. These two systems have basically different approaches to the question of litigation and how litigation is conducted.

In the so-called common law countries, of which the United Kingdom is the prime example together with the United States and Canada, Australia and New Zealand, litigation (whether civil or criminal) is conducted on the so-called 'adversarial' basis. In contrast, in the so-called civil law countries (the vast majority of the rest of the world and Continental Europe in particular) litigation (again both civil and criminal) is conducted on the so-called 'inquisitorial' basis.

What do these terms 'adversarial' and 'inquisitorial' mean? In an 'adversarial' system the role of the court is to act as a kind of umpire between the parties in dispute. It is there to hear both sides of the story and to decide which story to believe. The court adopts what is essentially a passive role and this in turn dictates the kinds of rules and procedures that govern the litigation.

In contrast, in an 'inquisitorial' system the role of the court is to ascertain the 'truth' and this results in the court playing a proactive role in the proceedings. This role in turn dictates the type of rules and procedures which govern the litigation.

Once one has grasped these two differing underlying philosophies in the role of the court one can then appreciate why, in a particular legal system, litigation is conducted in a particular way.

Clearly there are advantages and disadvantages in each of the above outlined approaches when looking at a legal system as a whole, but of course we are here only concerned with litigation in the intellectual property field. However, this field in itself cannot be treated as if it were homogeneous because, for example, the issues involved in litigating a patent are completely different from the issues involved in litigating a trade mark, and in the latter case particularly where 'passing off' is involved.

However, in one key area, namely cost, which must be of prime concern to any litigant, as a generalization costs are lower in countries which have a civil law based 'inquisitorial' system than in countries which have a common law based 'adversarial' system of litigation.

It has certainly been a commonly held view among legal practitioners in the United Kingdom that the cost of UK patent litigation is significantly higher than that in most civil law based countries such as Germany. This difference has been ascribed to various factors, some of which are concerned with the way in which the legal profession organizes itself (i.e. the distinction between barristers, solicitors and patent agents) and some of which have been concerned with the underlying difference between an 'adversarial' and an 'inquisitorial' based system.

Apart from the basic distinction between the two systems as indicated earlier, at the practical level this underlying difference manifests itself in an emphasis in the adversarial system on advocacy and the use of oral evidence. In contrast, an inquisitorial system relies much more heavily on written evidence and the role of the advocate is consequently diminished in comparison with an adversarial system.

However, since 1978 a bridge has come into existence between these two philosophies, in the sense that since that date the European Patent Convention has been in existence, the concrete manifestation of that Convention being the Europcan Patent Office in Munich, Germany. Although there is still no European Patent Court, as such, a large number of contentious matters relating to patents are dealt with by the so-called Boards of Appeal associated with the European Patent Office. These Boards of Appeal, which are multi-national in their composition in that they are staffed by nationals of the member states of the European Patent Convention, employ what is essentially an 'inquisitorial' system.

Many practitioners are of the view that in the intellectual property field, an 'inquisitorial' system is more suited to the resolution of disputes, particularly patents, than the 'adversarial' system.

Having, as it were, set the litigation scene by giving a very broad view of the two types of system involved, we shall now concentrate on the UK legal system insofar as it is relevant to the resolution of intellectual property related disputes.

The UK legal system
The recent Copyright Designs and Patents Act 1988 creates a new cheaper forum for trying patent actions, namely the Patents County Court which came into operation in 1990. This Court, as its name implies, is part of the existing County Court system which is generally geared to trying relatively low value civil (as opposed to criminal) disputes such as breach of contract and debt actions. The County Court already has specialist 'branches' such as the Divorce County Court.

The court structure in the United Kingdom, as far as patent litigation is concerned, is shown in Figure 9.2, which shows the various tribunals that can be involved in patent litigation and their relationship to one another.

The Patent Office's main function is to grant patents on patent applications lodged with it, after having satisfied itself there is a patentable invention in relation to the prior art. If it is not satisfied, then it refuses the application for a patent. Such a refusal can be appealed against to the Patents Court, as can other administrative actions taken by the Patent Office. The Patents Court is presided over by a judge who has a technical and specialist intellectual property background. The Patents Court is part of the Chancery Division of the High Court. Decisions of the Patents Court can be appealed to the Court of Appeal whose decisions, in turn, may be appealed to the House of Lords where either the Court of Appeal or the House of Lords has given leave to do so.

As stated earlier, a new lower tier for patent and designs litigation has been created by the Copyright Decisions and Patents Act 1988, namely the Patents County Court. Decisions of the Patents County Court can be appealed to the Court of Appeal and thence to the House of Lords with the leave either of the Court of Appeal or the House of Lords.

It is intended that the Patents County Court should provide a cheaper and more expeditious means for resolving patent and design disputes compared with the existing Patents Court. One reason why it should be cheaper is that a party to an action can have the whole case handled by a patent agent in contrast with having to employ a patent agent, solicitor and barrister if litigation takes place in the High Court. As far as operation of the new court is concerned, it is hoped by many practitioners that there will be some move away from the 'adversarial' system and towards the 'inquisitorial' system.

STRATEGY AND LITIGATION   195

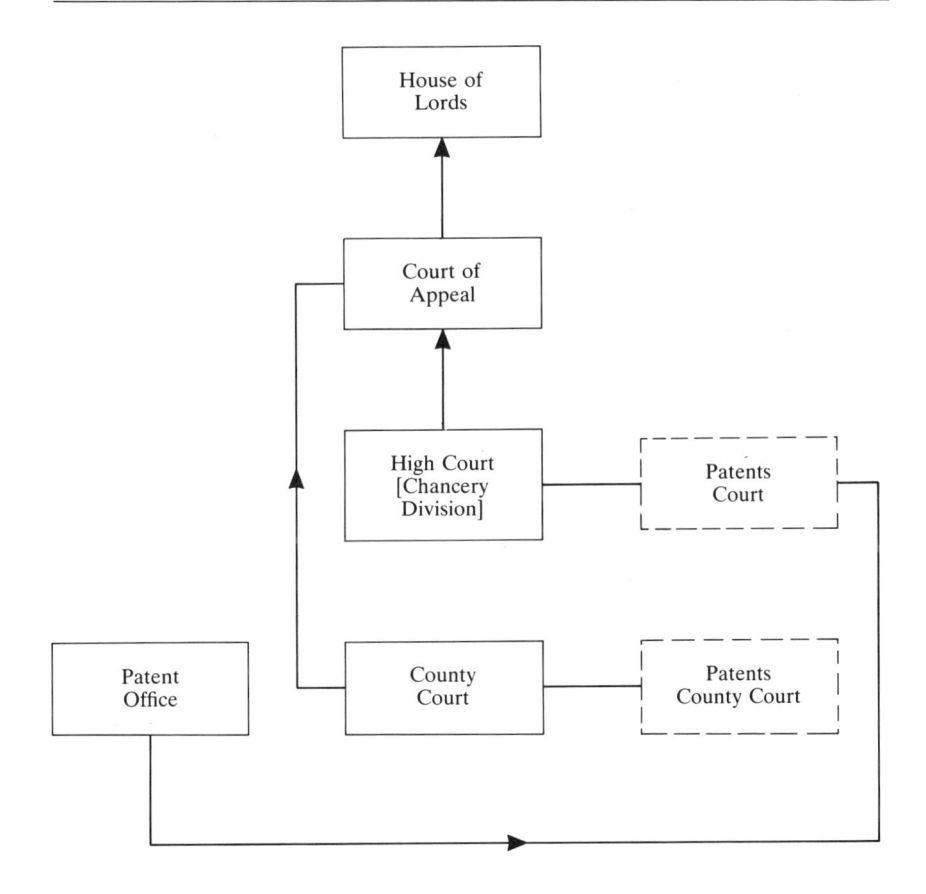

```
                    ┌──────────┐
                    │ House of │
                    │  Lords   │
                    └──────────┘
                         ▲
                         │
                    ┌──────────┐
           ┌───────▶│ Court of │
           │        │  Appeal  │
           │        └──────────┘
           │             ▲
           │             │
           │        ┌──────────┐      ┌─ ─ ─ ─ ─ ─┐
           │        │High Court│      │  Patents  │
           │────────│[Chancery │──────│   Court   │──┐
           │        │ Division]│      │           │  │
           │        └──────────┘      └─ ─ ─ ─ ─ ─┘  │
           │                                         │
 ┌────────┐│        ┌──────────┐      ┌─ ─ ─ ─ ─ ─┐  │
 │ Patent ││        │  County  │      │  Patents  │  │
 │ Office │         │  Court   │      │County Court│ │
 └────────┘         └──────────┘      └─ ─ ─ ─ ─ ─┘  │
      │                                              │
      └──────────────────────▶───────────────────────┘
```

Figure 9.2 **Patent litigation in the United Kingdom**

Figure 9.3 illustrates the relationship between the UK court structure, the European Commission in Brussels and the European Court in Luxembourg.

On the right-hand side of Figure 9.3 is a simplified representation of Figure 9.2, whereby appeals from the High Court (Chancery Division) or the Patents County Court can be made to the Court of Appeal and thence to the House of Lords with the leave of the Court of Appeal or the House of Lords.

On the left-hand side of Figure 9.3 is the European Court to which issues involving European law, that is, the Treaty of Rome, can be referred by any of the UK courts. As a practical matter, the UK courts tend to consider themselves competent to decide so-called Euro-points of law and therefore in the majority of cases no reference is in fact made to the European Court. In the context of intellectual property rights litigation

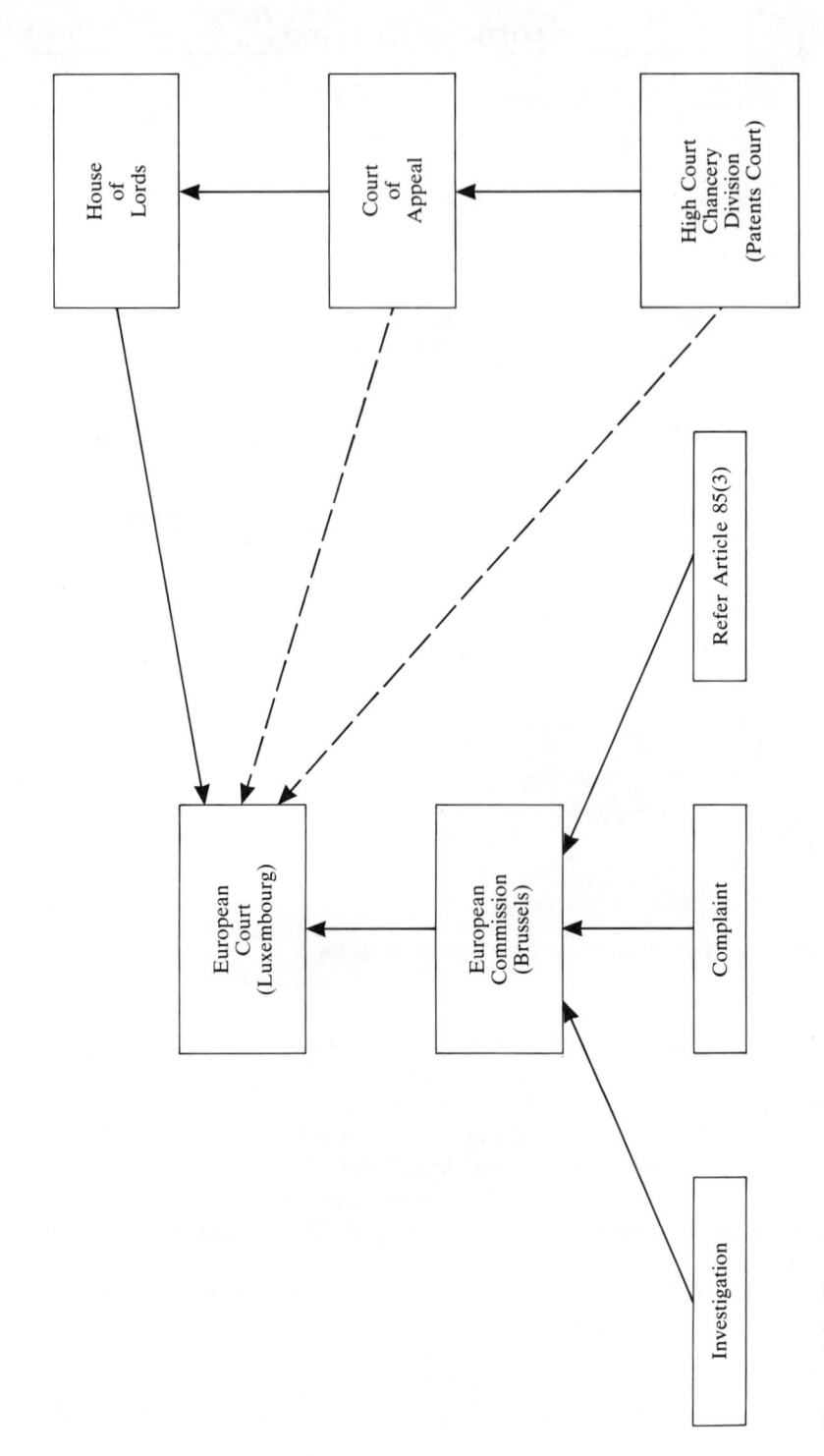

Figure 9.3 European court structure

this usually means that the so-called Euro-defences, which usually involve an allegation that to enforce an intellectual property right is contrary to Article 85 of the Treaty of Rome, are decided by the UK courts.

The European Court hears appeals from decisions made by the European Commission. These decisions can be as a result of investigations made by the Commission into the activities of companies or complaints against the commercial activities of companies—those complaints having been lodged by third parties with the Commission.

Steps in a UK patent infringement action
The following is a brief outline of the steps that go to make up a patent infringement action in the High Court. This outline is of necessity an oversimplification, but it is intended to give the reader who has no knowledge of the way a patent action is tried a chance to appreciate the essential structure of the action. This outline is from the viewpoint of the plaintiff, that is, the patent owner who is bringing the action.

1. A chartered patent agent would usually give the initial opinion as to whether the patent has been infringed and also an opinion on the strength of the patent in the light of known earlier patents and publications. The chartered patent agent would then instruct a solicitor specializing in intellectual property matters who would, in turn, instruct counsel also specializing in intellectual property matters. The role of the chartered patent agent is to act as the technical adviser on the patent; the role of the solicitor is to be concerned with the formalities and mechanics of the action; and the role of the barrister is to act as advocate at the trial of the action. Depending upon the importance of the matter a QC as well as a junior counsel may be instructed.

2. The so-called writ of summons, statement of claim and particulars of infringement are settled by counsel. The purpose of the statement of claim is to set out the details of the patent and the relief sought, for example damages injunction, delivery up and cost. The purpose of the particulars of infringement is to set out the acts of infringement being alleged and also the particular claims of the patent that are alleged to be infringed.

3. The defendant is then required to acknowledge service of the writ and to submit his defence, the latter normally including a counterclaim to revoke the patent on the basis that it is invalid for one of a number of possible reasons, the commonest being that the alleged invention is obvious in view of the earlier knowledge. Up to this point the proceedings have not taken up a lot of time, typically several weeks. However, it is the following steps which, because there is no real timetable

imposed by the court, can result in the time taken before the action reaches a trial running into several years.
4. Discovery, summons for directions and preparation for trial. The purpose of these steps is to try and ensure that neither party is taken by surprise at the trial by the evidence which the other side intends to submit and also to try and ensure that the real issues in the case are focused on before the trial. However, because of the court's essentially passive role the opposite of the latter objective is often achieved.
5. The trial. This can typically last for several weeks and in complicated cases considerably longer by running into several months. The characteristic of the trial, as indicated earlier, is that evidence is given orally and considerable emphasis is placed on the adversarial skills of counsel on both sides. It is also a characteristic of patent actions that even before the witnesses are examined orally considerable time is spent in court in reading out what is purported to be all the relevant documentation, that is, it is assumed that the judge has not seen any of the material to be submitted by either side prior to the hearing in court.
6. Judgment and any appeal. Judgment will not normally be given at the end of the hearing but there will be a delay of several months before the court delivers its judgment. If the unsuccessful party wishes to appeal against the court's decision it can do so as of right to the Court of Appeal. If there is to be a further appeal from the Court of Appeal to the House of Lords this can only be done with leave of either the Court of Appeal or of the House of Lords.
7. Damages. At the trial of the action the court would not in fact specify the amount of damages to be awarded to the winning party, in practice it being left to the parties to negotiate a settlement. Should they fail to do so damages would then be assessed as a separate issue by the court, this inquiry taking place several months after judgment has been given. This inquiry as to damages is usually delayed if there is an appeal.

Remedies
If, as the owner of intellectual property rights, you decide to resort to litigation what can the courts do for you? Or to put it another way what can you get the courts to do to the other party?

The courts have two broad powers. The first is the power to prevent the other party from either continuing or starting to infringe your rights. This is achieved by the granting of an injunction. The second power is to award damages against the infringing party in respect of the financial loss suffered by you as a result of the infringement.

One thing that the courts cannot do is to order an infringer to take a licence under your rights. As this is often the purpose of the owner of intellectual property rights in commencing litigation, it is a shortcoming of the legal system. However, it is often the case that the practical outcome of successful litigation by the intellectual property owner is that the infringer is willing to take a licence.

As far as injunctions are concerned there are a number of different types. From a practical point of view the most significant distinction is between those that can be obtained at short notice (so-called interlocutory injunctions, or interim injunctions) and those that are obtained following a full trial of the issues involved—this typically taking several years in the case of a patent action.

From a commercial point of view the interlocutory injunction is the most significant and serious because it enables the owner of intellectual property rights to obtain a relatively immediate benefit, and thus has the potential for putting the infringer out of business as far as the particular infringing product is concerned.

To obtain an interlocutory injunction the owner of the intellectual property rights has first to show that there is a case to answer. If the defendant can then show that there is an arguable defence then whether or not the intellectual property owner will get the interlocutory injunction will depend upon the so-called 'balance of convenience'.

This means that the court will look at the commercially relevant surrounding circumstances of both parties and ask the question: 'Would the granting of an injunction create a greater inconvenience to the defendant than the inconvenience caused to the plaintiff by the failure to grant an injunction?'

The question is thus answered not on the basis of the detailed legal considerations in the case but upon the commercial reality of the situation. For example, at one extreme is the situation where an owner of intellectual property rights is trying to establish itself in the market and is threatened by an infringer who is also thinking of entering the market. In this case it is probable that the court would grant an interlocutory injunction, on the basis that the balance of convenience is in favour of the intellectual property owner, because its whole business hinges on becoming well established in the market, whereas the infringer has not yet committed itself. In contrast, at the other extreme is the situation where an intellectual property owner has either not exploited the intellectual property at all or has exploited it by licensing third parties, and the infringer is already selling infringing products in the marketplace. In this situation the court would probably hold the balance of convenience to lie with the infringer and would not grant an injunction.

Two other general points must be borne in mind when considering the question of injunctions in general and interlocutory injunctions in particular. There is a general principle that the granting of any injunction is a discretionary remedy which the courts should only grant in those circumstances in which damages cannot adequately compensate the owner of the rights being infringed. The second general principle, which applies to interlocutory injunctions, is that it is critical that the owner of the rights should act immediately, that is, apply for the interlocutory injunction immediately on becoming aware of the other party's actual or intended infringement. In other words delay will prevent the owner of the rights from obtaining an interlocutory injunction. As to how much delay would be fatal to the obtaining of an interlocutory injunction, that will depend on the circumstances but we are talking about weeks rather than months. In some circumstances even days could be critical.

As far as damages are concerned, these are financial compensation for the infringement of the intellectual property rights. The assessment of these damages follows general legal principles. The main principles are: first, any loss should have resulted from the infringement of the rights in question; and, secondly, the loss should not be too remote from the acts of infringement. In practical terms this can mean that damages in intellectual property actions are likely to be assessed either on the basis of sales which the owner of the intellectual property rights can show would have been made if it hadn't been for the infringing acts of the other party or, alternatively, on the basis of a notional royalty applied to the sales of the infringing items by the other party.

As an alternative to claiming damages an owner of intellectual property rights can instead claim what is termed 'an account of profits'. This means that the plaintiff would claim the profit that the other party has made on the sale of the infringing items. Although, in theory, this may be an attractive financial alternative in certain circumstances, it is generally not one which the owners of intellectual property rights would opt for. The reason is that an assessment of profits made is an area open to considerable interpretation, if not argument.

Apart from the civil law remedies discussed earlier there is the possibility of criminal penalties in connection with copyright and trade mark infringement. These can take the form of fines or even a jail sentence.

UK litigation and the European Community

A party's freedom to exploit its intellectual property rights is constrained to a certain extent by the Treaty of Rome which in essence lays down the law for the European Community.

The effect of the Treaty manifests itself as far as UK intellectual property litigation is concerned by defendants attempting to rely on so-called Euro-defences. These Euro-defences are based essentially on the allegation that even if the intellectual property right in question is validly enforceable under UK national law, its enforcement should nevertheless not be allowed because to do so would result in contravention of the Treaty of Rome.

Euro-defences
These so-called Euro-defences fall under two headings. The first involves Article 85 of the Treaty of Rome and is concerned generally with ensuring the free flow of goods between member states. The second involves Article 86 of the Treaty of Rome and is concerned generally with preventing companies which have a dominant position in the marketplace from abusing that position.

This is, of course, an oversimplification but the essential thing to bear in mind is that there is an inherent conflict between the enforcement of national intellectual property rights and the objects of the Treaty of Rome. A similar conflict arises in the United States between the enforcement of intellectual property rights and the so-called anti-trust laws.

Parallel imports/exhaustion of rights
Reference has just been made to the impact of the Treaty of Rome on the ability of a proprietor to enforce intellectual property rights, for example patents, registered trade marks, copyright, etc. One of the consequences of the Treaty of Rome's basic philosophy that there should be free flow of goods between the member states of the European Community is that national intellectual property rights in individual Community countries cannot be used to partition the 'common market'. A consequence of this general philosophy is that if goods are put on the market in one Community country, either by the proprietor or by somebody licensed by the proprietor, then that proprietor cannot use any intellectual property rights that he or she might have in another Community country to prevent the import of that particular example of the product into that second country. This situation is variously referred to as being one concerned with 'parallel imports' and with 'exhaustion of rights'.

The classic situation which arises in practice is usually as a result of price differentials for a given product in different member states of the European Community. This price differential gives a commercial incentive for people to purchase the product in the cheaper country and then endeavour to sell it in the more expensive country and thereby make a profit. This has occurred in many fields including drugs and motor vehicles. Without the Treaty of Rome the owner of the relevant intellectual property rights, for example patents or trade marks, would be able to use those rights in the more expensive country to prevent such sales. However, with the provision of the Treaty of Rome such 'parallel imports' into the more expensive country cannot be prevented because the relevant intellectual property rights are deemed to have been 'exhausted' after they have in effect been used in the first cheaper country, that is, by the owner of those rights actually manufacturing the product or by licensing a third party to do so. Such imports are also commonly known as 'grey' imports to distinguish them from 'white' imports—those agreed by the proprietor of the rights—or 'black' imports—straightforward arm's length infringements of the proprietor's rights, that is, copies of the product itself. In other words a 'grey' import is the genuine article that is being sold in a territory in which the proprietor of the relevant intellectual property rights would rather it was not sold.

There have been numerous decided cases on these issues and the outcome of these can be summarized as follows:

1. Straightforward attempts to enforce intellectual property rights (in the absence of any agreement between undertakings) do not contravene the Treaty of Rome.
2. Intellectual property rights in one member state cannot be enforced against the importer of infringing goods from a second member state if those goods were put on the market in that second member state either by the potential enforcer or with his or her permission.
3. Intellectual property rights in one member state cannot be enforced against the importer of the infringing goods originating in a second member state if the goods were put on the market in the second member state without contravening equivalent intellectual property rights, which had a common origin with those intellectual property rights which it is attempted to enforce.
4. An attempt to enforce intellectual property rights in a first member state against goods imported from a second member state in which those goods were put on the market in that second member state without the contravention of the first mentioned industrial property rights would not be a contravention of the Treaty of Rome, provided that the first and second mentioned intellectual property rights did not have a common proprietor in their origins.
5. Intellectual property rights can be enforced to prevent the importation from a third country outside the EC into the EC.

Other types of intellectual property litigation
This chapter has only dealt specifically with patent litigation. There can also be litigation involving all the other forms of intellectual property rights covered in earlier chapters, for example trade marks, passing off, registered designs, unregistered design right and copyright as well as what are really contractual disputes concerning misuse of confidential infor-

mation. The court procedures are essentially the same as those already described with reference to patents.

Summary
This chapter looks at intellectual property rights from the point of view of a company's commercial objectives.

The way in which intellectual property rights are used varies from industry to industry but the three broad categories of use are: first, to obtain a commercial monopoly in a product; secondly, to obtain an income by licensing; and, thirdly, for purely defensive/insurance purposes. Which of these strategies is employed depends not only on the particular industry involved but on the position of the particular company in that industry and the underlying economics of its operation.

With research based activities it is often difficult to decide a right time to file a patent application. This is because there is a conflict between waiting until sufficient detailed information has been generated to support a valid patent and the need to file as soon as possible in order to forestall competitors. There is also the conflict between a researcher's desire to publish results and the need to keep the innovation secret until a patent application has been filed. These various conflicting requirements have to be resolved by the application of management judgment.

In many situations, particularly in larger companies, intellectual property rights should be looked at from a portfolio point of view rather than on an individual basis.

The approach to managing a trade mark portfolio in many ways is basically different from that of managing a patent portfolio (and registered designs). This is because the validity of trade mark registrations is dependent upon use of the trade mark in question whereas the same does not apply to the validity of patents or registered designs. Furthermore, whereas patents and registered designs have a finite statutory life, registered trade marks can last indefinitely.

Although intellectual property litigation can be embarked upon for a number of reasons the common background is usually the failure of a third party to respect an intellectual property right or the failure of the proprietor and a third party to reach agreement on the terms of a licence. What are the circumstances that would justify the expense and management time involved in engaging in intellectual property litigation? The answer depends upon whether the intellectual property right was obtained for the purpose of attempting to secure a monopoly in the marketplace of a product, or to generate an income by licensing or merely as a defensive/insurance measure.

In formulating a strategy for the obtaining and use of intellectual property rights it must be borne in mind at all times that their use and enforcement is now dominated by the overriding philosophy underlying the Treaty of Rome—namely, to promote the free flow of goods within the European Community.

Useful addresses

Chartered Institute of Patent Agents
Staple Inn Buildings
London WC1V 7PZ

Patent Agents handle registration of patents, trade marks and registered designs for clients

Institute of Trade Mark Agents
4th Floor
Canterbury House
2-6 Sydenham Road
Croydon
Surrey CR0 9XE

Trade Mark Agents handle registration of trade marks for clients

The Patent Office
State House
66–71 High Holborn
London WC1R 4TP
and
PO Box 111
Government Buildings
Cardiff Road
Newport
Gwent NP9 1RH

Part of the Department of Trade and Industry. Deals with granting of patents, registered trade marks and registered designs

Science Reference and Information Service
25 Southampton Buildings
London WC2A 1AW

Part of the British Library. Has available copies of all UK and foreign patent specifications and extensive IP reference material

Public Libraries in Aberdeen, Belfast, Birmingham, Bristol, Coventry, Glasgow, Leeds, Liverpool, Manchester, Newcastle-upon-Tyne, Portsmouth, Plymouth and Sheffield

Also have copies of patent specifications

Innovation Centre
The Design Council
28 Haymarket
London SW1Y 4SU

Information for designers and innovators is available

British Technology Group
101 Newington Causeway
London SE1 6BU

Support for innovation and technology transfer expertise available

Institute of Patentees and Inventors
505a Triumph House
Regent Street
London W1R 7WF

Advice for innovators available

National Computing Centre
11 New Fetter Lane
London EC4

and

Oxford Road
Manchester M1 7ED

Computer software escrow service

Advice may also be available from:
Chambers of Commerce
Regional offices of Department of Trade and Industry
Local Innovation Centres
Local Exploitation Brokers
Scottish Development Agency
Welsh Development Agency
Northern Ireland Local Enterprise Development Unit
Council for Small Industries in Rural Areas

Index

Account of profits, 200
Adapt (adaptation) of copyright, 39, 40, 45, 56
Aesthetic (*see* Eye-appeal)
Algorithm, 105–106
Anti-trust, 163–165
Architecture, 37, 49
Article 85, 163–165, 197, 201
Article 86, 163–165, 201
Artistic craftsmanship, 37, 49
Artistic work, 37, 40, 49, 104
Assign, 133, 152
Author, 40, 42–44

Biotechnology, 107
Black clause, 165
Block exemption, 165
Broadcast, 40

Cable programme, 38, 40, 54
Chip, 89–99, 113
Circuit layout (*see* Topography)
Commission, commissioned works, 48, 58, 93, 134
Commonplace, 80, 92
Compilation, 39, 54
Computer-generated works, 52–54, 134
Computer program, 50–52, 55–58, 105–106, 158
Computer program and escrow, 11, 161
Confidential (confidentiality), 1–14, 108, 145
Conversion damages, 47
Copy protection, 57
Copy (reproduce), 40, 45, 55, 82
Copyright, 35–59, 85
   assignment, 49, 134
   infringement, 44–48, 55–58
   licence, 158
   marking (copyright notice), 50, 58
   owner, 43, 134
   symbol, 50, 58
Co-owners (*see* Joint owner)
Criminal (law, offence), 2, 19, 46, 57, 58, 200

Damages, 118, 198–200
Database, 54
Decompilation, 56
Design document, 48, 53, 82, 83
Design right, 47–49, 74–87
   assignment, 85, 134
   infringement, 83–84
   licence of right, 84
   ownership, 53, 134, 147
Device mark (*see* Logo)
Discovery, 104
Distribution agreement, 158
Document (documentation), 55, 58
Dominant position, 163, 201
Double taxation, 167
Down-payment (*see* Lump sum)
Dramatic work, 38, 40
Drawing (*see* Artistic work)
Drug (*see* Pharmaceutical)

Electronics industry, 174
Employee, 7–11, 137–147
Employer, 7–11, 137–147
Escrow, 11, 161
European Community, 163–165, 201–202
European Community: directive on computer software, 51
European Court, 195–197
European Patent, 119–120
Exhaustion of rights, 94, 201–202
Exploitation, 151–170
   (*see* also Licences)
Export, 125
Ex-employee, 7–11, 109

Eye-appeal, 61-62, 64

Fair dealing (with copyright), 46
Film, 38, 40, 44
Franchise, franchisee, 16, 29, 157
Freedom to use, 113-114, 179
Functional article, 62, 64, 68, 76, 86

Game (patentability), 104-105
Generic trade mark, 25
Geographical name, 22
Germany, 158, 176

High Court, 125, 127, 141, 144, 194-197

Implied confidence, 6
Import, 83, 125, 202
Injunction, 44, 199
Innocent (infringer, third party) 12, 27, 50, 72, 84-85
Integrated circuit, 54, 89-98, 99
International convention
    copyright, 35, 51
    patents, 118-120
    trade mark, 31
Invention, 99-104, 138
    ownership, 139-141

Japan, 97, 121, 190
Joint author, 43
Joint owner, 43, 49, 135

Kit of parts, 70
Know-how, 2, 13, 157-158

Legal aid, 141
Licence, exclusive (exclusivity), 125, 153-154
Licence, of right, 47, 84
Licence, sole, 153-154
Licences, 3, 133, 151-165, 187-189
Literary work, 36, 40, 104
Litigation, 189-203
Logotype, 16, 135
Look and feel, 52
Lump sum, 13, 154-156

Marketing agreements, 158-159
Marking
    of design right, 85
    of patent, 127

of registered design, 72
of topography, 97
of trade mark, 26
Mask, mask work (*see* Topography)
Mathematical (numerical) table, 37, 39
Micro-organism, 117
Moral right, 43-44, 147
Motor industry, 173
Music, musical work, 38, 40
Must fit, 76-78
Must match, 77-78

New (novelty), patent, 107-109, 115
New (novelty), registered design, 65

Object code, 51, 56
Obvious (invention), 109-110
Original, (originality), copyright, 39-42
Original, (originality), design right, 78-80
Owner, ownership, 43, 48, 50, 58, 133-150

Parallel import, 201
Passing off, 17, 27-28
Patent, 99-132
    application, 113-122
    assignment, 134, 147
    claim, 117
    examination, 115
    foreign, 118-124
    infringement, 125, 197-198
    licence, 124-125, 157, 187-189
    litigation, 189-203
    owner, 124, 135
    portfolio, 181
    priority date, 115-118
    renewal fee, 127-128
    search, 114-115, 178-189
    specification, 116-117
Patents county court, 125, 141, 194
Petty patent (*see* Utility model)
Pharmaceutical industry, 124, 173
Pharmaceutical (drug), 106-107, 124
Photograph, 37
Piracy, 50, 90-91, 95
Printed circuit board, 92, 157-158
Product liability, 161-162

Registered design, 64-74, 85, 104

INDEX

application, 70–72
assignment, 85, 134–135
infringement, 70
owner, 134, 139, 147
priority date, 72
renewal fee, 71
search, 71
Renewal fee, patent, 127–128
Rental right, 46
Reproduce (*see* Copy)
Reverse assembly, reverse engineering, 2, 56, 91, 94
Royalty, 124, 154–156

Sculpture, 37
Secrecy (*see* Confidential)
Semiconductor products, 89–98
Service mark, 16
Set of articles, 66
Show-how, 13, 157–158, 167
Software (*see* Computer program)
Sound recording, 38, 40
Source code, 11, 51, 56, 161
Spare part, 76
Strategy, 122–123, 171–189
Substantial part, 45
Suggestion (scheme), 13, 145–146
Suggestion (unsolicited), 13
Surname (as trade mark), 23

Taxation, 166–168
Time shift, 47
Topography right, 89–98
  infringement, 94
  marking, 97

ownership, 93
registration, 92, 96
Trade mark
  class, 20
  examination, 22
  infringement, 26
  marking, 26
  owner, 135
  permitted user, 29, 156
  portfolio, 186–187
  registration, 21–24
  renewal fee, 24
  search, 22, 32, 186
  selection, 32
  specification of goods, 22
Trade marks, 15–34, 184–187
Trade secret, 7–11
Transient copy, 56
Translation (of copyright), 39
Treatment of human being
    (patentability), 106
Trial, 197–198

United States of America, 51, 96, 158, 161, 176, 190, 192
University, 135
Utility model, 123

VAT, 166–167
Video, 38, 47

White clause, 165
Word mark, 16
World patent, 120
Writ, 197